T0305313

ENERGY AND ENVIRONMENT IN INDIA

CENTER ON GLOBAL ENERGY POLICY SERIES

CENTER ON GLOBAL ENERGY POLICY SERIES

Jason Bordoff, series editor

Making smart energy policy choices requires approaching energy as a complex and multifaceted system in which decision makers must balance economic, security, and environmental priorities. Too often, the public debate is dominated by platitudes and polarization. Columbia University's Center on Global Energy Policy at SIPA seeks to enrich the quality of energy dialogue and policy by providing an independent and nonpartisan platform for timely analysis and recommendations to address today's most pressing energy challenges. The Center on Global Energy Policy Series extends that mission by offering readers accessible, policy-relevant books that have as their foundation the academic rigor of one of the world's great research universities.

Robert McNally, *Crude Volatility: The History and the Future of Boom-Bust Oil Prices*

Daniel Raimi, *The Fracking Debate: The Risks, Benefits, and Uncertainties of the Shale Revolution*

Richard Nephew, *The Art of Sanctions: A View from the Field*

Jim Krane, *Energy Kingdoms: Oil and Political Survival in the Persian Gulf*

Amy Myers Jaffe, *Energy's Digital Future: Harnessing Innovation for American Resilience and National Security*

Ibrahim AlMuhanna, *Oil Leaders: An Insider's Account of Four Decades of Saudi Arabia and OPEC's Global Energy Policy*

David R. Mares, *Resource Nationalism and Energy Policy: Venezuela in Context*

Agathe Demarais, *Backfire: How Sanctions Reshape the World Against U.S. Interests*

JOHANNES URPELAINEN

ENERGY AND ENVIRONMENT IN INDIA

The Politics of a Chronic Crisis

Columbia University Press / *New York*

Columbia University Press
Publishers Since 1893
New York   Chichester, West Sussex
cup.columbia.edu

Library of Congress Cataloging-in-Publication Data
Names: Urpelainen, Johannes, author.
Title: Energy and environment in India : the politics of a chronic crisis /
Johannes Urpelainen.
Description: New York : Columbia University Press, [2023] |
Includes bibliographical references and index.
Identifiers: LCCN 2022040008 (print) | LCCN 2022040009 (ebook) |
ISBN 9780231194808 (hardback) | ISBN 9780231194815 (trade paperback) |
ISBN 9780231551021 (ebook)
Subjects: LCSH: Environmental policy—India. | Energy policy—India. |
India—Environmental conditions.
Classification: LCC HC440.E5 U77 2023 (print) | LCC HC440.E5 (ebook) |
DDC 338.954—dc23/eng/20230118
LC record available at https://lccn.loc.gov/2022040008
LC ebook record available at https://lccn.loc.gov/2022040009

Printed and bound by CPI Group (UK) Ltd, Croydon, CR0 4YY
Cover design: Noah Arlow
Cover image: Getty Images

CONTENTS

CONTENTS

Notes

Bibliography

Index

ENERGY AND
ENVIRONMENT IN INDIA

INTRODUCTION

In the twenty-first century India will play a pivotal role in global energy markets and in protecting or destroying the global environment. India has significant, if perhaps uncertain, potential for economic growth in the medium run, and its huge population continues to grow. As a result, India drives some of the most important trends in the global energy economy. As the country grows larger and wealthier, Indians buy more televisions, computers, cars, air conditioners, and flights. These consumer choices shape demand for coal, oil, and natural gas—all fossil fuels that cause climate change—and natural resources.

But India's story is not just one of rapid growth. It is also one of persistent poverty, inequality, and environmental degradation. In 2019, when Americans already worried about robots and artificial intelligence replacing human workers, large swaths of India struggled with intermittent power. In some of the poorer states, such as Uttar Pradesh (population 200 million) and Bihar (population 100 million), villagers with electricity at home faced five to ten hours of power outages on a daily basis.[1]

At the same time, India's air pollution problems have already grown worse than those in China. When President Obama visited New Delhi in

January 2015, the media wrote about his losing six hours of his expected lifespan during the three-day visit.[2] The flashy headlines focused on a short visit by the president of the United States, but Delhiites have to deal with this problem every day. In fact, over a million premature deaths in India can be attributed to air pollution every year.[3]

This book tells the story of energy and environment in India. It not only reviews the evolving state of the natural environment and the dynamic patterns of energy and resource use but also offers a new perspective on the massive challenges that India faces in the coming decades. These challenges converge around securing a supply of abundant and affordable energy to fuel economic growth without uncontrollable, irreversible environmental degradation. The book focuses on energy as the lynchpin of India's most severe environmental crises: air pollution, groundwater depletion, and climate change.

All three crises threaten India's future. In each crisis, the production and consumption of energy plays a central role in turning a once beautiful country into a parched and smoggy dystopia. Although the crises are only a few decades old, they have rapidly become chronic in nature. They are widely recognized by experts, and their crushing impact on Indians is clear. And yet an unfortunate combination of public apathy and institutional dysfunction has made solutions elusive.

This book is intended for anyone interested in understanding India's energy and environment in the past, present, and future. It can be used as (1) a reference book for relevant facts, (2) a textbook for supervised or independent learning, and (3) a scholarly volume that aims to summarize, synthesize, and interpret existing material for an academic audience. The book covers both India's domestic energy and environment and India's role in global energy and environmental politics. Indeed, while domestic concerns tend to dominate over international diplomacy, the two are intertwined and must be considered in tandem. For example, at a time of climate disruption caused by greenhouse gas emissions, India, alongside other major economies, faces growing pressure to reduce its reliance on fossil fuels. These pressures give rise to domestic debate about India's role in global climate action and pathways to a more sustainable future.

While my primary goal is to synthesize existing material, I also attempt to explain India's challenges in energy and environment. Once described as a "flailing state,"[4] India faces a number of governance challenges that have made existing energy and environmental policy rather ineffective in dealing with the country's worsening environmental problems. In particular, the implementation of key laws, policies, and regulations across India's twenty-nine states remains plagued by administrative ineffectiveness. A mix of resource scarcity, weak incentives, corruption, and political opportunism has paralyzed the Indian frontline bureaucracy. From public transit planning to renewable energy finance, institutional deficiencies prevent India from realizing its full potential.

Because of these institutional failures, India has become a *captive society* in which the wealthy and the privileged find their own solutions to deal with energy shortages and the most salient consequences of environmental degradation. Wealthy Indians look for their own solutions to secure a reliable supply of energy and mitigate the worst effects of air pollution, groundwater scarcity, and extreme weather caused by climate change.

India's huge fleet of diesel generators—from small domestic engines to massive industrial power sources—not only reflects a failure of power sector governance but also contributes to it. When consumers can find a private, if perhaps expensive, solution to a government failure, their interest in systematic solutions through government policy is diminished. Polluting and expensive, diesel generators supply industry with power during outages. Groundwater pumps, though necessary for irrigation, contribute to alarming rates of groundwater depletion. Private electric pumps reach deeper and deeper to extract scarce groundwater resources in cities without municipal supply. Air purifiers and air conditioners protect the Indian middle class—in plain English, the wealthy—from air pollution and heat waves caused by climate change. These devices keep wealthy Indians' homes and offices free of the deadly smog and extreme heat that literally kill those working outside.

India's energy and environmental problems remain unaddressed partly because the middle class, which has the wherewithal and knowledge to contribute solutions, focuses on a relentless search for private solutions that exclude the poor and the marginalized. The prevalence of these private solutions reduces political pressure to act, as powerful people leave the state's public service system behind. The poor and the marginalized continue to suffer, but they also lack the political clout and mobilization capacity to force the government's hand. The pressures to reform Indian institutions that govern energy and environment are still weak, as the most powerful victims of environmental degradation have found private solutions that protect them from harm, while leaving the vast majority of the population vulnerable.

The good news for India, and the world, is that much can be done to solve these problems. Although India is among the most vulnerable and ecologically fragile countries, it is important to remember that only a few decades ago, industrialized countries grappled with equally serious energy and environmental issues. From renewable energy to electric vehicles, new technologies provide solutions to India's problems. As India becomes wealthier, more urban, and more educated, the opportunity for an environmental awakening emerges. Government, private sector, and civil society can and should take advantage of this opportunity to make India a sustainable society, ready to face the trials and tribulations of the twenty-first century.

GLOBAL ENERGY AND ENVIRONMENT: THE SHIFTING CENTER OF GRAVITY

India's ascent in global energy markets and as a player in global environmental politics has been a long time coming. The two critical determinants of economic clout, and therefore potential for environmental degradation, are population and income per capita. While India's population has grown rapidly for a long time, rapid income growth is a more recent phenomenon.

India's population reached half a billion—second only to China—as early as in 1966.[5] At that time, India's GDP per capita, measured in 2010 constant dollars, stood at US$320. Meanwhile, China's had barely reached

US$200. But as we move forward to the year 1990, China's GDP per capita had grown to US$730, while India languished at US$540. China almost quadrupled its GDP per capita in twenty-four years, while India's did not even double.

India's poverty can also be seen in a lackluster demand for modern energy. In 1990 India's per capita electricity consumption was 270 kilowatt-hours (kWh), while China stood at 510 kWh. For comparison, in 1990 Japan was at 6,850 kWh and the United States at 11,710 kWh. For every unit of electricity used by the average Indian, the ultra-efficient Japanese consumed 25. And as Todd Moss, at the time a senior fellow at the Center for Global Development (Washington, D.C.), noted in 2013, his refrigerator consumes 459 kWh a year—over twice the Indian per capita electricity consumption in 1990.[6]

Based on these numbers, it is no surprise that although the country is gargantuan in size, India's entry into the global limelight is a very recent phenomenon. Until the very end of the twentieth century, India was a minor player in the energy-environment nexus by almost any indicator except population. In table 0.1, I show some statistics on the Indian economy as compared to the world average in 1997, when the Kyoto Protocol on climate change was negotiated. With the singular exception of having a large population, India shrank into insignificance in the world economy and energy markets. India's GDP per capita was less than one-tenth of the global average; both CO_2 emissions and energy use per capita were less than

TABLE 0.1 Indian Economy in 1997

VARIABLE	INDIA	WORLD
GDP per capita, constant 2010 USD	671	7,695
GDP total, constant 2010 USD	669 billion	45,241 billion
CO2 emissions per capita, tons	0.98	4.08
CO2 emissions total, megatons	918	23,975
Population, billion people	1.00	5.88
Energy use per capita, kg of oil equivalent	399	1,624

Source: World Bank Development Indicators, https://datasets.wri.org/.

one-fourth of the average. As a result, India's total CO_2 emissions were less than 4 percent of the global total—hardly a country of importance for global climate diplomacy or energy markets. While India was the second most populous country on the planet, its per capita emissions were so minuscule that it did not yet register as a major emitter in global climate diplomacy. During the Cold War, India distinguished itself as a staunch opponent of colonialism and imperialism in global environmental politics. India's diplomatic stance reflected its closed economy and refusal to align with the industrialized West. When Prime Minister Indira Gandhi addressed the United Nations Conference on the Human Environment in Stockholm, Sweden, in 1972, she claimed the leadership of what was then known as the Third World:

> On the one hand the rich look askance at our continuing poverty—on the other, they warn us against their own methods. We do not wish to impoverish the environment any further and yet we cannot for a moment forget the grim poverty of large numbers of people. Are not poverty and need the greatest polluters? For instance, unless we are in a position to provide employment and purchasing power for the daily necessities of the tribal people and those who live in or around our jungles, we cannot prevent them from combing the forest for food and livelihood; from poaching and from despoiling the vegetation. When they themselves feel deprived, how can we urge the preservation of animals? How can we speak to those who live in villages and in slums about keeping the oceans, the rivers and the air clean when their own lives are contaminated at the source? The environment cannot be improved in conditions of poverty. Nor can poverty be eradicated without the use of science and technology.[7]

Prime Minister Gandhi had her facts right: India's environmental problems were caused by population growth and poverty, such as food security and growing biomass consumption. No wonder, then, that India's arguments on the global diplomatic arena focused on demanding more action from the industrialized countries and emphasizing how little India, and other less developed countries, had done to create the global environmental crisis. How could a country reduce its emissions when the vast majority of its population lived in abject poverty? Before India, it was China's turn to establish itself as the central player in global energy and environment. In 1978 Mao Zedong's successor, Deng Xiaoping, launched an ambitious reform program that was to bring communist China to the forefront of global capitalism.[8] Over the next three decades, China's economy grew by about 10 percent annually, resulting in an aggregate effect of a tenfold increase. By 2001 China's carbon dioxide emissions per capita had increased to 2.7 metric tons while India's remained stagnant at about 1 metric ton. In 2001 India was still very poor and therefore only a marginal player. While India's economy was just beginning to grow, China was already at the cusp of a phenomenal industrial expansion.

China will likely remain the largest consumer of energy and the largest source of carbon dioxide emissions for decades to come, but its importance is, perhaps paradoxically, already in decline. Although China's carbon dioxide emissions have grown significantly over the past decades, the potential for future growth is more modest. China's total energy demand was 3,053 megatons of oil equivalent in 2016. By 2040 it is expected to increase by 950 megatons of oil equivalent (Mtoe).[9]

In contrast, the IEA predicts that India will drive global energy demand in the coming decades. Drawing on *India Energy Outlook* (2021), India's primary energy demand is expected to grow by over almost 650 Mtoe by 2040.[10] This is both equivalent to one-fourth of expected growth in global energy demand over the same time period and 70 percent of India's entire primary energy demand in 2019, which was 929 Mtoe. While India would still remain a smaller consumer of energy than China, the difference would shrink significantly, and India would emerge as the driver of global energy demand.

The global pivot toward India is driven by an explosive combination of (1) population growth, (2) economic performance, (3) abject poverty, and (4) chronic institutional handicaps. In 1991 India, facing a balance of payments crisis, followed China's lead and began an economic reform program. From telecommunications to foreign direct investment, it embarked on a

TABLE 0.2 India Now and in the Future

VARIABLE	2016	2050
GDP per capita, USD PPP	6,600	25,900
Population, million	1,326	1.705
GDP, USD PPP billion	8,700	44,100

Source: Projections based on PricewaterhouseCoopers,
https://www.pwc.com/world2050.

liberalization spree. Between 1990 and 2010 the Indian economy grew by
6.6 percent on an annual basis—a major departure from the earlier growth
of 3.5 percent between 1950 and 1980. Unfortunately, this economic boom
contributed to a host of energy and environmental problems that remain
unsolved to this date and are the subject of this book.

To understand India's colossal size now and in the future, consider
table 0.2. Based on a future scenario study by the consulting firm PricewaterhouseCoopers, India's GDP per capita—measured in purchasing
power parity—would quadruple by the year 2050 while population would
grow by almost 30 percent. As a result, the Indian economy would be five
times as large as it is today. In a worst-case scenario, the environmental
destruction caused by such a massive economic expansion could be
enormous.

If anything, the great uncertainties surrounding India's future amplify
its importance for the world. In an ideal scenario, India would continue
making rapid progress toward eradicating poverty, but in a sustainable manner by taking advantage of clean technology. Alternatively, India could fail
to grow because of its mounting social problems. The COVID-19 pandemic
that started in early 2020 caused massive damage to the Indian economy,
showing that India's growth trajectory remains uncertain. Such a scenario,
of course, would be a human disaster for over a billion people. The third
possibility is that the Indian economy would grow, but the growth trajectory would be unsustainable and the ensuing environmental destruction
would drive the country and the world into a crisis.

Be that as it may, India's prospects and choices will be central to global energy and environment.

GOVERNING ENERGY AND ENVIRONMENT IN INDIA

The Hindi word *jugaad* can be roughly translated into English as "hack." India's long history of resource scarcity has given rise to a special kind of innovativeness that turns frugality into a virtue. In the field of energy, the ubiquitous diesel generator is a great example of this approach. North India was hit by the largest power outage in human history on July 30, 2012. And yet the most important factories, offices, and malls continued to operate with minimal inconvenience. At the time, about two-thirds of India's companies had a captive power source ready for use in an outage. In a country that had launched satellites and had a nuclear arsenal, about 70 gigawatts of captive generation capacity—roughly equivalent to seventy nuclear power plants—substituted for unreliable grid electricity supply.[11]

This capacity cost hundreds of billions of dollars, contributed to the country's trade deficit thanks to increased oil and diesel imports, and polluted the air. It was a measure of last resort, where the Indian state failed to provide a reliable supply of electricity from the national grid. And yet the ubiquity of the diesel generator also shows that enterprising Indians can find heterodox solutions to their power system problems against seemingly long odds. Where the government failed to create a viable power sector, Indian entrepreneurs stepped in and developed a supply chain that provided over a billion people with a reliable source of power.

The central role of the diesel generator in the Indian economy highlights the country's challenges. On the one hand, rapid economic growth has created unprecedented wealth and made India a dynamic marketplace of goods, services, and ideas. India's private sector has found innovative solutions to problems such as resource scarcity and unreliable public services. From information technology to telecommunications and medical services, the top end of the Indian economy has thrived in the postreform era. These solutions have brought the private sector back to life after decades of neglect under the stifling license *raj*, under which the Indian government withheld permits to prevent entry into industry. Indeed, they have begun to relax the resource scarcities that created the need for *jugaad* in the first place. On the other hand, India's insufficient capabilities for governance have given rise to an environmental crisis of massive proportions. Basic public services, such as electricity and water, are lacking. This makes both everyday life and industrial activity difficult. Environmental regulations, though impressive on paper, are rarely enforced and thus have little impact on pollution and waste. Air in India's cities is a toxic mix of pollutants from burned agricultural residue, cooking with biomass, coal-fired power generation, industrial emissions, diesel engines, and dust.

The diesel generator is but one example of the problem. Industries are now investing in rooftop solar with limited regulatory oversight, contributing to a utility "death spiral" as the best consumers of struggling distribution companies reduce their purchases from the electric grid.[12] Groundwater pumps deplete a scarce resource at a furious pace as farmers, industry, commerce, and households drill deeper into the aquifers to meet their water needs. Industrial and power plants violate emission regulations to maintain their competitive edge. In each case, India's limited governance capacity contributes to social problems, as private innovation generates environmental degradation.

In India's 600,000 villages, a billion people aspire for a middle-class lifestyle. If that aspiration is met without improved governance capacity, the number of winners in a captive society grows while the underlying social and environmental problems continue to worsen.

To be fair, India has seen success in some important government programs. Specifically, the Indian government has been successful where government purchases have been enough. Take India's LED lighting program, UJALA, which was launched in 2014. Already by end of April 2018, the program had resulted in the sale of a staggering 300 million LED lights, saving 38,570 gigawatt-hours of electricity per year and avoiding 7.7 gigawatts of peak demand.[13]

UJALA was essentially a bulk procurement scheme to bring down the cost of LED lights. The government correctly recognized that it had the wherewithal to massively reduce the cost of the lights and thus transform the domestic lighting market in one bold move. India's leaders leveraged the vast domestic lighting market to reduce the cost of LED lights through mass procurement. For a country with a large and growing domestic market but only limited industrial prowess, such a strategy was appropriate.

Renewable energy installations tell a similar story. According to the Ministry of New and Renewable Energy (MNRE), India had installed 46 gigawatts of solar power and 40 gigawatts of wind power by September 2021.[14] This is a massive increase from December 2014, when MNRE estimated that wind power stood at 22 gigawatts and solar at only 3 gigawatts.[15] Although COVID-19 slowed down India's progress temporarily, renewables have made impressive progress, and their long-term trajectory is promising thanks to low generation costs, improvements in battery storage, and policies at the national and state levels.

Where public capital to subsidize production or procure goods is enough, India's massive government programs can make a real difference. The government has had little success, however, in regulating and changing the behavior of firms, individuals, and communities. India's national air quality standards are continuously violated across the country, and emission norms for power plants and industry go unenforced. The government has not, despite decades of efforts and a series of dangerous droughts across the country, found a feasible way to regulate the use of groundwater in irrigation. These regulatory failures stand in stark contrast to the government's success in procurement and auctions.

These diverging fortunes reflect India's inconsistent performance. A dynamic economy has created a host of environmental problems, but the government's response has been inadequate. India's growing tax revenue has enabled successful schemes that are based on public spending, but efforts to regulate society for improved sustainability have largely failed.

The global implications of India's challenges are nothing short of momentous. On the one hand, India's pivotal role as the world's economic engine and the driver of energy demand means that our ability to stop global environmental destruction depends to a significant extent on decisions and behaviors in the country. If India's middle class continues to expand without new solutions to the country's environmental crisis, the entire world will suffer. On the other hand, India's failure to develop would be equally troubling. With a population in the billions, India's failure to develop would doom efforts to end global poverty.

OVERVIEW OF THE BOOK

This book has two goals. The first is to present an accurate and concise summary of energy and environment in India. In chapter 1 I present a broad historical overview of the field. I go back to ancient times and run through energy and environment from the Indus valley civilization and the Vedic age to the colonial period and independent India before the economic reforms in 1991. This historical overview is useful for understanding the basic relationships among population, economic activity, energy, resources, and the environment in India. I pay particular attention to the legacy of India's economic policies and the Green Revolution, which introduced high-yield agricultural crops and thus saved India from famine in the 1960s. These legacies, I venture, continue to play a major role in India's energy and environment landscape to this date.

Chapter 2, in turn, focuses on energy and environment in emerging India. While economists continue debate exactly how important the reforms of 1991 were for India's economic boom,[16] it is obvious that India's significance for global environment and energy began to grow rapidly at the end of the Cold War. India began to enjoy rapid rates of economic growth, while the population explosion continued almost unabated. These changes revealed that the Indian government and its states were wholly unprepared to deal with the consequences, and India's environmental degradation grew into crisis proportions. While the country has in recent years found innovative approaches to halting environmental degradation, the root causes of the problem remain unaddressed, and the future uncertain.

The second goal of this book is to understand India's governance challenges in energy and environment. To achieve this goal, I present the core of my argument in chapter 3. Drawing on Albert Hirschman's groundbreaking *Exit, Voice and, Loyalty* (1970) on how individuals respond to problems in organizations and societies, I explain and document India's institutional failures and growing dependence on captive solutions to societal problems, as the wealthy look for private solutions to collective problems. In the meantime, public service delivery remains trapped in a low-performance equilibrium.

Chapter 4 situates India in global environmental politics and energy markets, documenting its growing importance in environmental politics and energy markets over time, and showing how fundamental the change in India's position has been. I then explain the implications of the country's changing role for governments, the private sector, and civil society in the rest of the world.

In chapter 5 I reach for the crystal ball and consider potential future scenarios. I analyze uncertainties related to population numbers, economic growth, inequality, technology, and governance. I flesh out the implications of these uncertainties in a series of qualitative scenarios that assess India's energy and environment under optimistic and pessimistic assumptions about the future. These scenarios reveal huge differences between an India that manages to solve many of its fundamental problems and one that continues to expand economically and demographically but fails to govern the accompanying challenges. These considerations confirm India's pivotal role in achieving sustainable human development at the global level.

Taken together, these chapters provide an overview of energy and environment in India and explain the country's present predicament. I begin the analysis by going back in time, to precolonial India and South Asia.

1

FOUNDATIONS AND HISTORY

To set the stage for an analysis of India's contemporary environmental problems, this chapter describes some basic facts about Indian society and reviews the country's environmental history. In India, as elsewhere, government and society are both shaped by historical developments. From the deep undercurrents of precolonial India to the trauma of British colonialism and the trials and tribulations of central planning after independence, India has gone through a wide range of social arrangements that continue to affect norms, attitudes, and behaviors in the twenty-first century.

To summarize, India's environmental history before the reforms of 1991 can be divided into three periods. In the precolonial era, environmental problems reflected scarcity of natural resources and low productivity. As such they, could not be separated from the more general problem of poverty. When the British colonialists took over, India for the first time faced widespread environmental destruction due to the commodification, commercialization, and industrialization of natural resource use. After India gained independence in 1947, a race between technological progress and population growth under resource scarcity began. Social, economic, and political developments during these three periods set the stage for India's postreform environmental crisis.

THE BASICS

Figure 1.1 shows the nations of modern South Asia. This region covers modern India, Bangladesh, Bhutan, Maldives, Nepal, Pakistan, and Sri Lanka.[1] India as an entity has changed over the years. For thousands of years, the Indian subcontinent consisted of a diverse group of societies. During the British colonial era, India covered a vast area that included modern Bangladesh and Pakistan. From the Myanmar border along the Bay of Bengal to the city of Peshawar near Khyber Pass, fewer than two hundred miles from the Afghan capital Kabul, India covered the vast majority of South Asia's land mass. Today's India, though still large compared to most countries and clearly the hegemonic country in South Asia, is far more circumscribed in territory.

As the Indian National Congress fought for independence and the British colonialists began to plan their exit at the aftermath of the Second World War, efforts to reassure India's Muslim minority in what would be a Hindu majority country failed. The Muslim League, led by Muhammad Ali Jinnah, had already passed the Lahore Resolution in 1940 to demand a separate nation for Muslims. When the negotiations between the Muslim League and the Indian National Congress broke down, India was partitioned in 1947 into India and Pakistan, with modern Bangladesh as East Pakistan.[2]

In a chaotic and violent partition, over ten million people were displaced, and the refugee crisis threatened to overwhelm the two young nations. In the Census of India in 1951, 2 percent of India's entire population were refugees who had relocated from either East or West Pakistan. These wounds have yet to heal, and India and Pakistan consider each other enemies. They have fought multiple wars since 1947 and continue to dispute the status of Kashmir, the northernmost region of the Indian subcontinent. A curious

FIGURE 1.1 Modern South Asia. Throughout this book, the representation of India's borders is for illustration only and is not a comment on territorial sovereignty. Map by author.

consequence of the partition was that West and East Pakistan had no land connection. India's Muslim population was always split between the two distinct areas, and between them lay India's Hindi-speaking heartland. In 1971, after a civil war and India's intervention, Bangladesh declared independence and became an independent nation.

Today, India is a vibrant democracy with a population of 1.4 billion people and a GDP per capita of about US$2,000. A country of seemingly endless diversity, India listed eleven languages in the Census of 2011 with over 30 million primary speakers. In North India, Hindi is by far the most common language spoken at home, with over 500 million speakers. It is also the second or third language for over 160 million people. Other major Indian languages include Bengali (97 million primary speakers), Marathi (83 million), Telugu (81 million), Tamil (60 million), and Gujarati (55 million). About 80 percent of Indians are Hindus by religion, with the rest split between Islam (14 percent) and smaller religious groups such as Christianity, Sikhism, and Buddhism.

A particularly complicated but important feature of Indian society is the caste system.[3] While I cannot do justice to this complex issue here, it is useful to review the basics and explain how they might influence energy and environment. Historically, the caste system is based on a hierarchic organization of social groups called *varnas*, ranging from the lowest rung of "untouchables"—a practice that is fortunately slowly losing its relevance[4]—to the priestly Brahmins. Each primary caste group is divided into a huge number of localized *jatis*. Traditionally, the caste system both prescribes the primary occupation of the *jati* members and proscribes intercaste marriage, along with several other social interactions. These rigid structures have reduced social mobility and minimized the pace of socioeconomic change in society, as Indians were born into certain positions in society that were, until recently, very difficult to change.

The Constitution of India was written by Dr. B. R. Ambedkar, a prominent intellectual of the formerly untouchable Mahar caste. It bans caste-based discrimination and provides certain reservations for people belonging to certain castes or tribes. In a form of affirmative action, these Scheduled Castes (SC) and Scheduled Tribes (ST) have their reserved electoral constituencies, public employment, and social benefit schemes.[5] The idea behind these provisions is to provide opportunities for social groups that have historically faced discrimination and had few opportunities to improve their lot.

The caste system is worth noting in a study of energy and environment because caste-based discrimination raises the possibility of environmental injustice and inequality in energy access. As caste continues to restrict social mobility and create uneven opportunities, one must consider the possibility that the worst problems of energy poverty and environmental degradation are felt by lower-caste and tribal populations. For example, Kopas et al. find that air pollution from coal-fired power plants tends to find its way to relatively poor towns and villages with large lower-caste and tribal populations.[6] Such environmental injustices and inequities cannot be fully understood without referencing the historical evolution of the caste system.

Like Indian society, the country's economy is diverse. It is already the third largest economy in the world, behind only the United States and China, when measured in terms of purchasing power parity—that is, considering the low cost of goods and services in India. The most striking fact about India is the low contribution of industry to the economy. India has a relatively advanced service sector, which amounts to 54 percent of value added; industry, in contrast, produces only 30 percent of value added. This uneven pattern of development reflects both an advanced service sector, with major strengths in fields such as medicine and information technology, and the weakness of the industrial sector, especially the light industries such as textiles, which played such a critical role in China's escape from poverty.[7]

Within India, regional differences are significant. South India tends to perform better than North India on a wide range of social, economic, and governance indicators. The most troubled states are found in the Hindi-speaking Indo-Gangetic Plain. India's largest state, Uttar Pradesh, for example, has recorded an annual per capita growth rate of only 3.1 percent between 1995 and 2017, while the Indian average is 5.3 percent. Another large Hindi-speaking state, Bihar, has grown at 3.8 percent, although this twenty-year analysis hides recent improvements in performance.[8]

A key feature of the Indian economy is the monsoon. While Indian weather patterns are complex, their defining feature is the southwest monsoon season that typically brings rains to the country between early June and early September.[9] In the capital city of Delhi, in northern India, rains are rare in the winter (October–January) and hot season (February–April), with fewer than 30 millimeters of rainfall per month. In June, rainfall increases to 55 millimeters and then reaches 220 millimeters and 250 millimeters in July and August, respectively. As the monsoon comes to an end in September, average rainfall is 135 millimeters. This variation in rainfall, which could be exacerbated by climate change, is a key reason why surface and groundwater irrigation is so critical for India's agriculture.

India's monsoon- and irrigation-fed agriculture feeds the world's second largest population in an area of only 3.3 million square kilometers, or one-third of the United States. These numbers yield a population density of 455 people per square kilometer in 2018. That is a staggering number, as one sees by comparison to the world average (60), China (148), the United States (36), or even Japan, famous for its dense population and limited land availability (347). No other major economy comes close to India's density.

India's population trends give rise to both hope and despair. Beginning with the bright side, India's fertility rate—births per woman—has decreased significantly over time. In 1960 the average Indian woman gave birth to almost six children, though it bears remembering that many of them died as infants because of poor health care and nutrition. By 2016 this number had come down to about 2.3, or close to the estimated replacement rate of 2.2. These changes are in line with falling birth rates across the world and are critically important in an already crowded India. Yet India remains above the replacement rate, and population growth continues. Indeed, at the current rate, India's population will exceed 1.5 billion by 2030.

My rather cursory review of Indian fundamentals would not be complete without a comment on India's energy resources. According to BP's *Statistical Review of World Energy* (2021), India had few oil and gas resources. In 2020 the country had only 0.6 billion barrels of oil reserves, or 0.3 percent of the world's total. It had 1.3 trillion cubic meters of natural gas, or 0.7 percent of world total. The only fossil fuel that India had in some abundance was coal, of which it had 111 billion tons, or 10.3 percent of the world's total.

While India thus has relatively abundant domestic coal resources for power generation, it is almost entirely dependent on imports for oil and gas, compromising India's energy security and adding to its trade imbalance problem.[10] As we shall see, this heavy dependence on foreign energy has been an important driver of India's efforts to reduce reliance on fossil fuels over time.[11]

From an environmental perspective, India's energy security problem is both an important driver of action and a potential bottleneck. India's energy policy aims to minimize the growth of oil use to strengthen energy security, while encouraging the expansion of domestic coal production.

HUMANS AND NATURE IN PRECOLONIAL INDIA

Although my focus in this book is on the energy-environment nexus today, understanding India's contemporary plight is easier with some historical background. In this section, I briefly review the human-nature relationship in India before the arrival of the British colonialists. Key themes include resource scarcity and the role of the caste system in managing resources.

Nobody can say with certainty when humans first reached South Asia. Gadgil and Guha note that while human migrants could have arrived almost two million years ago, soon after they left Africa, credible evidence of human artifacts can be dated back to 700,000–400,000 B.C.[12] At that time, the Himalayan Mountains had risen and the South Asian pattern of monsoon, with dry winters and summers followed by months of heavy rain, was established. The Neolithic revolution prompted hunter-gatherers to domesticate animals and cultivate plants around 10,000 B.C., and in the coming millennia these practices spread to South Asia from the Middle East through what is now Pakistan.

Environmental constraints have shaped life on the Indian subcontinent in lasting ways. The first major civilization to emerge in the area was the Indus Valley Civilization (3300–1300 B.C.). Considered one of the three cradles of human civilization along with ancient Egypt and Mesopotamia, the Indus Valley Civilization was of the Bronze Age. It achieved a high level of urbanization, engaged in trade using bullock carts and boats, and created an extensive canal network. One important cause of the civilization's demise appears to have been shifts in river courses driven by the continuing rise of the Himalayas.[13] As major rivers, such as the Saraswati, changed course for natural reasons, urban settlements along them lost access to water and their populations were dispersed. Other possible contributors to the end of the Indus civilization include climate change, flooding, and salination of agricultural soil from irrigation. While the relative importance of different causes is hard to establish, it is clear that natural causes played a key role. When geographic and climatic conditions changed, urban settlements failed to adapt and lost their dynamism over time.

When the Indus Valley Civilization collapsed, Indo-Aryan people migrated into the northwestern parts of India and the Vedic age (1500–500 B.C.) began. The society was initially organized along tribal lines, but it consolidated toward the end of the Vedic age into kingdoms with administrative capabilities. Between 500 B.C. and A.D. 300, expanding agricultural production finally gave rise to surpluses that made nonagricultural activities possible. As a result, trade across the Indian subcontinent began to grow. These favorable economic developments, in turn, gave rise to India's first generation of empires. Of these, the early Mauryan Empire (320–180 B.C.) left a particularly important mark on South Asian development. Expanding from the Gangetic plains, the Mauryan Empire expanded further south, colonizing river valleys and investing in irrigation works that further contributed to agricultural surpluses. After the empire collapsed, it was replaced by a number of smaller kingdoms that were unified into the Gupta Empire in the third century A.D.

At this time, the Indian caste system was slowly gaining a foothold in the society.[14] The Vedic scriptures describe how a blood sacrifice produced four caste classes, or *varnas*: the priestly brahmin, the martial kshatriya, the trader vaishya, and the servant sudra. As tribes consolidated into kingdoms with monarchs, the *varna* hierarchy gained traction and social stratification increased. The other component of the caste system, *jati*, is related. It consists of a huge number of local caste groups that inherit specific occupations. In a specific area, for example, a certain *jati* might be responsible for buffalo rearing while another caste group would cultivate paddy. Marriages between *jati* groups would be regulated by complex customs that reduce the likelihood of large status differences between the groom and the bride's family.

The caste system was still far from comprehensive or ironclad. In the diverse Indian subcontinent, the caste system gained strength slowly over time and had little impact on large segments of the population in tribal and other communities outside the Hindu system. According to Bayly, "Caste is not and never has been a fixed fact of Indian life . . . it is possible to see a sequence of relatively recent political and ideological changes [between about 1650 and 1850] which brought these ideals into focus for ever more people in the subcontinent."[15]

Gadgil and Guha argue that the caste system, with its rigid endogamy and occupational specialization, was itself strengthened by a "resource crunch" in the second half of the first millennium A.D.[16] After the Mauryan and Gupta empires, agricultural productivity declined, possibly because of reduced rainfall or lower soil fertility. This decline contributed to economic stagnation under severe resource scarcity. As the caste system contributed to economic specialization, it regulated the use of scarce natural resources and protected villages from crisis. The caste system of highly specialized occupations allocated to different households by birth reduced resource competition. In each village, some caste groups even inherited the occupation of guarding common resources. Thus the strengthening of the caste system may have been an organic response to resource scarcity.

The Gupta Empire was followed by the classical and medieval periods. At this time, the first estimates of the Indian population began to appear. Cassen, warning that we "only have the sketchiest idea of the population size before the nineteenth century," notes a seventh-century estimate of 37 million from Hiuen Tsang, a Chinese Buddhist traveling through India, as the first "plausible" estimate of population.[17] To put this number in context, for every Indian at that time, there are over thirty-five today. It bears remembering, then, that India's high population density is a relatively recent phenomenon.

When the Mughals conquered India and the Central Asian ruler Babur started his empire in 1526, they claimed the surplus from grain production and taxed animals "above a certain number," but not forests.[18] The Mughal Empire, by and large, respected local customs and property right systems. Overall, then, the Mughal Empire's imprint on natural resources was, with the exception of agriculture, quite limited. Of particular import and in stark contrast to British conduct in the colonial era, the demand for timber was limited, and India's forests were mostly used by hunter-gatherers and farmers for their subsistence. The systematic exploitation and eventual destruction of Indian forests were yet to come with the British colonialists.

COLONIAL EXPLOITATION OF
NATURAL RESOURCES

The arrival of the British Empire in India changed everything. In a few centuries India went from a localized, largely subsistence economy structured by caste to a commercial, industrial system that tried to satisfy the British Empire's seemingly unlimited hunger for resources.

When the East India Company began gaining a foothold in India in the early seventeenth century, European influence on the subcontinent was still minimal. The Portuguese had established a trading center in Kerala in 1505, and in 1510 the colonialists established a stronghold in Goa that was to hold until 1961, fourteen years after India's independence. The Dutch East India Company traded along the Indian coast, but over time their presence diminished as they shifted their attention to the Dutch East Indies, known today as Indonesia. A milestone for the British East India Company was the Battle of Swally in Surat, Gujarat, in 1612, where British troops achieved a decisive victory over their Portuguese opponents. Following a commercial treaty with the Mughal emperor Jahangir in the same year, British commercial influence in India began to expand. By 1717 the Mughal emperor had waived all customs duties for trade with the British, and trade in textiles and other goods and commodities boomed. Between 1757 and 1858 the British East India Company was dominant in India, as it acquired the right to collect taxes and even established a capital city in Calcutta, known today as Kolkata.

The British Empire disrupted the traditional pattern of natural resource use in India, "their political victory equipping the British for an unprecedented intervention in the ecological and social fabric of Indian society."[19] Whereas resource use in precolonial India was still overwhelmingly directed toward local subsistence needs, the British colonial administration extracted large surpluses for commercial use. Precolonial India had rich natural resources and abundant forest cover, and the British set to replace this socionatural system with a system built around scientific forestry, agrobusiness, and industrial exploitation of nature.

As a result, markets instead of communities began to govern natural resource use. For the first time, commodity prices in London shaped the exploitation of nature in India. Forests, in particular, saw rapid depletion in the hands of the British.[20] As forest resources dwindled on the British islands, the demand for timber for navy and industry from the colonies grew dramatically. One example of this pattern is Britain's voracious appetite for teak, the best timber for shipbuilding. As the British merchant fleet's tonnage increased from 1,278 to 4,937 thousand tons between 1778 and 1860, the vast majority of the required wood came from the colonies, with India playing a major role.

The British Empire took direct control of India after the 1857 mutiny. An uprising by sepoys—Indians serving in the British armed forces—in Meerut, forty miles northeast of Delhi, erupted into a series of rebellions in North and Central India. The ultimately unsuccessful resistance led to the Government of India Act of 1858, which dissolved the British East India Company and created the India Office to rule what was now a fully colonial India. After the failed mutiny, the official British *raj* began, as the British Crown, represented by Queen Victoria, took direct control of India from the British East India Company.

Besides extensive commercial exploitation, the British also constrained traditional forest uses with rules and regulations.[21] In 1865 the Indian Forest Act was the "first attempt at asserting state monopoly." In 1878 a more comprehensive revision claimed all land that was not cultivated for the state and imposed severe restrictions on the use of forest resources. Families were allowed only a limited quota of timber and firewood, while the sale of forest products was strictly prohibited outside the state monopoly. The Indian forest department became a profitable entity that reaped revenue from the sales of timber, firewood, and other forest products. Between 1869 and 1925 the Forest Department's revenue grew tenfold and surplus thirteenfold.

By this time railroads had emerged as a key mode of transportation in India, connecting different regions at an affordable cost.[22] Both the construction of railways and the fuel for locomotives in India's vast railway system had a destructive effect on forests in the Indian subcontinent. The rail network expanded from 1,349 kilometers in 1860 to 51,658 kilometers by 1910. This expansion led to rapid deforestation, as the massive need for Indian timber strong enough for railway sleeper construction—teak, sal, and deodar—necessitated expeditions far into the remote Himalayas for suitable wood. Areas around India's massive railway network were rapidly cleared, and timber was extracted from farther away.

When the British conducted their first official Census of India in 1881, India's population, standing at 254 million, had only grown sevenfold over the past millennium.[23] For comparison purposes, the Indian government reports that 238 million people lived within the boundaries of contemporary India in 1901.[24] Due to low agricultural productivity, and perhaps the colonial extraction of surplus through taxation and loot, India's demographic pattern followed the Malthusian pattern of slow expansion. According to the Malthusian trap theory, any gains made in the availability of food and other necessities will generate population growth, which again results in resource scarcity. In this system, any improvements in productivity or resource access are negated by a larger population, and true socioeconomic development is impossible. Despite high fertility rates, mortality related to scarcity of food, contagious diseases, and a total lack of health care kept population growth at a low level.[25] Indeed, some of the worst famines in Indian history hit the population during British rule. These include the Great Famine of 1876–1878 and the Indian Famine of 1899–1900, each of which killed up to ten million people.

In the colonial era, Indian industry was weak and, in many sectors, actually declined from the precolonial era, before the British East India Company began expanding its control of India in the seventeenth century. Between 1600 and 1871 India's agricultural output per capita decreased, leading to a decrease in GDP per capita from almost US$700 to about US$500 over three centuries. Industrial production, led by textiles, continued to grow until the end of the eighteenth century and all but collapsed when the Industrial Revolution gave British producers a huge advantage.[26] The Indian economy stagnated and failed to keep up with the industrial powerhouses of Europe.

To summarize, the colonial era left an abiding impression on India. The exploitation of natural resources accelerated, as it became more commercial and systematic. India's GDP per capita plummeted, however, as industrial and agricultural production stagnated. While the debate among economic historians on the long-term impacts of colonialism in India continues, with some benefits from infrastructure, commerce, and administration, it is clear that both indirect and direct British rule led to economic degradation on a grand scale, while much of the surplus went to British tycoon's profits or to support the continued wars with other major powers in Europe and around the world. The colonial trauma left, as we shall see, a lasting impression on Indian society.

ENERGY AND ENVIRONMENT IN INDEPENDENT INDIA, 1947–1991

In the pre-reform era, 1947–1991, India's most important environmental problems were related to poverty and resource scarcity, instead of pollution. The environment could not be separated from livelihoods in a predominantly agrarian society, and a typical environmental problem might be land degradation instead of, say, air pollution or climate change. Environment as such was not a notable concern, with the exception of the degraded forests left behind by the British. Here I briefly review India's energy and environment at this time.

In 1947, when India gained independence, the country's economic development was limited to a small number of urban areas that the British colonial administration developed into centers of industry and commerce.[27] "India at Independence inherited an economy whose main features reflected two centuries of subservience to British interests and, particularly in the twentieth century, the development of its own capitalism."[28] In 1947 over half of total national income came from agriculture while manufacturing stood at 12 percent. Equally important, half of all manufacturing came from informal, small-scale enterprises. Heavy industry was virtually nonexistent, and three-fourths of the workforce was still in agriculture.

India's population in the Census of India in 1951—the first conducted after independence, under the Census of India Act of 1948—was 361 million. If we compare that number to 238 million within modern Indian boundaries in 1901, we see a relatively rapid growth rate of 52 percent over four decades. At this time, infant mortality began to decrease, if perhaps slowly, as improvements in public health reached India, with Protestant missionaries and their health facilities playing an important role.[29] The catch, of course, was that population growth made the accumulation of wealth difficult, especially under the colonial rule.

No wonder that the average Indian was not much better off at the time of independence than in the early years of the twentieth century. According to Maddison (2010), India's GDP per capita in 1950 was US$619 (1990 prices). This number falls well below the country's GDP per capita in 1913, US$673, suggesting modest negative growth in the final decades of the British Empire. While these numbers must be approached with caution, as accounting for the dominant informal sector with any precision was impossible, they do reveal that the final decades of colonial rule in India did not produce major economic gains. Population grew at a faster pace than before, but the lot of the Indian population did not improve. At the time, then, India's economic and population dynamics could still be described as Malthusian in nature.

The theory applies quite well to India's first years of statehood. When availability of food improved, the population grew and food again became a problem. India's tiny modern industrial sector was of limited import to the country's vast population, and most people survived on subsistence farming or manual labor for major landowners. Specifically, although advances in nutrition and basic hygiene brought down child mortality—defined as share of children dying before the age of five—from over 50 percent to below 30 percent by 1951, the availability of food was still a fundamental constraint on the population, with no obvious solutions on the horizon.[30]

Before economic reforms, India's energy consumption was minimal. In 1971, the first year for which I was able to find data, energy consumption per capita was only 268 kilograms of oil equivalent.[31] The vast majority of Indians used traditional biomass for cooking and, in colder areas such as the mountains, heating. For their lighting needs, Indians would use small amounts of kerosene. Only a tiny middle class in the urban areas would have regular access to electricity, clean cooking fuels, or mechanized transportation.

Very few countries in the world today consume such small amounts of energy per capita. In fact, the only countries listed in 2012 by the World Bank Development Indicators as having a lower level of per capita energy consumption than India in 1971 were Bangladesh, Niger, South Sudan, and Yemen.[32] India's energy economy in 1971, in other words, is a thing of the past. The kind of energy poverty that characterized India during the first three decades of independence has almost entirely disappeared from the world.

India's autarkic and heavily regulated economy was never able to generate the kind of dynamism that would produce environmental degradation on a large scale. There was no industry to speak of; automobiles were a rarity; power plants were a handful at best. For the first two decades of Indian independence, the kinds of environmental problems that now prominently feature in public debate were not even on the political agenda. India's overwhelming problem was poverty stemming from primitive technology in agriculture, industry, and commerce.

While the first five-year plan, 1951–1956, mostly compiled existing projects into a roster with few new additions, it did attempt to lay out governmental priorities.[33] Unfortunately, the government failed to prioritize key issues by considering everything essential. India's scarce resources were allocated across a wide range of sectors in a way that failed to produce concrete progress in any of them. India's first prime minister, Jawaharlal Nehru, attempted to find a shortcut to industrialization, with inspiration from the Soviet Union.

It was only with the second five-year plan that the Indian government decided to double down on heavy industrialization in a systematic manner. Again, however, the lack of resources made actual implementation very difficult. In the 1960s India had a rude awakening as the combination of rapid population growth and poor harvests prompted a food security crisis. The third five-year plan pivoted back to agriculture, but poor economic performance, combined with costly wars with China and Pakistan, produced disappointing results.[34]

The Green Revolution was a development of major import to India, as it brought modern environmental concerns to public view.[35] While India's first government under Prime Minister Nehru had declared agriculture a top priority, between 1947 and 1960 India had grown increasingly dependent on U.S. food aid. Agricultural productivity had not kept up with population growth, and the country faced a very real threat of famine. In the northwestern Indian states of Punjab and Haryana, a solution finally emerged in the mid-1960s. The introduction of new high-yield varieties of crops, especially wheat and rice, made it possible for India to expand food production and become self-sufficient. The Indian government, with foreign support, invested heavily in rural infrastructure to help farmers gain access to these new crop varieties, distribute fertilizer, and encourage groundwater irrigation with electric pumps.

The results were easy to see, and the agricultural revolution expanded across India over the span of a few years. Food production surged, and the threat of famine subsided. India was now able to feed its population. However, food production was imbalanced across Indian states, and the government had to develop an elaborate system of procurement to ensure that surplus states transferred their grain to states in need. By the 1983–1984 growing season, "76.0 percent of the land under wheat and 54.1 percent of the land under rice were devoted to [high-yield varieties]." By that time, yields in some parts of India had grown two- or threefold as compared to 1965, and they began to grow again in the mid-1980s.[36]

These agricultural extension investments were critically important for the environment because high-yield varieties came at a cost of greater inputs. Writing in *Foreign Affairs* in 1969, Wharton aptly notes that the Green Revolution's success "will produce a number of new problems which are far more subtle and difficult than those faced during the development of the new technology."[37] These problems include dependence on large quantities of insecticide, fertilizer, and water. While great improvements in yield per acre did reduce land use pressure, excessive use of water and chemicals contributed to serious environmental problems, ranging from groundwater scarcity to soil degradation and contamination of drinking water supplies.[38] In India, these problems were recognized almost immediately, with Veeman writing about "groundwater problems which are emerging in northern India" as a consequence of the Green Revolution already in 1978.[39] Today, these problems have grown into crisis proportions.

The Green Revolution did not end the race between population growth and productivity improvements. As the Indian population continued to grow and land mass remained fixed, a certain degree of technological progress was necessary to compensate for the inevitable decrease in land per capita. Population growth translated into lower land availability per capita, and improvements in agricultural productivity were necessary to offset the resulting decrease in per capita food availability. In this sense, the Malthusian trap was still sprung. The main difference was that technological progress was now faster than before.

Where technological progress dominated, agricultural surplus contributed to social and economic development more broadly. Where population grew fast but technology stagnated, rural development stalled. Overall, GDP growth ranged from a decadal average of 3.3 percent in the 1960s to 5.2 percent in the 1980s. While these numbers may not look too bad, they were driven by population growth. India's GDP per capita (2010 prices) grew only from US$304 to US$536 between 1960 and 1990, with an anemic annual growth rate below 2 percent.

The story of Palanpur, a village in the state of Uttar Pradesh, over four decades offers important insights into this rat race between technology and population. Drawing on five socioeconomic surveys of this village between 1957 and 1993, Lanjouw and Stern (1998) identify three "primary drivers" of economic development, or lack thereof, in the village. These drivers are population growth, progress in agricultural technology, and nonfarm employment.

Population growth, naturally, puts pressure on the village's natural resources. The village population has doubled between 1957 and 1993, meaning that per capita land availability is half of what it used to be. To make up for this deficiency, the agricultural productivity of land would need to double. Such a change would not leave the village any better off than before.

Against this relentless logic of population growth, economic development originates from improved agricultural technology and nonfarm economic opportunities. In agriculture, a key improvement was the rapid expansion of irrigated land from about half of the total to virtually all of it as early as 1974, on the wings of the Green Revolution. Other key improvements included modern cultivation practices and, more recently, mechanization. As for nonfarm economic opportunities, the percent of adult males working in cultivation or livestock as their primary occupation decreased from 81 to 54, while regular or semiregular wage employment increased from 3 to 14 percent.

Between these countervailing trends, Palanpur's per capita income increased by only 20 percent between 1957 and 1983. This change amounts to a compound growth rate of well below 1 percent. At such growth rates, it would take villages like Palanpur several centuries to escape extreme poverty. Palanpur's story, then, is a powerful illustration of the Malthusian trap in which much of India found itself. Despite improvements in agricultural technology and increased availability of off-farm employment, shrinking land availability per capita all but canceled out these gains. Indeed, even without any growth in off-farm employment, the Green Revolution alone should have produced major gains in agricultural income, if only population growth had remained modest. Alas, technological progress barely kept ahead of population growth. Despite, or perhaps because of, government efforts, Indian industry stagnated.

The government attempted to kick-start the sector with capital investments in heavy industry. The combination of scarce capital, limited demand from the broader economy for heavy industry products, and autarkic trade policies made expansion difficult.[40] According to Chibber, however, the problems ran deeper than structural imbalances and poor planning.[41] India, unlike the stalwarts of the developmental state in East Asia, failed to industrialize because its policy interventions fell prey to rent seeking and

bureaucratic paralysis. Where countries like South Korea used state intervention to spur productivity growth in private industry, the Indian state's
developmental programs failed in the face of stiff resistance from industrialists. India's import substitution strategy made lobbying for specific subsidies and resistance to coordinated industrial policy a rational strategy for
India's great business houses. As a result, industrialization failed, and the
Indian economy languished for four decades after independence.

Environmental problems of the time reflect this state of affairs in a poor,
predominantly agricultural society. When the Delhi-based Centre for Science and Environment (CSE) published its first *Citizen's Report on the State
of India's Environment* in 1982, India's environmental concerns were still
largely traditional in nature and today's pressing issues were only slowly
emerging. In fact, the report recognized that "atmospheric pollution has
long been regarded as probably the least important of all the environmental problems in the country, concentrated mainly in the major cities and
industrial towns."[42] As we shall see, things are a little different in India
today.

The report had it right, as a cursory review of the relevant statistics shows.
While systematic pollution data is not available, many of today's drivers of
bad air quality were simply not there. In 1981 India had only 5.4 million
vehicles—including two-wheelers and three-wheelers—on its roads.[43] With
such a tiny fleet, transportation would not have been an issue, except perhaps in some of the larger cities, despite a complete lack of emission control technology or regulations.

Thermal power generation capacity, mostly coal, remained below 20
gigawatts.[44] This capacity is about one-tenth of where India was thirty-five
years later. Again, even though these power plants were very inefficient and
had no end-of-pipe emission control technologies, their overall impact was
limited simply because of scale. For a country of India's size, 20 gigawatts
of thermal capacity is simply not enough to make much of a difference, even
without any environmental technology at all.

Aklin et al. offer a snapshot of Indian energy access in 1987, at the end
of the prereform era, using National Sample Survey data. At that time, only
one-third of the rural population had electricity at home. Cooking fuel

access was far worse, with only 6 percent of all rural households being able to access liquefied petroleum gas (LPG), the dominant clean cooking fuel in India.[45] Again, these numbers show how little progress India had made in reducing rural energy poverty.

The CSE report in 1982 did emphasize indoor air pollution as an environmental problem. With over 90 percent of India's population dependent on firewood for their daily cooking needs at the time, the *Citizen's Report* played a pioneering role in recognizing smoke from cooking as a major threat to public health. Because indoor cooking with firewood produces large amounts of smoke, Indian households did suffer from air pollution in their homes and, where population densities were high enough, in the nearby areas. As we shall see, residential solid fuel use remains a major environmental problem in India.

To summarize, before the great Indian economic reforms that began in 1991, the country's environmental problems were directly related to poverty. Until the Green Revolution, low agricultural productivity made life harsh and perilous for the rapidly growing population. After that time, India averted the threat of famine, yet the relentless logic of population growth under land scarcity continued to drive Indian rural population into poverty. Air pollution was mostly a product of residential biomass burning. The Green Revolution gave rise to an alarming pattern of groundwater depletion, which Indian researchers began to observe as early as in the 1970s. But the most profound environmental problems were yet to come.

ENVIRONMENTALISM IN THE INDIAN SOCIETY

Environmentalism and environmental thought are not new to India. Already in ancient times, the challenge of natural resource governance featured prominently in the densely populated Indian subcontinent. In the colonial era, the clash of indigenous and colonial natural resource regimes gave rise to widespread social conflicts that contributed to calls for independence. Indeed, the British exploitation of India's natural resources amounted to massive environmental and economic losses over time, and even today's environmental discourse reflects this historical experience to a notable extent.

In precolonial India, both natural resource conflicts and indigenous environmental protection were important themes. In their study of India's environmental history, Gadgil and Guha note that by the time of India's great empires, natural resource scarcity had emerged as a major societal concern.[46] The combination of local hunting-gathering and organized surplus extraction for commerce and elite consumption put unprecedented pressure on natural resources, and social norms began to reflect the increased scarcity. In the sphere of religion and philosophy, both Buddhism and Jainism emphasized the sanctity of life, encouraged vegetarianism, and applauded modest and prudent living. In the long run, perhaps more significant was the emergence of India's caste system. The rigid stratification of families into specialized castes "traditionally moderated or largely removed inter-caste competition through diversifications in resource use and territorial exclusion. . . . This unique system of cultural adaptation to the natural environment was devised by Indian society in response to the resource crunch."[47]

More generally, Hindu religious tradition has left an abiding impression on Indian environmentalism. India has a homegrown environmentalist movement that has borrowed from its Western counterparts but has not lost its original approach. As Misra argues, "Environmental movements in India have been non-violent and firmly embedded in social and political structures. Unlike western environmental activist movements, they are strongly tied to human rights, women's rights, social justice and equity. . . . This distinct character of Indian environmental movements is linked to the Hindu ecological vision of life." He goes on to explain that Hinduism is based on a "form of utilitarian conservationism, as opposed to protectionist conservationism." Hinduism links ecological conservation to spiritually significant themes, as "Hindus seem to value and preserve those elements of nature that have ritual significance in the Hindu way of life."[48] In this telling, spiritual considerations are an important driver of environmental concern among the Hindu majority of India.

In the colonial era, natural resource conflicts were greatly aggravated, and indigenous environmental protection came under severe stress. Calling colonialism an "ecological watershed," Gadgil and Guha note that the British aggressively exploited Indian forests, and teak in particular, to enable a vast maritime expansion.[49] The colonial administration also put a heavy emphasis on expanding arable land and cleared vast areas for commercial agriculture. So while the traditional patterns of resource use were mostly localized, which limited the scale of ecological destruction, the British colonial administration transplanted an industrial approach that commodified and commercialized India's vast natural resources. This new pattern enabled widespread ecological destruction, as areas with abundant resource endowments or high potential for commercial agriculture were rapidly exploited to meet the empire's seemingly unlimited need for raw material and income.

At the time of India's independence in 1947, Mahatma Gandhi's environmental thought played an important role in the Indian discourse. Famous for his opposition to industrialization and the Western lifestyle, Gandhi saw economic growth in its modern form as an obstacle to moral and spiritual development.[50] Among the many famous Gandhi quotes, these words summarize his position particularly well: "The world has enough for everyone's need, but not for everyone's greed." In Gandhian thought, the pursuit of material gain is ultimately futile, and modern forms of economic development ultimately counterproductive.

While Gandhi remains a widely admired freedom fighter in India, the relevance of his antigrowth philosophy has decreased over time. The Indian government is firmly committed to the idea of rapid economic growth, industrialization, and modernization. Gandhian thought still has support among many popular movements and intellectuals, but the Indian government and business elites have a strong preference for technological modernization and economic development.

A key moment for India's environmental movement was the March 1973 Chipko "tree hugger" movement consisting of "unlettered peasants threatening to hug trees to prevent them from being cut."[51] In the mountain state of Uttarakhand, then part of the larger state of Uttar Pradesh, thousands of peasants mobilized to protest environmentally destructive forestry practices. Following heavy flooding in the Alaknanda River, enabled by deforestation, the movement succeeded as the government enacted a ban on commercial forestry for a decade.

The Chipko movement became a hit in the global environmental scene. As Rangan notes, "Chipko was a social movement that emerged . . . in the Garhwal Himalaya. Today, transformed by a variety of narratives, it exists as a myth."[52] The tree hugger movement struck a chord because it dealt with some of the major environmental issues of our time, demonstrated the power of the weak, and gave hope to a wide range of grassroots movements around the world. It also underscored a key feature of Indian environmentalism of the time: a focus on local livelihoods.

Another major mobilizer of environmental activism in India was the Sardar Sarovar dam on the Narmada River in the western state of Gujarat.[53] India's largest dam, it was initially planned in 1979 but only finished in 2017. The World Bank withdrew its support to the dam in 1994, after the Save Narmada Movement mobilized to resist the environmental and social impacts on the tribal population. With hundreds of thousands of farmers under threat of displacement, the local tribal population formed an alliance with Western environmentalists and convinced the World Bank to withdraw its support.[54]

The Narmada dam also became a major theme in global environmental activism. Environmental researchers and activists have written hundreds of papers on the dam and the movement resisting it. To this date, environmentalists invoke it as a powerful symbol of the folly of modernist "technopolitical dreams."[55] Again, the narrative of marginalized communities, fighting for their survival and livelihood against environmental destruction brought on by the powerful Indian state, proved irresistible.

These developments gave rise to three distinct ideological trends in Indian environmentalism during the socialist decades between independence and the economic reform era: Gandhian, appropriate technology, and ecological Marxism. As already noted above, the Gandhian view "relies heavily on a religious idiom in its rejection of the modern way of life. . . . Gandhians are concerned above all with the stranglehold of modernist philosophies (rationalism, economic growth) on the Indian intelligentsia."[56]

In contrast, the appropriate technology movement "strives for a working synthesis of agriculture and industry, big and small units, and western and eastern (or modern and traditional) technological traditions." Drawing inspiration from works such as E. F. Schumacher's *Small Is Beautiful*, this movement believes that capital-intensive development is a dead end for both environmental and social reasons. The movement focuses on "the creation and diffusion of resource conservation, labour intensive, and socially liberating technologies."[57] This movement does not reject modern technology but argues that for a country like India, technologies that do not require large capital investments are more appropriate. The combination of poverty, abundant labor, and resource scarcity would lead the appropriate technology advocates to reject the path of heavy industry that India's first prime minister, Jawaharlal Nehru, advocated.

Finally, argues Guha, the "third and most eclectic strand embraces a variety of groups who have arrived at environmentalism only after a protracted engagement with conventional political philosophies, notably Marxism."[58] This group embraces economic modernization and is unequivocally hostile to social tradition. It argues that ecological sustainability is possible only under a socialist mode of production. This group is far removed from Gandhian thought and appropriate technology, insofar as it embraces modern technology on a large scale. It attributes ecological degradation to the lack of integrated planning and perverse incentives in capitalist societies and sees centralized planning under socialism as a way to combine rapid economic growth with sustainability.

Environmental conflicts in postindependence India were the most pronounced in the realm of natural resources.[59] As we have seen, the energy and industrial sectors were still very small, and contemporary problems such as air pollution and climate change barely registered. In contrast, resource degradation had already emerged as a major theme. Both tribal and nontribal communities across India remained heavily dependent on forests, fisheries, and other natural environments for basic livelihoods. When state or private resource extraction activities threatened these fragile and uncertain livelihoods, social conflicts erupted as locals fought for their rights under an administrative system that was ill-equipped to handle the conflict and deal with the associated social problems.

India's postindependence environmentalism had limited space to operate, and its successes were ad hoc. It is true that the Chipko tree hugger movement and the movement against dams achieved some high-profile victories, but India's own economic stagnation did far more to protect the environment than these movements. Until the beginning of the economic reforms, India's primary environmental problem was natural resource scarcity under a large and growing population. But because per capita consumption remained low, environmental degradation did not reach the extreme levels we see today.

As we shall see, India now faces a rather different set of environmental problems. Air pollution, climate change, and groundwater depletion are increasingly central to the country's future. In the case of climate change, argue Dubash et al., India's environmental discourse has changed with the introduction of new ideas from a younger, more international generation.[60] Modern environmental discourse in India is much more heavily influenced by global environmental narratives than in the past. Younger environmentalists have often studied in English, spent time abroad studying and working, and regularly attend international conferences.

From a contemporary perspective the Gandhian, appropriate technology, and Marxist environmental movements may seem somewhat outdated. None of them begins with the notion of sustainable development in a market-based economy, where clean technology and smart policies and regulations are integral to environmental protection. As we shall see in the next chapter, these themes play a major role in postreform Indian environmentalism.

2

ECONOMIC GROWTH AND ENVIRONMENTAL DEGRADATION

I ndians love cricket, but these days a winter test match in Delhi can be a health hazard. When India faced Sri Lanka in a test match at Delhi's Feroz Shah Kotla stadium in December 2017, Sri Lankan fast bowler Suranga Lakmal was escorted off the ground on the fourth day as air pollution levels exceeded the World Health Organization's guidelines by a factor of twelve.[1] While Mr. Lakmal could escape the deadly Delhi smog after a few days, tens of millions of Delhiites have to deal with the problem every day. Air pollution levels vary over time, but they rarely fall to safe levels in this sprawling metropolis.

To help understand how polluted Delhi air is in the winter, figure 2.1 shows monthly mean levels of air pollution in Delhi from January to December 2016 on an hourly basis. The unit is the Air Quality Index (AQI) that aggregates different pollutants under one measure. The WHO typically considers values below 50 as good, over 100 as unhealthy, and over 300 as an emergency. In a healthy environment, values above 50 would be rare, and values above 300 never seen.

In Delhi, the mean value in that year was 119, and the index fell below the safe threshold value of 50 only 36 percent of the time. Of all the

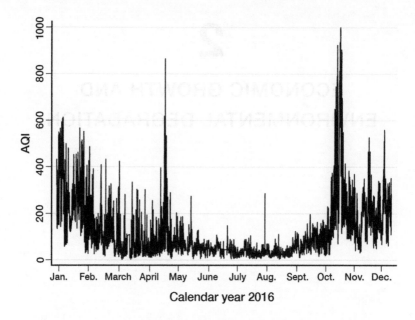

FIGURE 2.1 Air quality index (1–999) in Delhi, India, January to December 2016. The measures are hourly, and higher values indicate more pollution.

Data source: U.S. Embassy in India.

observations, 8 percent were above 300, which is considered hazardous for the entire population. The rest of the time, the WHO would advise people to stay inside and use an air conditioner or air purifier. Two-thirds of the time, being outside was not advisable, and one-tenth of the time the city was a dangerous gas chamber.

Delhi's air pollution problem is but the most visible symptom of India's environmental problems, as other major cities around the country suffer from the same problem. When I visited Lucknow, the capital of India's most populous state, Uttar Pradesh, in January 2018, I could not believe my eyes when I saw that the locals were not wearing masks. During the first two weeks of the year 2018, the average AQI in Lucknow was 390. From January 1 to 15 there was not a single day that fell below the emergency threshold.

Unfortunately, air pollution is not the only environmental problem that has reached crisis proportions in India. If anything, climate change presents an even more significant challenge for the future. India is one of the most vulnerable countries to the negative effects of climate change.[2] A combination of high population density, limited natural resources, and widespread poverty means that heat waves, droughts, floods, and sea level rise have a disproportionate impact on India.

While India is a major producer of greenhouse gases, third behind China and the United States in the world, the country's vast population still has low per capita emissions. When it comes to climate change mitigation, there are really two Indias. The middle-class India is quite similar to the affluent West, with high per capita emissions driven by a high living standard. The other India has over a billion people, but they lead lives that produce few greenhouse gas emissions. Within India itself, the stark contrast between luxury and survival emissions is readily seen.

The third environmental problem that I highlight in this chapter is groundwater depletion. Groundwater is very important for the country, as Indian agriculture is heavily dependent on irrigation.[3] In June 2017 the Central Ground Water Board of India conducted a thorough assessment of the country's groundwater resources.[4] The prognosis was not good. Overall, India's groundwater draft remains below replenishment, but as many as 1,034 of the 6,584 assessed blocks were overexploited and faced a long-term decline in groundwater resources. Combined with widespread poverty and a rapidly expanding population, India's water situation is a direct and grave threat to food security.

The totality of India's environmental problems leaves the country in a position far worse than the rest of the world. Every year researchers at Yale University construct an Environmental Performance Index (EPI) for countries of the world.[5] India was number 177 among the 180 countries under consideration. Only the Democratic Republic of Congo, Bangladesh, and Burundi performed worse. Besides a very poor performance in air pollution, India scored the worst of all countries in environmental health more generally—air quality, water and sanitation, and exposure to heavy metals.

In other words, India's population of 1.3 billion people suffer more from environmental hazards than the people of any other nation in the world.

This Indian environmental crisis cannot be understood without considering the momentous impacts of the economic reforms that began in 1991. Following these reforms, the Indian economy began a phase of rapid expansion. As a result of rapid economic growth, India's energy and resource consumption has exploded. In two decades' time, India went from abject poverty to a toxic mix of extreme poverty and spectacular wealth. The environmental impacts have been massive. Rapid economic growth under minimal environmental and energy policy has exposed India's massive population to an unprecedented level of environmental stress and hazard.

ECONOMIC PERFORMANCE AND POPULATION GROWTH IN THE REFORM ERA

July 24, 1991, was a decisive day in India's economic history. Facing a deep economic crisis, India saw its foreign exchange reserves almost run out that summer and was at one point forced to airlift fifty tons of gold as a collateral for a loan from the Bank of England.[6] It was against this backdrop that Manmohan Singh, then India's finance minister and later prime minister, presented a budget that was to change the Indian economy for decades to come.

India's desperate situation at the time was caused by a combination of a troubled world economy, excess spending, and a stagnant domestic economy with few realistic growth prospects. In the 1980s India's economy had been fueled by external debt. When the Soviet Union collapsed and oil prices doubled due to the U.S. invasion of Iraq in early 1991, India was in a lot of trouble. The demand for its exports crashed while the cost of imports skyrocketed. Already heavily in debt, India came close to being unable to serve its debts and pay for its imports. India stood at a crossroads, as the already strained socialist economy came to a grinding halt. Money was running out.

The government's actions changed the face of India under the leadership of Finance Minister Singh and Prime Minister Narasimha Rao, both from the Indian National Congress. The government reduced India's prohibitive import tariffs, deregulated markets, dismantled public monopolies, reduced taxes, and made foreign direct investment easier. As author James Crabtree puts it in *The Billionaire Raj*, "Import tariffs and limits on foreign investment were cut. Hundreds of fiddly licenses were junked. Industries closed to private competition, from iron and steel to telecoms, were suddenly opened up."[7] The reforms were daring and unprecedented, and they were the first step toward India's wholesale economic transformation. Their impact on energy consumption and production was equally significant.

The reforms were a great shock to a society that had for decades lived in a stagnant economy with rigid licensing arrangements, rationing of even basic commodities, and few opportunities for economic development. For the first time, the Indian economy embraced competition and allowed a new generation of entrepreneurs to pursue profits. For the first time, aspiring businessmen—and, increasingly, businesswomen—could take risks and try innovative schemes to make money. The government, of course, hoped this pursuit would give a massive boost to the Indian economy. Policy makers were ready to relinquish, at least partially, their political control of the economy in expectation of better performance, an end to dependence on agriculture, and fewer economic crises. This expectation turned out to be accurate.

The reforms that followed over the next three decades were at least equally far-reaching. From privatization of state-owned companies to power sector reforms and, most recently, the creation of a unified Goods and Services Tax (GST), the Indian economy has become significantly more open. For example, while international trade amounted to only 17 percent of India's GDP in 1991, that number stood at 40 percent in 2016 and had reached a high of 58 percent in 2012. Doing business in India is still not easy, but the stifling license *raj* of the olden days is long gone. In 2018 the World Bank ranked India seventy-seventh among 190 countries for ease of doing business.[8]

There is a broad consensus among economists about the importance of these reforms to India's rapid economic growth. The first decade of reforms—1992 to 2002—saw an annual growth rate of 6 percent on average. While the growth rate in the 1980s was only slightly lower, at 5.7 percent, "it can be argued that the 1980s growth was unsustainable, fueled by a buildup of external debt that culminated in the crisis of 1991."[9] Although it might initially seem that India's growth story started well before the reforms, the reality is that the reforms, instead of the earlier debt boom, unleashed India's hidden economic dynamism. There is a world of difference in the long-run sustainability of new incentives and opportunities through carefully planned structural reforms, as opposed to a temporary surge in public credit. The former changes the nature of the game; the latter gives a temporary boost but inevitably comes back to haunt the debtors.

On the other hand, India's economic growth did not rely on the kind of rapid industrialization we have seen in China. In fact, India's industrialization remains limited to this date. Between 1991 and 2016 the share of industrial value added in GDP actually decreased from 30.3 to 28.9 percent. By comparison, China's industrial value added remained above 40 percent between 1976 and 2015. It fell below that threshold only in 2016 when China took its economic transition to the next level, away from industry and toward a service economy. Despite a more open and competitive economy, Indian industry has not become competitive at the global level.

Indian companies excel in many services, however. Key areas include information technology, health care, entertainment, and telecommunications. Indian service industries benefit from a large skilled workforce and the prevalence of English as a language of higher education, especially in the South. Many Indian firms in information technology and customer service use English as a working language or to serve customers from across the world.

India's economic growth has resulted in one of the most unequal societies in the world, in a pattern that reminds one of Russia's oligarchs. India's "bollygarchs" control vast fortunes. To be among the richest 1 percent in India only requires assets worth US$33,000, and yet the same 1 percent owns a full half of the country's assets.[10] According to the World Inequality

Dataset, the bottom 50 percent of India—over 650 million people—earned only 15 percent of the nation's income.[11] The Gini coefficient, which measures inequality and ranges from 0 to 100, with higher values reflecting more uneven distributions of income, stood at 0.83 for India in 2018.[12] That number ranks India as one of the most unequal countries in the world. Finally, India's rapid economic growth was amplified by continued population growth. For the past half a century, India's population growth has been almost linear. From 450 million Indians in 1960 to 870 million in 1990 and 1.32 billion in 2016, India's population growth has shown few signs of abatement. Although birth rates have decreased rapidly, from 5.91 births per female in 1960 to 2.40 in 2015, the combination of lower infant mortality and a growing number of women has ensured that the population continues to grow. Not only is the average Indian much wealthier than before, but the number of Indians has also grown very rapidly.

The compound effect of rapid population and economic growth has turned India into the world economy's future engine. India's per capita growth rate is not in the double digits and population growth is slowing down, but together these two forces have contributed to a steady and accelerating expansion. Even though the Indian economy's performance has fluctuated over time, reaching a nadir during the COVID-19 public health crisis that started in early 2020, the Indian economy has a lot of room for expansion in the long run. This expansion, in turn, plays a key role in explaining India's energy and environmental problems.

RAPID GROWTH IN ENERGY AND RESOURCE CONSUMPTION

Rajasthan is a beautiful state with a rich history in northern India, close to the Thar Desert. It can, however, become an inferno during the hot season before the monsoon rains bring relief. Just ask the residents of Phalodi, who experienced India's hottest day on record on May 19, 2016. The mercury rose to 51 degrees Celsius—that is, 124 degrees Fahrenheit.[13] The worst heat I have experienced in India was 48 degrees Celsius, and I had air-conditioning both in our vehicle and at my hotel, if perhaps intermittently. To add another three degrees, considering that the vast majority of Indians cannot afford the luxury of artificially cooled air, is a public health crisis.

The Indian market for air conditioners is booming.[14] If an American household in the 1950s suburbs considered a car their first and most important durable asset, an Indian family in Rajasthan now looks at air-conditioning in the same way. When temperatures begin to approach 50 degrees Celsius, life without air-conditioning is no longer just somewhat uncomfortable. It is literally deadly, as extreme heat contributes to a wide range of health problems especially among older, already fragile Indians.

Only 8 percent of India's 250 million households today have air-conditioning, but this number is expected to reach 50 percent by 2050, as growing wealth encourages families to seek relief from India's intense heat—which, in turn, will only get worse because of global warming. Considering that air-conditioning is the most energy-intensive of all residential energy services, this sixfold increase in air-conditioning would have a huge impact on electricity demand in India.

The air-conditioning saga illustrates some of the key impacts of India's economic dynamism. For one, growth of energy demand has been robust over the past three decades. In 1990 the average Indian used only 351 kilograms of oil equivalent (kgoe) per capita; by 2019 the number had almost doubled, to 680 kgoe. Electric power consumption increased from 273 to 884 kWh between 1990 and 2019. Although India is not heavily industrialized, household and commercial demand for energy are rapidly growing.

In the future, this growth in energy demand will likely continue.[15] In June 2017 NITI-Aayog, the successor to India's Planning Commission, published a draft national energy policy built on detailed scenarios of future energy demand up to the year 2040.[16] The results were impressive, if also daunting. Under business as usual, India's total energy consumption would rise from 4,926 to 15,820 terawatt-hours (TWh). By 2040, if all goes well on the economic front, India's economy will more than double compared to today. At the same time, its population will surpass that of China. Urban population will increase by a staggering 315 million people. As a result, India alone will be responsible for one-fourth of growth in global energy demand. Indian energy consumption will double as a result, with massive potential for environmental impact.

The COVID-19 pandemic that started in 2020, however, could reduce India's energy demand growth. The Indian economy was hit hard by the pandemic disruptions and the forced return of migrant workers from the urban to rural areas. As a result, in the International Energy Agency's *India Energy Outlook* (2021), the baseline scenario has India's energy demand growing only 70 percent instead of over 90 percent by 2040.

India's resource consumption has also grown exponentially. Consider, for example, India's changing dietary preferences. According to agricultural scientists, meat consumption takes its toll on the environment.[17] Meat-based diets typically consume more energy than plant-based nutrition, as animals first consume feed and then convert it into meat in an inefficient manner.

If humans instead ate plants without the conversion step, they would recover the same nutrients at a far lower resource requirement. Less energy, water, and land would be used. Less methane, a potent greenhouse gas, would be produced. While meat consumption in India was only 4.4 kilograms per capita in 2017, demand for meat, eggs, and milk is growing at a rapid pace.[18] Over two-thirds of all Indians eat at least some nonvegetarian foods, and meat consumption is growing because higher wealth levels allow people to substitute more expensive meat for less expensive plant-based food. As this trend continues, India's already fragile food security situation will grow worse.

The same trends can be seen for many goods and services across the board. The Indian aviation industry is undergoing explosive growth, with domestic and international flights increasing from about 50 million in 2008 to almost 150 million in 2018.[19] Passenger vehicle sales are also growing fast: according to the Ministry of Road Transport and Highways, the total number of vehicles on India's roads grew from 82 million in 2006 to 230 million in 2016. As noted, air conditioners are increasingly popular among India's middle class.

The patterns of growth in energy and resource use are unevenly distributed across India.[20] In 2012 the average household used only 10.7

kilowatt-hours of electricity per month; in urban areas, the consumption was 23.8 kWh per month. Both numbers are very low—the average German household consumes over 250 kWh a month—and yet the rural-urban inequality is striking.[21] In urban India, a combination of higher incomes and easier access to high-quality electricity service and modern cooking fuels contribute to growth in energy demand. In rural areas, both affordability and access to energy remain problematic.

The rural-urban difference also holds for LPG, which is by far the most popular modern cooking fuel in the country.[22] In 2019 annual consumption of this fuel was only about 90 kilograms per household in rural areas and about 110 kg per household in urban areas. Urban households consume more than their rural counterparts because of both higher incomes and ease of access to modern energy from markets and public distribution channels.[23] These rural-urban differences have shrunk over time, but the fact remains that energy poverty is a far more serious problem in India's 600,000 villages than in its towns and cities.

As India's villages fall farther behind cities and towns in economic development, the already wide gap in rural and urban energy demand will continue to grow. Considering this trend, future patterns of urbanization will play a critical role in shaping India's overall energy demand in the residential, commercial, and industrial sectors. From the power sector to petroleum imports, urban India will drive future trends in energy demand. While urbanization may improve the efficiency of energy use due to higher population densities and better infrastructure, any efficiency reductions will pale in comparison to rapid increases in energy demand. Growing energy demand is not a bad thing itself in a country like India, as long as the energy is used in a productive manner, but it does pose a major challenge for central and state governments in terms of energy security and sustainability.

Similar inequalities are found in comparisons across states. Despite India's socialist legacy, regional differences today are highly salient. In 2016 per capita electricity consumption across India's states ranged from lows of 272 and 585 kWh in Bihar and Uttar Pradesh, respectively, to as high as 2,028 and 2,279 kWh in Punjab and Gujarat. These differences are illustrated in figure 2.2. The eastern and northeastern regions of India stand out

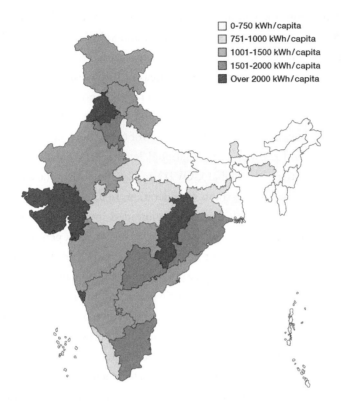

FIGURE 2.2 Per capita electricity consumption in Indian states in 2016.

Data source: Data.gov.in, State/UT-Wise Details of Per Capita Electricity Consumption from 2012–13 to 2016–17, https://data.gov.in/resources/state-ut-wise-details-capita-electricity-consumption-2012-13-2016-17-ministry-power. Map created with MapChart, http://www.mapchart.net/india.html. All India average: 1,122 kWh/capita.

as laggards. Whereas regional averages for the 2016–2017 financial year in the western and southern regions were 1,432 and 1,533 kWh, respectively, they were only 694 and 392 kWh in the eastern and northeastern regions. These stark regional differences highlight variation in economic performance and human development across the diverse Indian peninsula.

To summarize, India's economic growth has brought about an explosion in resource and energy use. While Indian per capita consumption remains low, the sheer size of the population and economy make India a major player in global energy and commodity markets. If economic growth continues at a brisk pace, these patterns will result in an explosion of demand in the future. The changes have been uneven across rural and urban areas, however, as well as between states. Some areas of India, especially major economic centers such as Mumbai, have seen rapid economic progress. Meanwhile, vast rural areas in North India, and the state of Uttar Pradesh in particular, have grown only slowly. The robust pattern of economic and energy demand growth at the national level masks equally important regional variation. The global COVID-19 pandemic that started in 2020 hit India very hard and warrants consideration. In its 2021 outlook for India, the International Energy Agency downgraded its projection for India's energy demand growth by 2030 from 50 percent to 25–35 percent.[24] While India's economic and energy future remains uncertain, even the downgraded numbers would make the country pivotal to global climate change.

Unfortunately, the Indian economic boom and the resulting growth in energy demand have come with large and growing environmental and human costs. The most important environmental problems related to energy use in contemporary India are summarized in table 2.1. The combination of air pollution, climate change, groundwater depletion, and energy poverty is a major threat to the future well-being of Indians. Each of these problems presents a serious risk to India's social and economic development. The salient and growing regional differences across India highlight the importance of sophisticated energy and environmental policy, as the

TABLE 2.1 India's Environmental Problems Related to Energy

PROBLEM	STATUS
Air pollution	Worst air quality in the world
Climate change	Third largest source of carbon dioxide; fourteenth most vulnerable to climate change risk
Groundwater depletion	30 percent of the country facing critical groundwater shortages
Persistent energy poverty	Poor quality of rural electricity service; majority of households continuing to use traditional biomass for cooking

challenges faced can vary dramatically depending on the overall level of development and quality of governance. In the rest of this chapter, I will review these issues in turn.[25]

AIR POLLUTION

India's air pollution crisis is perhaps the most immediate and most visible consequence of the booming economy. The country has the world's worst air quality and the highest number of deaths from diseases related to air pollution. Unfortunately, the government has made very little progress in controlling air pollution and ensuring clean air for the Indian population. The problem has complex origins, as air pollution cannot be attributed to any single source. From power plants and industry to residential biomass burning, India's air pollution problem is the composite of many different sources.

Because air pollution is a combination of particulate matter and noxious gases, which come from many different sources, it presents a complex governance challenge. In India, the National Air Quality Index (NAQI) includes particulate matter, nitrogen oxide, ozone, carbon monoxide, sulfur dioxide, ammonia, and lead. These pollutants come from a range of economic activities, from residential biomass burning to power plants and construction sites. Natural sources, such as dust, also make significant contributions. The air pollution problem in India has grown worse over time, as shown in figure 2.3. Between 1990 and 2015 India's average PM2.5 concentrations, measured in micrograms of particulate matter per cubic meter of air, rose from 60 to almost 80, with most of the growth occurring since the year 2010. For reference, the WHO considers an annual mean of 10 the highest permissible safe value.

What is more, a WHO study in 2018 found that out of the twenty most polluted cities in the world, 14 are in India.[26] The northern city of Kanpur in the state of Uttar Pradesh had the worst air quality, with an annual mean of 173 for PM2.5. Delhi's value was 143. Even air pollution is unevenly

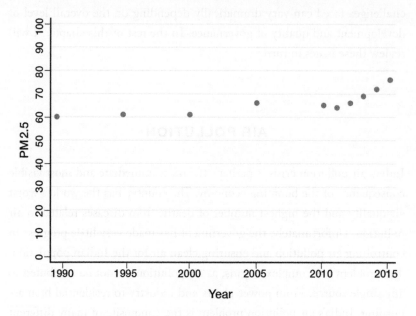

FIGURE 2.3 Air pollution in India, 1990–2015.

Data source: State of Global Air, https://www.stateofglobalair.org/.

distributed across India, with the poorer and less well governed North bearing the brunt of the burden. All the heavily polluted cities were in the northern parts of the country. Air quality is significantly better in the South.

The public health impacts of India's air pollution crisis are severe. Air pollution contributes to blood pressure, heart disease, stroke, pulmonary disease, lung cancer, and pneumonia. In 2015 almost seven million people in the world died from diseases related to air pollution, and almost 30 percent of these deaths—1.8 million—were in India.[27] Considering that about ten million people die in India every year, every fifth of the deaths could be attributed to air pollution. Furthermore, of these deaths, three-fourths are rural.[28] Even though urban air pollution problems receive most of the media attention and coverage, the reality is that rural areas are also heavily polluted.

The economic losses are significant, too. According to the World Bank, in 2013 India lost almost 8 percent of its GDP to air pollution.[29] Besides the direct cost of deaths, air pollution also contributed to health-care expenses, illnesses, and lowered productivity. With 1.4 million deaths from air pollution in 2013, India lost a staggering US$505 billion in welfare and US$55 billion in labor output that year. Overall, air pollution makes Indian lives shorter, less healthy, and less productive.

Why is India's air so dirty? Before we delve into specific drivers, a note on geography is in order. In northern India, air pollution does not have an escape route. Because of geographic and wind patterns, the air above the Indo-Gangetic plain does not circulate much. As Singh writes of North India's "meteorological misfortune," "While there are several contributory sources of air pollution in the region, pollution levels remain at critical levels to a considerable extent due to geographic and meteorological conditions."[30] Unfortunately, the capital city of Delhi, with its vast urban population, is located in this region.

Imagine being in a room with no air-conditioning, open windows, or open doors. Then add lots and lots of cigarette smoke, and the situation resembles that of North India:

> Temperature inversions and stable wind conditions are characteristic features of winters in North India. While calm wind conditions prevent the dissipation of pollutant emissions, the temperature inversion layer tends to trap pollution, thereby increasing the observed pollutant concentrations. . . . The Indo-Gangetic plain is essentially landlocked. According to Sachchidananda Tripathi, senior scientist at IIT-Kanpur, the Himalayas prevent polluted air from escaping to the north creating the so called "valley effect." Other studies have pointed out that the formation of low pressure troughs across this region causes winds to converge, resulting in trapping of local, as well as pollution from outside.[31]

Another way to understand this problem is to emphasize that the phenomenon is highly specific to North India. In the coastal areas of South India, strong winds blow pollution away to the sea where it cannot hurt humans. In North India, particulate matter, whether produced locally or brought in by the winds, gets trapped along the vast area between Punjab and West Bengal. There is no escape route, and hundreds of millions suffer from polluted air. It is the difference between someone smoking with the windows open or closed. There is smoke in the air in both cases, but with windows closed the situation is a lot worse.

Geographic and atmospheric conditions alone do not create pollution. Rather, they create a conducive environment for air pollution to grow in tandem with population and economic activity. Indeed, Singh notes that Los Angeles faces a similar meteorological challenge, as a so-called temperature inversion traps air into the valley.[32] Despite this misfortune, Los Angeles does not look like a gas chamber today—though decades ago, in the worst days of the California smog, it may have. Therefore it would not be wise to blame North India's geographic misfortune for the smog. Rather, geography is an amplifier: it raises the stakes by ensuring that emissions remain where they are produced, instead of escaping to the sea.

Table 2.2 lists the key human drivers of India's bad air quality. As the table shows, India's air pollution crisis has multiple drivers and would therefore require a holistic solution. I will discuss each driver in turn and then

TABLE 2.2 Sources of Air Pollution in India

SOURCE	GLOBAL BURDEN OF DISEASE (GBD) 2018	GUO ET AL. 2018
Transportation	2.1%	1.9%
Power plants	7.6%	6.8%
Industry	9.9%	19.7%
Dust (mineral and construction)	38.8%	4%
Biomass burning (residential and agriculture)	29.4%	67.4%
Diesel generators	1.8%	N/A

Note: The contribution estimates are based on GBD (2018) and Guo et al. (2018). The total does not add up to 100 percent because the final one-tenth of concentrations originate from complex chemical interactions that cannot be traced back to any specific source. Note that Guo et al. (2018) do not separately estimate the contribution of diesel generators.

assess the relative importance of the different sources. I also comment on some key barriers to solving the problems, though a full analysis of the governance issues will have to wait until the next chapter.

Traffic is a natural starting point. At different times during the day, India's urban areas have a seemingly unlimited number of vehicles on the road. Between 2001 and 2016 the total number of vehicles registered in India surged from 55 million to 230 million, amounting to a compound growth rate of almost 10 percent. Importantly, the vast majority of these vehicles are two-wheelers: their number grew from 39 to 169 million. As a share, they actually grew from 70 percent to 73 percent, as poorer households were increasingly able to afford mechanical transportation.

This growth's effect on air pollution is substantial in some urban areas, even though the overall contribution across India is limited. In Delhi, for example, vehicular emissions are responsible for up to 30 percent of all PM2.5 pollution.[33] Because Indian cities are typically not walkable and public transportation is limited, growing income levels translate into rapidly growing automobile ownership and use. India already sold over three million cars in 2017. With growing household wealth, the potential for increased automobile ownership and use is massive.[34]

On the other hand, India now follows the European Union's automobile emission standard and has enforced Stage IV standards since April 2017. These standards reduce air pollution by forcing manufacturers to install catalytic converters. Enforcement is straightforward because units without catalytic converters can no longer be sold, but the effect can be delayed because the standards apply only to new units. Older, more polluting cars may remain on the road for years to come. The good news here, of course, is that the Indian automobile fleet is still very small relative to overall population. With twenty-six million cars and two million jeeps in 2016, India in fact has a very low level of automobile ownership—even though it might not feel that way in India's crowded metropolitan cities.

Electric vehicles (EVs) have major potential in India, where much of the transportation demand is concentrated in densely populated urban areas and the rapidly falling costs of renewable power enhance the competitiveness of electrified transportation. As India's electric grid continues to decarbonize with renewables, electric vehicles offer a potentially transformative solution to the problem of vehicular emissions. While India's electric vehicle fleet is minuscular at the time of this writing, interest in electrified transportation is growing rapidly, and in 2017 the Indian government announced the target of all new vehicle sales being EVs by 2030. These targets, however, have not yet translated into a comprehensive policy.

India's EV future faces a number of high but not insurmountable barriers. A May 2017 joint report by NITI-Aayog and the Rocky Mountain Institute—a U.S. nonprofit focusing on sustainability—emphasizes the importance of key investments and a change of approach.[35] These include investing in charging infrastructure, capitalizing on domestic manufacturing opportunities in the EV value chain (e.g., batteries), and developing an integrated approach to transportation planning based on the idea of mobility as service. Instead of focusing on inputs, such as roads and railroads, a service-oriented approach would first assess people's mobility needs and then develop innovative approaches to meet those needs. The solutions could be infrastructural, but they could also include reducing the need for mobility (e.g., telecommuting).

This approach would be a major paradigm shift from conventional planning, which focuses on building transportation infrastructure and often adopts a narrow technical perspective. As long as Indian transportation planning begins with infrastructure, instead of mobility needs, the output is additional infrastructure investment instead of planning for smart mobility. Such an approach is hardly suitable for meeting the needs of a rapidly growing and mostly poor population in or around densely populated urban centers.

Of the problems associated with Indian transportation, governance is the most fundamental and difficult to solve. A true EV revolution will require coordinated efforts that make electric transportation convenient and affordable. Because the EV sector is immature and dynamic, any one-off scheme that does not address underlying governance problems would not set India on a sustainable trajectory over time. Having an institutional foundation for smart mobility is essential for adapting to the complex challenges ahead.

Another important modern source of air pollution is power generation. While India's per capita consumption of electricity remains low, the total size of the power sector is massive, and two-thirds of it is fueled by coal. Despite rapid recent growth in renewable power generation, coal remains by far the most dominant fuel. According to a study by researchers at ETH Zurich in Switzerland, India's outdated coal-fired power plants cause more premature deaths than those of any other country.[36] The combination of high population densities, outdated or lacking pollution control equipment, and low-quality coal makes Indian power plants the deadliest in the world.

Indeed, India's own emission norms are already quite stringent. In December 2015 India announced new standards for four key air pollutants— sulphur, nitrogen, particulate matter, and mercury—for power plants. This was the first time the country had sulphur, nitrogen, and mercury standards, and the particulate matter standard for coal-fired power plants now ranges between 30 and 100 milligrams per cubic meter instead of the earlier 150– 350. These standards are comparable to modern standards in the United States and European Union.

Unfortunately, many Indian coal-fired power plants do not comply with the country's emissions standards. In December 2017 a report by the environmental group Greenpeace revealed that 60 percent of India's coal-fired power plants flouted the new emission standards executed in December 2015.[37] These numbers suggest that before India begins to implement new emission standards, the first order of business would be to enhance compliance with regular inspections and sufficiently severe penalties for noncompliance. In principle, monitoring compliance with emission norms is not very difficult, considering coal-fired power plants are relatively large stationary sources. Regular, unannounced inspections or real-time emission monitoring systems would do the job. The challenge lies with inspectors' incentives to accept bribes, political incentives to avoid harsh penalties on influential tycoons, and more generally lack of effective environmental governance in the power sector.

The economic costs of pollution control are significant, too. A study by the Centre for Science, Technology and Policy estimates that 80 percent of the plants need to invest significant amounts of money, up to US$150,000 per megawatt of capacity, to meet the 2015 national standards for emissions.[38] As a result, retail electricity prices could increase by 9–25 percent. While this is a relatively high cost, the total benefit in reduced mortality and morbidity is higher. In India, the economic case for reducing air pollution from coal is, if anything, unusually strong. A densely populated country with a growing economy and per capita income, India pays a high price for untreated emissions from coal.

An important step would be the closure of the oldest and most inefficient plants. While India underwent a massive coal capacity expansion between 2010 and 2016, going from about 80 to almost 200 gigawatts (GW) in five years, India already had about 50 GW of capacity in the year 2000, well before the air pollution debate began or modern emission standards were introduced.[39] As a result, the average Indian coal-fired power plants was twenty-three years old in 2017, though it bears remembering that older plants tend to be much smaller. About 85 percent of India's coal-fired power plants have subcritical combustion technology, meaning that coal burns at lower temperatures and generates fewer kilowatt-hours per ton burned than using modern, supercritical or ultra-supercritical technologies.

India's troubled power sector contributes to air pollution not only from coal-fired power plants, but also from its general failure to deliver reliable electricity to the population. Because India's electricity supply is often unreliable, diesel generators with a total capacity close to 100 GW—think of a capacity equivalent of 100 modern nuclear power plants—also contribute to air pollution. Diesel generators are less efficient and lack emission control technology, so they also contribute to air pollution. They are also very difficult to control because of their widespread use and small size. Unfortunately for over a billion Indian lungs, these generators are literally everywhere in India. A 90-percent reduction in generator use would save thirty thousand lives a year by reducing PM2.5 concentrations by 0.4 units.[40]

Industry and construction are other major contributors. Industrial emissions from India's growing production of cement, steel, chemicals, and other products are burgeoning. Construction activities release fine particulate matter into the atmosphere as sand, bricks, gravel, and stones are turned into buildings and infrastructure. Although India is not heavily industrialized, low efficiency and lacking environmental regulations mean that industry has an oversized impact on air pollution. In North India, for example, industry is only second to the residential sector (e.g., cooking with traditional biomass) as a source of air pollution.[41]

Natural sources of dust aggravate the air pollution problem. Besides human sources such as construction and industry, dust is naturally prevalent in the region because of large arid areas such as the Thar Desert. When dust mixes with pollutants, particulate matter levels spike and create the atmospheric conditions over Delhi and other North Indian cities that some commentators have described as a gas chamber. Although dust itself is not a health threat, when it mixes with other air pollutants the problem is aggravated.[42]

But much of India's air pollution problem actually stems from the country's 600,000 villages. A major cause is the use of biomass for cooking and, during the cold season, for heating. Firewood and other forms of biomass remain by far the most important fuel in Indian cooking, especially in villages. The vast majority of rural Indian households continue to use biomass as their primary cooking fuel, despite growing access to cleaner alternatives such as LPG. Every night, hundreds of millions of people eat dinner cooked on a *chulha*, a traditional and highly inefficient stove that typically burns firewood and produces huge amounts of smoke. First, this smoke pollutes the home. Then, it escapes and pollutes the local air.

Every fourth death caused by air pollution can be attributed to smoke from cooking with traditional biomass.[43] In 2015 it is estimated that 267,000 Indians died from outdoor air pollution originating from residential biomass use, primarily for cooking purposes. This outdoor air pollution problem is common to both rural and urban areas, as cooking with firewood remains common in periurban and semiurban areas, while emissions from millions of *chulhas* around the country can travel long distances between villages and cities.

Notably, this number does not even include deaths and disease from indoor air pollution. The aforementioned 267,000 deaths are all attributable to the massive amounts of smoke that escapes kitchens and homes to the atmosphere when biomass is burned for cooking, or perhaps heating.

Needless to say, the situation is far more alarming for the people inside these homes.[44] According to a study by the Indian Council of Medical Research, almost half a million deaths can be attributed to indoor air pollution.[45] When people cook inside their homes, they are directly exposed to large quantities of pollution from the impure combustion of biomass.

Reducing people's reliance on firewood presents an immense challenge.[46] Because cooking requires large amounts of energy, the cost of replacing firewood—a free or inexpensive fuel source—with clean cooking fuels is high for poor rural households. In India, the primary modern cooking fuel is LPG. Unlike firewood, LPG is never available for free, and instead households must pay to refill their cylinders for cooking. Affordability and accessibility present major barriers to ending the practice of fuel stacking, which according to public health specialists is necessary to reap the full health benefits of clean cooking fuels. We will explore these issues in greater depth.

India's agricultural sector also contributes to air pollution. When India's farmers begin burning their agricultural residue after the harvest season, air pollution levels spike in New Delhi and other cities on the Indo-Gangetic plain. While this problem is highly seasonal, it is responsible for the dramatic "gas chamber" conditions in northern Indian cities in the fall. When the situation spiraled out of control in early November 2016, the chief minister of Delhi, Arvind Kejriwal, was quick to blame agricultural residue burning in surrounding states:

> Delhi has its set of sources of pollution such as road dust, vehicular pollution and open burning but these existed even a month ago. According to our assessment, the pollution and smoke are coming in a large quantity from neighbouring states because of crop stubble burning. . . . I was in Punjab and Haryana and there is smoke in the air just like here. How we can tackle the problem, only the Centre [Government of India] can say.[47]

This practice of "stubble burning" is a relatively new problem.[48] When India solved its impending food production crisis with new plant varieties during the Green Revolution, these advances gave rise to large-scale production of wheat and rice in the semiarid areas of North India, and the state of Punjab, often known as India's bread basket, in particular. With wheat sown in the dry winter season and rice during the monsoon, farmers have only a narrow window of opportunity to clear their rice residue before sowing the wheat. The simplest solution to this problem is to burn the residue, which results in air pollution. When many farmers burn their residue at the same time, air pollution levels spike.

The problem was made worse by the introduction of combine harvesters, which did a very good job at cutting, threshing, and cleaning the rice plants but also left behind a lot of residue. This residue, left behind by over twenty-six thousand combine harvesters in India, must be removed because otherwise the machines planting the next crop would get stuck. For farmers, there is no easier way to do this than pouring kerosene on the field and lighting it all up.

How can India deal with these problems? At the policy level, the answer might be found in a source apportionment study conducted in 2018 by researchers at Louisiana State University in collaboration with the environmental group Greenpeace.[49] The goal of such a study is to attribute air pollution to different causes. The researchers then conduct simulations to see how policy measures, such as new environmental regulations, change air pollution levels in the future. In this case, the Louisiana State University study finds that a combination of twelve different policy measures could reduce the average concentration of PM2.5 from 32.8 to 20.1 micrometers. The policies include power plant emission controls, avoided emissions from canceled coal-fired power plants, reduced use of biomass in households, reduced crop burning, reduced municipal waste burning, vehicle emission standards, reduced oil consumption growth, improved kilns for brick production, oil sulfur limits, industrial emission limits, dust control in construction, and the reduction of diesel generator use.

Of these, the most important measures are industrial controls, power plant controls, and reduced solid fuel use. These three solutions would together have a significant impact on air quality. Compared to the baseline exposure of 32.8 micrometers, the Louisiana State University team estimates that new emission standards for the industry would reduce air pollution by

2.95 micrometers, while power plant controls and reduced solid use would cause reductions of 1.83 and 2.27 micrometers, respectively.

Another study, by the International Institute for Applied Systems Analysis (IIASA) and the Council on Energy, Environment and Water (CEEW), finds that if India were to fully enforce all air pollution controls enacted in 2018, as opposed to those reflecting the 2015 policies, it would reap significant gains by 2030.[50] Specifically, almost 210 million people would breathe clean air. By 2050, however, further population and economic growth would cancel out some of these gains.

The most important takeaway from these analyses is the urgent need to enforce current policy. In the coming decade the most important question for India is whether policies on paper are enforced. The future will undoubtedly reduce the cost of clean technologies and open new opportunities for action, but strategizing about the introduction of zero-pollution technologies at this time is not relevant for policy. While the IIASA-CEEW study is correct to note that current policy would not suffice to maintain adequate air quality to 2050, the first step is to enforce current policy and reap sizable gains by 2030. After that, new technology and better living standards would enable the government to adopt more stringent policies. Unfortunately, addressing India's air pollution problem turns out to be politically challenging.

Although air pollution is on the political agenda, the Indian state does not treat it as a major emergency requiring urgent action. Unlike a terrorist attack or an explosion, air pollution is a creeping problem that slowly but surely inflicts major damage on people's health.

A good example of the resulting lack of urgency is the government's National Clean Air Programme (NCAP) of 2019. While the plan aims to reduce air pollution by up to 30 percent in 102 cities relative to 2017 levels, it does not contain specific sectoral targets or implementation measures. Total funding available for implementation, US$91 million over two years, is a drop in the bucket. Although the amount was increased fivefold in the 2020 budget, the total still amounts to little compared to the scale of the problem. So while the NCAP does raise the profile of and offer a framework for addressing the problem, it has very little to contribute by way of solutions. A modest budget and vague plans for narrowly defined urban areas are hardly enough to address a systemic problem that runs across rural and urban India in multiple sectors. A better alternative, if a truly national plan with integrated solutions is not in the cards, might be a plan to address the most important and politically most manageable sectors in North India.

Besides the creeping and often diffuse nature of the problem, India's response to air pollution is also constrained by the lack of awareness and the media's near obsessive focus on the capital city of Delhi. In the Census of India for 2011, 74 percent of India's population above the age of seven was literate. The standard for literacy is low, however, and only a small minority of Indians are fully equipped to read and grasp scientific facts about air pollution. In a country where illiteracy and semiliteracy remain widespread, popular awareness of the air pollution problem is also hampered by a lack of basic scientific knowledge. For many Indians, the idea that air can be polluted and contribute to poor health is difficult to grasp. When our research team conducted surveys on air pollution in the state of Uttar Pradesh, many of our respondents had difficulty understanding the idea of air quality, as they confused it with temperature.

The media's focus on Delhi at the expense of other population centers, some of which are more polluted than Delhi, further reduces awareness of air pollution as a social problem. It bears repeating that solving even Delhi's air pollution problem is not possible without addressing multiple sectors in rural and urban areas on a large scale in North India. By focusing on Delhi, the Indian media does a disservice to Delhiites too.

In early 2020 many urban citizens of North India saw clear skies for the first time in decades. The COVID-19 public health crisis brought economic activity to a grinding halt, and air pollution levels collapsed. As a result, people were able to see the imposing Himalayan Mountains. Such moments can contribute to a bottom-up demand for improved air quality, but an effective government response requires a sustained and systematic effort over long periods of time.

To summarize, air pollution has caused a major public health crisis in India. With over a million premature deaths per year, Indians suffer greatly from polluted air. The problem is difficult to solve not only for geographic reasons, but also because the sources are complex, and governing them requires a lot of institutional capacity. A lack of public awareness of the problem means that politicians and government agencies face only limited pressure to act.

CLIMATE CHANGE: INDIA'S CONTRIBUTION

India is both a contributor to and a victim of climate change. Due to its vast population and growing economy, it is responsible for about 7 percent of global emissions, and this number is rapidly growing. At the same time, the average Indian's per capita emissions are very low and raise difficult questions about equity in the global climate mitigation effort. The same people who produce few greenhouse gas emissions are highly vulnerable to the negative effects of climate change and, at least for now, lack the wherewithal to adapt effectively to this looming threat.

In 2018 India already was the world's third-largest emitter of greenhouse gases. The country emitted a total of 2.6 gigatons of carbon dioxide, the vast majority of it from energy use, and another 1.1 gigatons of other greenhouse gases, most important methane from agriculture and waste. India's CO_2 emissions have about quadrupled between 1990 and 2019, while non-CO_2 emissions have grown by one-half.

Globally, India's share was at about 7 percent, and well below its global population share of one-sixth. While China (11 gigatons) and the United States (5 gigatons) have far higher emissions than India, the total EU emissions of 3.5 gigatons are comparable to India's. Every year, India approaches other major powers, as Indian emissions today grow far faster than those of any other major emitter. This is no surprise, considering that India begins from a low level of per capita emissions.

While India's overall emissions are large, the per capita situation is very different. On a per capita basis, India's 2 tons pale in comparison to those of other major emitters. The average American emits 15 tons, Chinese 7.7 tons, and European 7 tons. The average citizen of the world emits about 4.2

tons. If we conceive of equity as everyone having an equal share of the carbon budget, India stands out among the major emitters as the only one with a plausible claim to increasing its emissions under international climate cooperation. All other major emitters produce too many emissions per capita, whereas India still has some room for expansion.

India's historical responsibility for emissions is also limited. An analysis by Carbon Tracker shows that since 1750, India has emitted an estimated 51 gigatons of carbon dioxide equivalent into the atmosphere.[51] That is less than German (90) or British (77) emissions over the same time, even though these countries together have about one-tenth of India's population today.

This already complex reality masks some variation across different strata of the Indian society.[52] In India as of 2010, the poorest two-thirds produced about 1.2 tons of carbon per year. For the remaining one-third, per capita emissions ranged from 4.2 tons to as high as 40 tons per capita. While India's poor majority produces about half of India's carbon dioxide, the other half is produced by people with carbon footprints similar to those in China, Europe, and the United States.

For India's very poor majority, reducing emissions to any significant extent is almost impossible. These households use very little modern energy to begin with. Their emissions come from biomass burning, agriculture, and very small amounts of electrical energy. As they grow wealthier and begin to use energy services that wealthy people take for granted, their emissions will continue to grow. With today's technology, it is not yet plausible to achieve zero-emission growth when the baseline is this low. Even in the highly unlikely scenario of the Indian power sector completely relying on zero-carbon power for future growth, the other sectors—agriculture, transportation, industry, and buildings—would continue to see rapid emission growth. The COVID-19 pandemic caused a temporary dip in emissions in 2020, but it seems highly unlikely that emissions would not continue their growth in the future—if perhaps at a lower rate because of a weaker economy.

Of the total 3.7 gigatons of CO_2 equivalent, about 2.6 gigatons is CO_2 itself and the rest consists of other gases, such as methane. Energy generation is responsible for over 90 percent of India's carbon dioxide emissions.

In turn, of all carbon dioxide emissions, coal is responsible for about two-thirds and oil for one-fourth, while natural gas contributes only about 5 percent. Emissions from both coal and oil are projected to grow in the future, though coal's relative importance will slowly decrease while oil's relatively importance will grow. While coal is today the dominant driver of India's carbon dioxide emissions, much of the growth potential is in oil and gas. The energy-related emissions are, in turn, dominated by electricity (and, much less important, heat) generation at about half of all emissions. About one-fourth comes from industrial energy use in manufacturing and construction, and the rest consist of other fuel combustion, transportation, and fugitive emissions.

The sectoral breakdown of greenhouse gas emissions is quite similar to its global counterpart. Globally, about 34 percent of all greenhouse gas emissions came from electricity and heat generation, whereas their share in India was 31 percent. Transportation and manufacturing produced 27 percent globally and 23 percent in India. The most important difference between India and the rest of the world is that Indian agriculture is responsible for 20 percent of all greenhouse gas emissions in the country, mostly because of methane emissions, whereas globally agriculture is only 10 percent of the total. The comparison is shown in table 2.3.

Let us now consider Indian end use emissions, sector by sector. We begin with the power sector. Similar to China, India is heavily reliant on coal for meeting its electricity needs. For India's carbon dioxide emissions, coal-fired power generation is the sine qua non. In 2018 India had 197 gigawatts of coal-fired power generation capacity and an average capacity factor of 61 percent. Figure 2.4 shows the growth in India's coal-fired power generation over time. Coal consumption has grown rapidly, from about two quadrillion British thermal units to a peak of fifteen in 2012. Although the growth is not as spectacular as in China, the expansion of coal consumption is nonetheless the most important driver of India's growing greenhouse gas emissions. Growing per capita incomes have increased the demand for electricity in households, industry, and commerce. Until very recently, almost all that new demand was met with additional coal-fired power generation.

TABLE 2.3 Comparing Sources of Greenhouse Gas Emissions: India Versus Global (2014), in Gigatons of Carbon Dioxide Equivalent

SECTOR	INDIA GT	INDIA %	GLOBAL GT	GLOBAL %
Electricity and heat	1.08	34	15.31	31
Manufacturing and construction	0.53	16	6.23	12
Transport	0.23	7	7.55	15
Other fuel combustion	0.31	10	4.11	8
Fugive emissions	0.04	1	2.62	5
Industrial processes	0.19	6	3.16	6
Agriculture	0.63	20	5.25	10
Waste	0.06	2	1.52	3
Land use and forestry	0.12	4	3.15	6
Bunker fuels	0.02	1	1.13	2
Total	**3.22**		**50.03**	

Source: Climate Watch, http://cait.wri.org/.

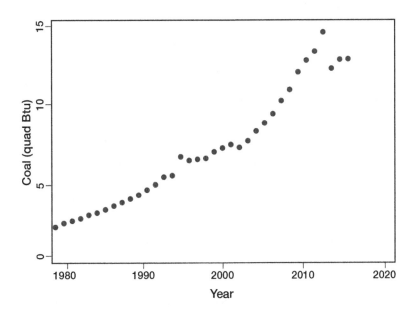

FIGURE 2.4 Coal consumption in energy use in India, 1980–2015.

Data source: United States Energy Information Administration, https://www.eia.gov/international/overview/world.

Future trends point in the right direction, but change is slow. Renewable energy has recently begun to reduce investment in coal-fired power generation. Thanks to falling generation costs, favorable policy, and a mature industry, India has become a global leader in renewable energy deployment. The government's target of 450 gigawatts of renewable power generation capacity by 2030 has come with government tenders that allocate large, utility-scale renewable energy projects to lowest bidders under certain quality criteria.

There is a significant difference between slower growth and actual reductions in coal-fired power generation. India's industry and commerce remain heavily dependent on coal-fired power generation for their daily needs, and there are few signs that the central and state governments, which own about half of the country's power generation capacity, would shut down coal-fired power plants anytime soon unless they approach the end of their useful lifespan. For India, a more likely scenario is one of slow growth in coal-fired power generation, mostly relying on existing capacity with modest replacements of the oldest and most inefficient plants. Most of the new capacity will be renewables—wind and solar power—but until battery storage and other technological advances make wind and solar dispatchable, and thus available in any season and at any time of the day, massive reductions in coal-fired power generation are unlikely, considering India's growing electricity demand.

A common misconception about India's coal-fired power generation is that because huge numbers of planned projects have been canceled, India is rapidly moving away from coal. The reality is that in 2019 Indian coal-fired power plants ran at 55 percent of their theoretical capacity. The government's own long-term goal is to increase this number to 85 percent. If the government were to only replace retiring plants with new ones to keep the capacity at about 200 gigawatts, Indian coal-fired power generation could increase by 40 percent.

A report by Rahul Tongia and Samantha Gross published by Brookings India offers a useful baseline for India's demand for coal-fired power generation.[53] They assume that India's electricity demand will grow at a 6.45 annual compound rate, from 1,149 billion kWh in 2017 to 2,574 billion kWh by 2030. At this growth rate, total need for power generation would grow by 120 percent. If India were to reach 350 GW of renewable capacity and run it at a typical 22 percent capacity factor, coal-fired power generation would have to grow by 80 percent to meet the demand gap left by renewables. If coal-fired power generation were to stabilize at 240 GW, its average capacity factor would have to increase to 77 percent from 56 percent in 2017. Thus even rapid increases in renewable energy capacity would not be enough to stop growth in coal-fired power generation.

An insightful analysis from the Institute for Energy Economics and Financial Analysis illustrates the profound importance of India's peculiar load profile for electricity demand over the day.[54] Because India is one of the hottest countries in the world and industrial electricity demand is limited, the Indian power demand peaks sharply late at night, when people are at home and switch on air conditioners, coolers, fans, and other electric appliances. The exact shape of the demand curve over a typical day varies between seasons, but the common denominator is an evening peak after the sunset. Demand tends to be lowest during the early morning hours, when most people are in bed, and then peak once in the morning and again in the evening, with another low point in the afternoon. This pattern is shown in figure 2.5.

The implications of this load profile for renewable energy integration are far-reaching. While India is fortunate to benefit from both wind and solar power, we have seen earlier that most of the current growth is in solar power, whereas the wind sector is more mature and has less future potential. The problem is that India's load profile implies any growth in solar power generation does not coincide with the greatest need after sunset. India's load profile is already heavily concentrated at night, and growth in air-conditioning could contribute to an even more uneven twenty-four-hour pattern, with sharper peaks when families gather in homes and switch on their air conditioner.

A variety of demand-side management solutions could reduce pressure on the Indian power system at peak time. Improvements in air conditioner efficiency could be a critical piece of the puzzle. Changes to default settings can make indoor temperatures follow outdoor air temperatures. Such

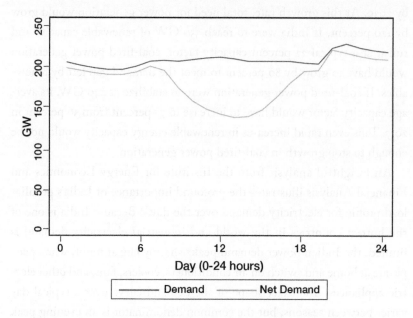

FIGURE 2.5 Typical daily demand and net demand (excluding renewables) in India.

Source: Soonee et al. (2019).

changes could be encouraged with dynamic electricity pricing, such that consumers pay higher prices when demand is high and supply is low. Unfortunately, India does not yet have a dynamic pricing system.

The most important technological solution to variable power is storage. To support India's ambitions to install 500 gigawatts of renewable power capacity by 2030, expanded storage capacity is essential. According to NITI Aayog and the Rocky Mountain Institute, annual demand for battery storage could range from 106 to 260 gigawatt-hours across all sectors of the economy.[55] Both the central and state governments are now developing policies to promote battery storage. India also has formulated a National Hydrogen Mission and a National Hydrogen Policy, with a focus on producing green hydrogen with renewable power. India has recently seen success with standards-based strategies for energy efficiency.[56] The Bureau of Energy Efficiency (BEE), which was formed in 2002 to oversee the implementation of the Energy Conservation Act of 2001, prepared an Energy Conservation Action Plan that focused on standard setting. The act gave BEE a powerful mandate to set standards for new buildings and appliances, and to impose energy consumption norms on large consumers such as industry. BEE's standards have proven successful, as they avoided over five gigatons of power generation capacity between the years 2007 and 2010, according to the IEA.[57] Because India's construction needs and appliance sales are already substantial and rapidly growing, standards for new buildings and appliances can be powerful. They are also relatively easier to enforce than complex policies, which is important given India's limited institutional capacity.

Overall, India's energy efficiency has continued to improve at an impressive rate. According to the World Development Indicators, in 1991, when the reform era was just beginning, India spent 8.5 megajoules of energy for every dollar of output (2011 constant prices, adjusted for purchasing power parity). By 2015 this energy intensity had decreased to 4.5. Between 2000 and 2017 India's energy efficiency policies, which cover 23 percent of energy use, avoided a 6 percent increase in total energy use.[58]

As for supply-side solutions, carbon capture and sequestration remains a distant dream for India. As Gupta and Paul note, India's approach to this technology can be described as "cautious," even though avoiding future emissions in the power sector and industry will be very difficult without this technology, considering coal's continued dominance.[59] Without a high carbon price, energy and industrial companies simply do not have the incentives to invest in expensive technologies regardless of their climate mitigation merits.

Although the Indian government and Indian industry have expressed interest in applications of carbon capture, they have not yet been tried on a commercial scale. This is not surprising, as India does not currently have policies that would put a price on carbon. There is no business case for carbon capture without such policies. Carbon capture is a largely precommercial and very expensive technology, so it would require a high carbon price or other policies that constrain carbon emissions from the Indian power sector. Concerns with air pollution would not drive such policies. Today, no such policies are on the horizon.

The fundamental challenge, then, is one of a gradual but rapid transition away from coal and toward sustainable energy sources. A steady expansion of renewable energy, along with policy measures and new technology, to deal with the problem of intermittency—modern renewables are available only when the sun shines and the wind blows—can over time mitigate and reduce India's reliance on coal. While there is little that India can do to rapidly transition from a coal-based power sector to a renewables-based power sector, a gradual transition is both feasible and desirable. The long-term benefits of reducing dependence on coal include climate change mitigation, air pollution, and energy security.

Transportation is another important and rapidly growing source of carbon dioxide emissions. Although I noted earlier that oil is responsible for only 25 percent of all fossil fuel combustion emissions in India, and much of this consumption falls outside the transportation sector, the trend is clear: in 2016, for example, oil consumption grew by 10 percent. This growth pattern is shown in figure 2.6. While growth in electricity consumption remains uncertain, oil consumption will continue to grow fast unless India makes major strides in electric vehicles, public transit, and better mobility planning.

Growing demand for motorized transportation and air traffic, as well as diesel generator use, contribute to the rapid growth trend. These sectors expand as Indians purchase cars, trucking increases, and aviation becomes increasingly affordable:

> In India, urban road passenger transport consists of road passenger and road freight transport travel demand. Road passenger transport is made up of passenger-carrying vehicles such as motorcycle, scooters, cars, and buses, whereas road freight transport demand consists of trucks and heavy diesel vehicles which carry only goods. Similarly, rail transport also consists of passenger and freight travel demand. The [annual] growth rate of road passenger transport demand (which is passenger kilometers traveled) is 11% from 1831.6 billion passenger kilometers in 2000 to 6351.2

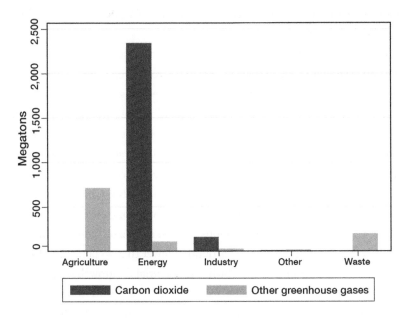

FIGURE 2.6 Oil consumption and production in India, 1,000 barrels/day.

Source: BP (2018b).

billion passenger kilometers in 2012. For road freight transport demand, the growth rate is 8% from 467 billion tonnes kilometer in 2000 to 1212.4 billion tonnes kilometers in 2012.[60]

With the exception of an extensive railway network, India's public transportation is not able to meet growing demand for mobility. Across India's cities, including metropoles like Delhi and Mumbai, public transportation is in a sorry state.[61] While private vehicle ownership has surged, the bus fleet has fallen farther and farther behind. In 1951 there was a bus in India for every nine vehicles. By 1991 there was a bus for every fifty vehicles; by 2011 this number had reached ninety. Even as massive population growth and rapid urbanization have made the case for public transport ever more compelling, the role of buses in urban transit has declined. Indian cities lack a coordinated approach to developing public transport, as authority is fragmented across multiple agencies. Transport planning is not combined with land use planning.

India's market for electric vehicles also remains nascent. In 2018 the share of electric vehicles in new sales of cars and two-wheelers was below 1 percent. The Indian government hopes to increase this share to 30 percent by 2030 and to have all new sales in EV instead of the internal combustion engine. It remains unclear how this goal will be met. Except for modest conventional subsidies, India does not have an integrated plan for developing an EV system with charging infrastructure and competitive markets.

While India is not the industrial powerhouse that China is, there is enough inefficient and polluting industrial activity for concern. The Indian industry emitted only 164 million tons of CO_2 and 32 million tons of CO_2 equivalent in fluorinated gases, contributing fewer than 10 percent of India's total greenhouse gas emissions.[62] Still, the potential for growth here is large. As China's labor costs continue to rise, India can draw foreign direct investment in industry. In September 2014 Prime Minister Modi launched the Make in India scheme to expand industrial production in India. To the extent that the scheme succeeds and such investment goes to energy-intensive and resource-intensive sectors, the potential for environmental degradation will grow. On the other hand, growth in Indian manufacturing could also play a globally significant role in promoting battery storage, electric vehicle development, and other new clean technology industries without powerful incumbents.

Indian industry has varying prospects for climate mitigation. Busby and Shidore examine three major segments of the industry. They note that the Indian steel industry operates at low levels of energy efficiency, meaning that technological improvements alone can help bend the emission curve. In contrast, the Indian cement and fertilizer industries already operate close to the global technology frontier.[63] India is not, overall, a heavily industrialized country, but demand for steel, cement, chemicals, and other basic industrial goods will continue to grow with the economy.

In agriculture, forestry, and land use, most emissions originate from livestock and rice. If agriculture is responsible for about one-fifth of all greenhouse gas emissions, within agriculture livestock is responsible for about

60 percent and crops for about 40 percent.[64] Of all crop emissions, rice alone was responsible for about one-half.

As agricultural production grows to keep up with population growth and changing diets, notably increased consumption of meat, India will need mitigation solutions. The good news for Indian agriculture is that solutions are readily available.[65] Three simple, cost-saving measures—efficient use of nitrogen fertilizer, adopting zero-tillage farming, and improving the management of rice water—would together reduce emissions by over 40 megatons annually. All these solutions are consistent with a more efficient future for Indian agriculture and bring many cobenefits, from cost savings to reduced groundwater depletion.

The challenge with implementing these agricultural measures is the highly fragmented nature of the sector. Indian farmers are an incredibly diverse group, ranging from large landowners producing cash crops for exports to marginal farmers who barely manage to grow enough food to feed their own families. This fragmentation makes implementation of climate-friendly solutions difficult at scale, as farmers face different challenges and incentives. To summarize, India's contribution to climate change today is still modest, yet it is growing fast. Historically, India's primary source of greenhouse gas emissions has been coal burning, but in the future much of the growth will come from increased petroleum consumption. India's greenhouse gas emissions will undoubtedly continue to grow, but the rise of renewables along with new opportunities in electrified transportation, energy efficiency, and farming practices give hope for a more climate-friendly future.

CLIMATE CHANGE: INDIA AS A VICTIM

India is not only a source of greenhouse gas emissions, it is also among the most vulnerable countries to climate change. A special report on South Asia by the Climate & Development Knowledge Network (CDKN) in 2014 paints a dire picture of the future. It notes flood damage, food and water shortages, and heat waves as particularly important threats. The report states, "Climate change poses a moderate threat to current sustainable development and a severe threat to future sustainable development. . . . Added to other stresses such as poverty, inequality or disease, the effects of climate change will make sustainable development objectives such as food and livelihood security, poverty reduction, health and access to clean water more difficult to achieve in many environments and societies."[66]

India's vulnerability to climate change has two closely related sources. First, South Asia as a region is sensitive because of geographic and atmospheric conditions, as well as its high population density. Second, India remains a very poor country, with most people directly or indirectly dependent on agriculture for their livelihoods. The South Asian condition means climate change will bring rapid changes to the region; poverty means India will have great difficulty adapting to these changing circumstances:

> Agriculture is a key driver of economic growth in Asia including in South Asia. Projections indicate that floods, droughts and changes in seasonal rainfall patterns could negatively affect crop yields, food security and livelihoods in vulnerable areas. Projections indicate that rural poverty in South Asia could continue to be more widespread than urban poverty for decades to come. Indeed, rural poverty in parts of South Asia could rise because of poor rice harvests, and high food prices and living costs.[67]

Or, as Srinivasan puts it, "In India, climate change will have more adverse impact as compared to many other countries. This is because India has a higher population density, larger spatial and temporal variability of rainfall, and more poor people who are vulnerable to climate variability."[68]

One major problem is heat waves and droughts.[69] In a tropical country where two-thirds of the population are farmers or work in agricultural labor, extreme weather events can be devastating. Not only do extreme temperatures have a direct negative impact on human health through dehydration, strokes, and similar problems, but droughts also present a chronic and worsening threat to food security. Indeed, over the past sixty years the Indian monsoon itself has grown more erratic and declined in many areas.[70]

Although India's agriculture is now mostly dependent on groundwater, the monsoon remains an essential source of free water for growing plants. As the monsoon grows more erratic, farmers must either use less water or put more money into pumping groundwater, making the country's groundwater depletion problem worse.

In India, farmer suicides have for decades been a major social problem in rural areas. Every year more than 100,000 farmers commit suicide, and many commentators attribute these deaths to economic distress, such as defaults on bank loans.[71] A study conducted by researchers at the University of California, Berkeley, found a strong association between temperature and farmer suicides in India. Using forty-seven years of data for suicide records and climate data, it found that reduced crop yields due to higher temperatures increase the suicide rate. Over the past three decades, the research attributes 59,000 suicides to global warming.[72] While the specific causes of this association are unclear, the combination of direct distress from extreme heat and damage to crops appears to contribute to India's farmer suicide problem. Indian agriculture is already under serious stress, and climate change might well be the straw that breaks the camel's back.

Sea level rise and floods present another major vulnerability. The United Nations Global Environmental Outlook (GEO-6) estimates that by 2050, 40 million Indians will be threatened by sea level rise.[73] At the same time, more than 200 million Indians will live in low-elevation coastal zones by 2060 and over 60 million in flood plains.[74] These populations face a direct threat from sea level rise and may need to migrate to other parts of India, further contributing to environmental problems associated with high population densities and lack of planning.

For India, climate change thus presents a major future threat. According to a study conducted in 2015 by the Indian Institute of Management in Ahmedabad (IIM-A) and the Council on Energy, Environment and Water (CEEW) in New Delhi, India needs to invest an additional trillion U.S. dollars to adapt to climate change until 2030—over US$60 billion annually.[75] From that time, the need to invest will likely grow even further. Although both the central and state governments in India are already investing in adaptation, the gap between what is needed to achieve goals such as poverty alleviation remains wide. Climate change continues because of little progress in mitigation and carbon abatement across the world.

A report by Moody's Analytics further confirms India's high vulnerability to climate change.[76] Among the twelve largest economies, India fares by far the worst, with a projected reduction of 2.5 percent in GDP by 2048 in an aggressive scenario that sees global temperatures increase by over 4 degrees Celsius by 2100. This reduction may seem small, but it bears remembering that the models used to assess climate-related damages fail to consider second-order consequences such as social conflict and inequality. More significant than the predicted GDP loss is the fact that no other major economy faces such a high level of vulnerability to climate change

Within India, regional inequality in vulnerability to climate change is stark.[77] In particular, North India compares poorly to the South and the northeastern mountain states. The reason for this poor performance is a combination of (1) climate sensitivity from droughts, heat waves, and water scarcity and (2) low adaptive capacity due to widespread poverty and a lagging economy.

Case studies from two districts—Jhalawar in Rajashtan and Anantapur in Andhra Pradesh—show these dynamics in action. In both cases, droughts have caused substantial crop reductions, and farmers have failed to adapt to the situation because of weak institutional structures that would allow measures such as shifting to drought-resistant crops or increasing irrigation. The situation is further compounded by forces of economic globalization, which make farmers vulnerable to commodity price fluctuation.

The link between rural poverty and climate change is critically important. Large segments of the Indian population remain directly dependent on harvests, and no sector of the economy is as vulnerable to climate change as agriculture. While adaptive measures are available, impoverished farmers lack the resources to adopt them. To the extent that climate change exacerbates rural poverty, it also undermines adaptive capacity, triggering a vicious cycle that is hard to break.

This gloomy outlook notwithstanding, India's capacity to respond to climate-related disasters appears to be improving. Consider the eastern state of Odisha, which is relatively poor and highly vulnerable to climate disruptions. When it was hit by the Orissa Cyclone in October 1999, about ten thousand people died as a result. Over one million homes were destroyed, and crop losses were widespread. Overall, it was a real calamity.

Odisha was hit in April 2019 by another very powerful cyclone, Fani. This time, however, government officials were prepared. Meteorologists tracked the cyclone, and state officials evacuated over 1.2 million people on short notice. A thousand emergency workers and 43,000 volunteers worked on the evacuation, and the state government launched a massive information campaign, including 2.6 million text messages, to inform people in the affected areas of the need to evacuate. Fewer than one hundred people died because of Fani.

Odisha's experiences with two powerful cyclones twenty years apart are important because they show that India's capacity to respond is improving. A combination of better technology—both meteorological (satellites) and communications (widespread mobile phone penetration)—and higher incomes and state capacity has enabled Odisha officials to respond to natural disasters in a far more effective manner than before. In 1999 the state government was not able to predict the cyclone's trajectory and effectively communicate to the population that evacuation was necessary. In 2019 the state government succeeded in both tasks and likely saved a large number of lives. While reconstruction was still costly and the cyclone caused a lot of suffering, the most important kind of loss— human lives—was almost entirely avoided. This success story should be a source of inspiration and hope for anyone who worries about India's ability to withstand rapid climate disruption in the coming decades. Technology will continue to improve, and economic growth appears to be robust for now.

To be sure, India's growing economy enhances the country's ability to adapt. As India's wealth levels continue to grow, technology, from sea walls to drought-resilient crops and air conditioners, will help mitigate the worst impacts of climate change. But the highly unequal nature of India's growth story so far raises concerns. It is far from clear that India's vast majority, most of whom are rural and poor, can cope with the extreme temperatures and other effects of climate change in the future.

In the worst case, however, climate change could become a major contributor to this gap. If climate change reduces economic growth and increases poverty, India's ability to generate resources for adaptation is curbed. That lack of adaptation could, in turn, further undermine prospects for economic development and poverty alleviation.

This vicious cycle is a major threat to India's future well-being. Adaptation is costly, and failure to adapt is a major threat to economic development. India needs to grow fast enough to allocate resources to adaptation, and this adaptation needs to be planned and implemented for a high level of effectiveness. If the economy stops growing or the fruits of such growth do not add to adaptive capacity, perhaps because of inequality or corruption, India will face the vicious cycle of slow economic growth due to climate disruption. The resulting damage would have global repercussions, considering how important India is as a future engine of the world economy.

For India, climate change is a bitter pill to swallow. Indians are not, as a nation, historically responsible for climate change, and yet they suffer some of the worst impacts because of South Asia's unique geography and high population densities. The very poverty that makes India a historically unimportant contributor to climate change makes adaptation a daunting challenge. Within India, the wealthiest one-third now contributes as much as half of total carbon. Under these conditions, there is a latent domestic political conflict over climate change. While poor farmers suffer from droughts and heat waves, the middle class contributes to these problems and protects itself with energy-hungry air-conditioning. As a result, the gap between the experiences of the wealthy and the poor could widen and generate hostility.

India today is not prepared for the alarming impacts of rapid climate disruption, yet its own contribution to the problem, while at most moderate today, is expected to continue to grow. Indian climate politics will become more salient and contentious in the future, as the simplistic narrative of climate change as a future problem caused by wealthy white people will lose traction in the face of a rapidly changing reality.

To summarize, India's role in global change is complex. India's massive size makes it an important contributor, and its emissions grow faster than those of any other major emitter. And yet per capita emissions remain so low that it is hard to conceive of a future in which Indian emissions would not continue to grow for decades, barring unprecedented technological progress. But while India can make a compelling case for protecting its carbon space, it is also exceptionally vulnerable to climate change. Already today, record heat waves and droughts highlight India's vulnerability and raise the political salience of climate change as an issue.

GROUNDWATER DEPLETION

When I visited Punjab to interview farmers in 2015, I saw the environmental consequences of bad policy in India. The state gives farmers free electricity for groundwater pumps, and many farmers had bought devices that automatically switched on their massive pumps the very second electricity became available. These devices ensured that major landholders, who could afford large pumps, could maximize the immediate benefits of free electricity and deplete scarce groundwater resources as fast as possible. Some of them told me that they were not worried about the problem because they did not expect their children to stay in the village. For them, it made more sense to use all available groundwater now and let future farmers worry about the resulting crisis.

India's agriculture is heavily dependent on groundwater for its irrigation. Surface water now amounts to less than one-third of India's irrigation need, as much of India's productive agriculture is in semiarid areas and cannot survive without copious amounts of groundwater.[78] In Punjab, the state known as India's bread basket, the annual rainfall available for agriculture in 2013 was only 9.51 million acre-feet. Considering only rice production, this left the state with a deficit of 39.23 million acre-feet for agriculture alone. Only about one-fifth of the water required for rice production was met with rainfall.[79]

Unfortunately, India's groundwater resources are being rapidly depleted.[80] When the Central Ground Water Board conducted its groundwater resource assessment in 2013, it found that out of the 6,584 assessment units that span India, "1034 has [sic] been categorized as Over-exploited, 253 as Critical, 681 as Semi-critical." In other words, over 30 percent of India already faced a critical groundwater situation. Equally troubling, the areas under threat were heavily concentrated in a few states. In Punjab, only 26 out of 138 blocks were considered safe; in Rajasthan, only 44 out of 248 blocks were safe. In the South, the state of Tamil Nadu had only 429 safe blocks out of 1,139. In these states, groundwater depletion has reached dangerous levels across large areas.

The depletion is driven by irrigation for agriculture, so depleted areas tend to play an important role in producing food for the Indian population. Indian agriculture is heavily concentrated in key producing states, such as Punjab and Haryana in the North. The irony here is that these states are semiarid, and their agriculture is already dominated by groundwater irrigation, as opposed to canals or rainfall.[81] Figure 2.7 shows the extent of baseline water stress in India. Based on research conducted by the World Resources Institute in 2019, the figure shows the ratio of water withdrawal to supply in percentage. Any aquifer with a ratio in excess of 40 percent is considered high. A ratio in excess of 80 percent is extremely high and indicates an imminent threat. According to this research, over one-half of India is now classified as being under high or extremely higher water stress.

The origins of India's groundwater crisis can be traced back to the Green Revolution, which saved India from famine in the 1960s.[82] When high-yield varieties of different crops, most importantly wheat and rice, arrived in India, productivity increased dramatically—and so did agricultural inputs. By increasing the productivity of land, the Green Revolution relaxed the most important constraint to growth in food production. In the state of Haryana, for example, average grain yields per hectare grew from 630 kilograms to 1,370 kilograms between 1966 and 1992—more than a doubling of agricultural productivity.[83]

The trouble with the Green Revolution was, and still is, the huge amounts of fertilizer and water that high-yield plant varieties consume. In 1966 India consumed only 0.8 million tons of fertilizer; this number climbed to 16.8 million tons by 2004.[84] Meanwhile, groundwater irrigation increased from

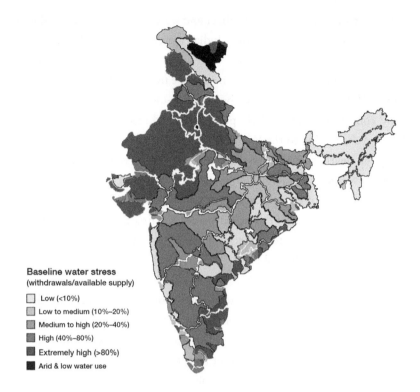

Baseline water stress
(withdrawals/available supply)

☐ Low (<10%)
▨ Low to medium (10%–20%)
▨ Medium to high (20%–40%)
▨ High (40%–80%)
▨ Extremely high (>80%)
■ Arid & low water use

FIGURE 2.7 Water stress in India: withdrawal as percentage of supply.

Data source: World Resources Institute, Aqueduct 3.0. (2019), https://www.wri.org /aqueduct. Data missing for Andaman and Nicobar and Lakshadweep Islands.

below 25 cubic kilometers per year in 1960 to over 250 cubic kilometers in 2010, exceeding any other country by a wide margin.[85]

Recognizing this need for massive inputs from the very beginning, the Indian government embarked on an epic rural electrification drive.[86] Government policies that encouraged the trend included heavily subsidized credit for agricultural investment, public investment in transmission and distribution, and electrification targets for both villages and pumpsets. In many states, agricultural producers expanded their political influence and secured heavily subsidized electricity for irrigation.[87] The results were clear: between 1965 and 1980 the number of electrified pumpsets in India climbed from less than one million to almost eight million.

This voracious appetite for fertilizer and water has, over time, produced a very generous system of subsidies. Indian agriculture is heavily subsidized for virtually every input, from fertilizers to electricity and market access through agricultural cooperatives. In 2007 the total subsidy on fertilizer had reached INR 225 billion (US$5.7 billion, end-of-year exchange rate). As a result, consumption of fertilizer per hectare had reached 105 kilograms as of 2004.[88] According to the World Development Indicators, in 2016 it was 166 kg, or clearly above the world average of 141 kg. In the United States, the 2016 average was 139 kg.

The evolution of electricity subsidies in Indian agriculture sheds light on the political origins of the subsidy issue. The first time a state politician promised free electricity to farmers was as early as in the 1970s, in the southern state of Andhra Pradesh:

> In its efforts to get re-elected in 1977 after the tumultuous time of Emergency, the Congress Party offered a flat-rate tariff and electricity subsidies to farmers as an election promise. Electricity subsidies became even more prominent in the elections of 1983, the first elections in Andhra Pradesh in which a regional party was able to challenge Congress rule. . . . The emergence of electricity subsidies in Andhra Pradesh and other states in the late 1970s has to be seen in the context of the Green Revolution, which started in the mid-1960s, and the debate about declining terms of trade that emerged in the 1970s. The provision of surface-water irrigation and electricity for groundwater irrigation was an essential condition for the Green Revolution. When electricity connections for pump sets were first introduced, they were metered, and farmers had to pay a volumetric price.[89]

Since then, electricity subsidies have become commonplace in India. From Punjab to Andhra Pradesh and, most recently, Telangana, farmers enjoy free or heavily subsidized electricity.[90] Agricultural electricity subsidies encourage farmers to use large amounts of groundwater for irrigation and to invest in thirsty but profitable crops such as rice. As groundwater levels continue to decline, the energy needed to pump a liter of groundwater grows, contributing to additional political pressure to continue electricity subsidies. This vicious cycle drives India toward a groundwater crisis.

In addition to these two subsidies, India's farmers benefit from the minimum support price (MSP) system. The Indian government sets the prices of agricultural products, and these prices are uniform across Indian states. They encourage farmers to cultivate crops with high administrative prices. Perversely enough, water-thirsty crops—in particular rice—tend to be profitable under the Indian system. The Indian minimum price support system, which does help farmers by offering stable and predictable prices, thus contributes to groundwater depletion because it is not tailored to the resource situation at local levels. The central government sets the minimum price, regardless of whether the soil and other conditions are suitable for a specific crop in an area. This uniformity results in groundwater depletion, as farmers do not have an incentive to choose crops that are suited for their land in the long run.

In essence, the Indian government is responding to a raging fire by pouring gasoline all over it. Groundwater depletion is already a serious concern for farmers, and government policies offer relief but in a way that makes the problem worse over time. India's central and state governments have not only failed to stop the alarming trend of rapid groundwater depletion but have instead contributed to a rapid downward spiral that threatens Indian agriculture, food security, and society as a whole.

The future trends are alarming. A comprehensive analysis by Zaveri et al. finds that even those areas that will benefit from higher rates of precipitation because of climate change will grow increasingly dependent on groundwater extraction in the future as irrigated area grows due to greater food production.[91] In other words, the rapid growth in demand for food, because of both population growth and changing dietary preferences such as increased meat consumption, dominates over benefits from increased precipitation. The situation, of course, is far worse where climate change is expected to undermine farm production through droughts and heat waves.

As a result, barring major policy changes or technological breakthroughs, groundwater depletion will likely continue to accelerate in the future, putting India's food security at risk and elevating the risk of domestic and regional conflicts over water resources. In an evaluation of this problem, Sekhri finds that a lack of groundwater access is already contributing to rural poverty and irrigation disputes in rural India.[92] As droughts are prolonged and groundwater reserves already under stress, the potential for social conflict, and potentially civil war, will continue to grow. Groundwater scarcity, then, must be considered among the greatest threats to human security in South Asia over the coming decades.

As these problems grow more severe, the potential for large-scale social conflict, including violence, increases. Water is a necessary input for food production, and there is no substitute for it. As India's groundwater levels fall while population grows, the country's food security deteriorates. In the worst-case scenario, India may return to the bad old days of looming famines thwarted by massive food imports. Today such a scenario is not yet in the cards, but a continued failure to curb groundwater use for irrigation combined with population growth, a more resource-intensive lifestyle in an expanding middle class, and rapid climate change could transform the situation in the coming years.

Solutions to the problem are elusive. Technological fixes, such as drip irrigation, are unlikely to shape the fundamental incentives as long as the cost of water is low because of the price distortions that extreme subsidies produce. Effective solutions, such as changes in administrative prices, electricity subsidy reductions, or constraints on groundwater use, seem to be as difficult as ever. It might be that a widespread crisis of water access is required for a true course correction, and at that point much of the damage would already be done.

PERSISTENT ENERGY POVERTY

If India's environmental degradation had in fact lifted 1.3 billion out of energy poverty, perhaps the sacrifice would have been worth it. Alas, energy poverty remains a persistent problem in India. Especially in rural areas,

TABLE 2.4 Energy Poverty in India

VARIABLE	2001	2011	2017	2019
Household electrification (%)	55	67	84	97
LPG as primary cooking fuel (%)	19	29	61	71

Sources: 2001/2011 Census of India; Saubhagya Dashboard; PMUY Dashboard; Agrawal et al. 2021.

Indians neither have access to reliable electricity nor use clean cooking fuels that minimize indoor and outdoor air pollution.

Table 2.4 offers some basic data on India's energy access problem. The table shows two key trends. First, progress in household electrification has been rapid. Already in 2017, India had electrified 84 percent of its households, and by 2019 this number had reached 97 percent. Second, there is still a long way to go for LPG adoption. Although exact figures are not available, it is safe to say that the majority of Indian households now have access to LPG, though exclusive use remains another matter altogether.

Electricity is the more visible face of energy poverty. For decades, India's household electrification rate in rural areas grew only slowly.[93] I have already noted that rural electrification was initially all about agricultural production and the Green Revolution. The rural electrification drive that enabled the Green Revolution notwithstanding, rural electrification rates grew only from 24 to 55 percent between the years 1987 and 2001. At this time, household electrification was not a priority for the government, which focused on economic reform. India was still a very poor country at the time of the Census of India in 2011, and affordability is the single best explanation for low household electrification rates at the time.[94]

All this changed in 2004 with the Rajiv Gandhi Rural Electrification Scheme (RGGVY) initiated by the INC government led by Dr. Manmohan Singh. The Indian government devised this scheme to electrify all villages in India and to offer free connections to households below the national poverty line. It scheme brought rural electrification back to the limelight, though the focus was still mostly on village infrastructure instead of household connectivity.[95] As a result, household electrification rates climbed from 55 to 67 percent in a decade, with almost all that growth recorded between 2005 and 2011. With near universal village electrification and free connections available to the poorest, progress in rural electrification was finally made.

In 2014 the BJP government headed by Narendra Modi continued these efforts, though under a different label—one simply cannot image a BJP leader running a scheme named after Rajiv Gandhi, the son of Indira Gandhi and a popular Congress leader who was assassinated. The Deen Dayal Upadhyaya Gram Jyoti Yojana (DDUGJY) basically continued village electrification and offered free connections for households below the poverty line. The focus at the time was still very much on village electrification, and households were a secondary consideration.

In 2017 the new Saubhagya—Hindi for "good fortune"—scheme both expanded the number of households that qualify for free connections and allowed everyone else to pay a heavily subsidized connection fee of INR 500 (US$7) in ten installments. This scheme set the goal of achieving universal rural electrification among all households willing to pay their monthly bills. It also provided for solar home systems in the most remote villages. The novelty in Saubhagya was the government's emphasis on household electrification. Now that virtually all villages had an electricity connection, the government's attention turned toward electrifying households. Saubhagya began with the assumption that villages now had the distribution infrastructure they needed, and the logical next step would be to encourage households to sign up and begin using electricity.

The government's efforts have begun to pay off: India's rural electrification rate has grown rapidly. In October 2017 India's electrification rate reached 84 percent, and the government planned to electrify every household in India by 2022. In January 2019 the government declared that all households willing to pay for electricity were connected. This would put India's rural electrification rate above 90 percent, though exact numbers are impossible to obtain until the 2021 Census of India.

More difficult is the problem of quality of rural electricity service.[96] While electrification rates continue to increase, having a connection does not guarantee access to a reliable, steady supply of power. A 2014–2015 survey of six states found, for example, that in Bihar (100 million people) and Uttar Pradesh (200 million people) the rural median of daily hours of power was about twelve hours. By 2018 the situation had improved significantly, as a follow-up survey by the same research team found that the median had increased to sixteen hours. This is a significant improvement, though the fact that half of rural households in these six states receive fewer than sixteen hours shows that India still has a long way to go.

The causes of India's rural electricity service problems are found deep in the governance of the power sector. When India began to enjoy the fruits of its groundwater irrigation boom, farmers became dependent on access to affordable inputs such as water and fertilizer that the high-yield varieties required. As described earlier, politicians began to campaign in state elections with populist promises of free or heavily subsidized electricity. Given that agriculture is responsible for as much as one-fourth of India's total electricity consumption, the effect on India's electricity distribution companies, most of which are state-owned, was devastating. The allocation of free or heavily subsidized electricity to farmers and other users resulted in significant losses, as electricity distribution companies supplied power at a price below the actual cost. State governments were forced to frequently bail out electricity distribution companies that were unable to pay their bills.

The consequences of poor service quality are potentially serious. Researchers have found that intermittent electricity supply is an important obstacle to productive growth among rural enterprises.[97] Under low service quality, rural consumers are also unwilling to pay higher electricity prices because they do not feel the service is worth the cost.[98] They may refuse to pay their bills, bribe the collector to reduce the bill, or even steal electricity from the grid. A long-term solution to India's rural electricity woes would require higher prices, measures against electricity theft, and effective billing and payment collection. These measures are hard to implement unless consumers value the service they obtain and develop a social norm against theft and nonpayment.

In a study that our team at the Initiative for Sustainable Energy Policy (ISEP) conducted with Smart Power India Foundation, we investigated these issues in a comprehensive survey of ten thousand rural households and two thousand rural firms across four states of North India: Bihar, Uttar Pradesh, Rajasthan, and Odisha.[99] We found that both households and enterprises consume minuscule amounts of energy. Both the average household and the average firm consumed only about 40 kWh per month, including both electrical and nonelectrical sources, despite the fact that 75 percent of households and 65 percent of firms were connected to the national grid. The typical household and firm would both mostly use electrical energy for lighting and mobile charging, and perhaps running a fan.

While poor quality of service is not the only reason for such low consumption, it is an important obstacle to address. According to our research, improving daily hours of supply by 1 percent increases electricity consumption by the average household by 0.8 percent, holding constant other factors such as household wealth and education.

Whether India can continue to improve electricity service in the coming years remains unclear. Persistent problems in the power sector suggest that the vicious cycle of poor technical and financial performance in the distribution companies could continue, and perhaps grow worse, over time. An effective solution to this problem would have to ensure that electricity distribution companies obtain a fair return, so that they have the motive and means to improve service quality. But given that the electricity distribution companies are mostly under state governments' political control, achieving such a goal will require political decisions that impose costs on farmers and other beneficiaries of underpriced electricity.

There are two perspectives on this issue. One emphasizes the challenge of "electricity as a right," whereby "the social norm that all deserve power regardless of payment . . . generates losses, rationing and unmet demand for electricity."[100] When people see electricity as something that they deserve regardless of payment, the distribution system becomes financially unviable, and service quality is compromised.

Another perspective adopts a more dynamic perspective and emphasizes the social contract between government and the people. Where electric utilities are state-owned, an ideal social contract would be a quid pro quo that delivers high-quality service in exchange for high payment rates. Whereas private companies sell electricity service against a price, public utilities would provide a social good but impose a price that the public considers equitable. The problem is that this system has two equilibria: one with high-quality service and payment, and the other with low-quality service and nonpayment. It is very hard to break the latter equilibrium, as government cannot afford to improve service without payment, and people feel little pressure to pay for low-quality service. What is worse, coordinating measures against power theft across a large number of often poor and uneducated consumers is very difficult, especially when politicians succumb to the populist temptation of promising free electricity for everyone.

There is a ray hope in recent studies that suggest the possibility of replacing the vicious cycle with a virtuous one. Blankenship, Wong, and Urpelainen conduct survey experiments in Uttar Pradesh and find that high levels of social trust increase willingness to pay for service quality improvements.[101] In a similar vein, Kennedy, Mahajan, and Urpelainen find that improved service quality is associated with higher willingness to pay for electricity connections among nonelectrified households across six Indian states.[102] These results highlight the importance of a virtuous cycle based on improved service quality, reduced power theft, and higher willingness to pay. As this cycle continues, the trust relationship between government and citizens improves, making further improvements based on cost-recovering pricing possible.

According to these studies, improvements in rural electricity service could increase people's willingness to pay their bills. As service quality improves, the logic goes, people both begin to consider the government's payment request as more legitimate and ascribe a higher value to a continued, reliable service. Under these conditions, the government could increase electricity tariffs and impose penalties on theft and nonpayment without major political backlash. After all, the government is now upholding its end of the social contract by providing adequate service.

Indian states have experimented with schemes to trigger such a virtuous cycle, but practical implementation has proven challenging. In Maharashtra, one of India's largest states and the home of the finance capital

Mumbai, linking power supply to payments has been a success.[103] The state has classified electricity feeders by the percent of power supplied without payment, with the best class having a percent below 20 and the worst class having a percent above 60. When the distribution company engages in load shedding—planned, scheduled blackouts—it first cuts power to feeders with poor payment records. This scheme has two benefits, one mechanical and the other behavioral. The mechanical benefit is that electricity now goes to feeders with consumers who pay, so losses drop without any change in behavior. The behavioral benefit is that as consumers around feeders learn about the scheme, they have a collective incentive to reduce their losses so that they can receive better electricity service.

Enforcing such a scheme is, however, not straightforward. When researchers from the Energy Policy Institute at the University of Chicago studied an experiment on a similar scheme in the state of Bihar, they found frequent noncompliance with the rules. In fact, at any given time, at least 50 percent of the feeders participating in the study failed to comply with the supply schedule given to them.[104] While weather and technical problems were common reasons, equally important were officials' instructions to disobey the rules or public protests that forced the distribution company's hand. In this context, the virtuous cycle failed.

In contrast, distributed renewable energy—solar mini-grids, home systems, and the like—have so far played a limited role. Although these resources could, in principle, replace the grid in remote locations with low population densities and limited energy demand,[105] they have faced a number of challenges in India. Due to high population densities and aggressive government policy, the electric grid has reached almost every village.[106] When grid infrastructure is already present and household connections either inexpensive or free, households have few reasons not to draw electrical energy from the grid.

Although distributed renewables could still play a role as secondary sources, to be used during a blackout, this role is inherently more circumscribed than the more romantic notion of "leapfrogging" the grid.[107] First, because the vast majority of households also have grid electric connections, they use their backup source only selectively. If they pay by kWh, they minimize their consumption; if they pay a fixed fee or purchase a system, they minimize capacity to provide only emergency services, such as lighting. Second, a secondary power source is not affordable for most households. When distributed renewables play a secondary role in a system saturated by domestic connections that are characterized by low reliability of service, the new technology moves from leapfrogging for the people to a solution in which relatively wealthy rural households who value reliability invest. The poor now have grid electric connections but must deal with a low quality of service.

In the first quarter of 2019, India installed about 260 megawatts of rooftop solar, and cumulative rooftop installations stood at about 3.5 gigawatts.[108] This is quite a low number, as rooftop now amounts to only 12 percent of all solar installations and 9 percent of the 40 gigawatt target for the year 2022. Similarly, distributed renewables lag behind.[109] In 2018 the only distributed solar technology with widespread penetration was solar lanterns, with sales of about 7 million units.[110] In contrast, sales of solar home systems by private players barely exceeded 100,000—a drop in the Indian Ocean.

The problem of clean cooking receives less attention in the media, even though in many ways it is a more serious issue. The vast majority of Indians— two-thirds in 2011—used some form of traditional biomass, overwhelmingly firewood, as their primary cooking fuel. This dependence on wood fuel is a serious social problem. As noted, it produces absurd amounts of indoor air pollution and kills half a million Indians every year. Collecting the firewood also requires a lot of time and effort, which could be used more productively if employment opportunities were more readily available.

Notably, women and children in particular spend significant amounts of time collecting firewood and cooking with it. Because men tend to work outside in the fields or other activities while women cook and take care of the children, indoor air pollution is a particularly serious threat to women and children. For women, direct exposure to air pollution from traditional biomass is a major health risk. For small children, the developmental effects of this air pollution are terrifying. The need to collect firewood also undermines female participation in the labor force and contributes to children's absences from school and poor performance because of exhaustion.

The good news is that the use of LPG in India has grown quite fast over time. In the Census of India in 2001, only 19 percent of households—and only 15 percent in rural areas—considered LPG their primary cooking fuel. In 2011 that number had increased to 29 percent. But that improvement does not mean that people are no longer using biomass. Instead, the vast majority of Indian households with access to LPG now engage in a behavior called "fuel stacking."[111] Even though these households have LPG at home, they continue to use firewood. In fact, many consider LPG a secondary fuel that is used only when tea or small snacks need to be quickly heated. In such a setting, households continue to use large quantities of firewood.

The causes of this "fuel stacking" behavior are complex, but LPG's lack of affordability is a key issue.[112] Firewood remains, for all practical purposes, either very affordable (when purchased from the market) or free (when collected, often by women and children). For households to stop using firewood altogether, they would have to accept the high cost of doing so, even when disposable cash is in short supply. That is a tall order, considering how scarce money is for rural Indian households.

The high cost of LPG, then, means that firewood is only partially displaced. While access to clean cooking fuels improves, the continued practice of fuel stacking means that traditional biomass continues to burn in most households. In fact, only about one in five households with LPG in the ACCESS survey states had switched to the exclusive use of LPG.

In recent years, Prime Minister Modi's flagship scheme to help rural households gain access to LPG has been the Ujjwala scheme. Under this scheme, free LPG connections are provided to households below the national poverty line, as per the socioeconomic caste census of 2011. The initial goal of the scheme was to reach 50 million targeted households and thus bring India close to universal access to clean cooking fuels. By January 2019, however, over 60 million households had received an LPG connection under the Ujjwala scheme.

While the Ujjwala scheme has contributed to a great increase in LPG connections, fuel use remains at a disappointingly low level. The distribution of free LPG connections has created a large number of consumers who use minimal amounts of cooking gas. The reason here is simple: free connection encourages many households to sign up for LPG, regardless of whether they can afford refills over time. In the past, households would pay for an LPG connection only if they expected to be able to refill their cylinders over time. Otherwise the LPG connection fee would be money wasted.

The official Ujjwala portal reports that, as of July 2019, over 70 million households—30 percent of all Indian households—had received a connection through the scheme.[113] Equally important, according to government statistics, 82 percent of all Ujjwala beneficiaries had returned for at least one refill by March 2019.[114] The average number of refills per year, according to IndianOil chairman Sanjiv Singh, is only about three.[115] This number does not compare favorably to the pre-Ujjwala LPG connection average of seven, which itself is not enough for exclusive cooking with LPG. Exclusive cooking with LPG typically requires about one large cylinder—14.2 kilograms of LPG—per month.

This is very bad news from a public health perspective. Recent medical studies show that modest reductions in indoor air pollution produce few public health benefits. Only major reductions, possibly achieved through complete abandonment of traditional biomass, would produce robust gains. The relationship between exposure to air pollution and health is such that only large reductions from India's dangerous baseline levels would move the needle, and such reductions would require minimizing cooking with traditional biomass.

India's energy security challenges add a few layers of complexity. On the one hand, Cameron et al. find that higher LPG prices because of climate policy—in this case, modeled as a carbon price—would have a severe negative effect on clean cooking across South Asia. Specifically, stringent climate policies in the region would increase the cost of LPG by 38 percent. And if LPG costs were to increase, be it because of climate policy or for any other reason, people's incentive to continue biomass use would grow.[116]

On the other hand, increased LPG use would further increase India's import dependence on foreign petroleum products and thus expose hundreds of millions to higher levels of energy security risk. In 2018 estimated Indian LPG imports were over 12 million tons while total consumption was about 23 million tons.[117] While this consumption is still small relative to overall petroleum consumption, its use in households means that hundreds of millions are now directly exposed to price shocks unless the governments decides and manages to keep LPG price down as international petroleum product prices fluctuate.

What about sustainable alternatives to LPG? So far, India's experience with improved cookstoves, which use biomass but burn it in a more efficient, cleaner manner, has been a major disappointment. According to Khandelwal et al., who conducted a sweeping review of India's experience with improved cookstoves, government programs have failed to address rural women's real needs.[118] For decades, various programs have had little success in promoting the adoption and use of improved cookstoves. Problems with the technology and programs supporting it include mismatched priorities (e.g., fuel efficiency versus convenience of cooking), inappropriate design, lack of after-sales maintenance, and basic program implementation.

While induction stoves do not yet play a major role in India, interest in them is growing. As LPG use spreads, researchers and energy access advocates are already looking for ways to reduce the recurring cooking cost, enhance energy security, and limit dependence on fossil fuels. In principle, an induction stove meets all conditions, as long as the electricity it uses is provided by clean energy sources—whether from the grid or in a distributed manner, such as through a solar mini-grid. For India, however, induction stoves do present a challenge because the twenty-four-hour load profile is already heavily biased toward an evening peak. If a hundred million households were to cook using induction stoves, which have wattage in the kilowatts, the evening demand peak would become even sharper. This is hardly a desirable outcome, as it would further complicate renewable energy integration and increase pressure to ramp up coal-fired power generation.

To summarize, India's energy access problem remains severe. While progress in both household electrification and LPG connections has been impressive, the improvements mask grim realities of low service quality in electricity, driven by fundamental political economy problems in the power sector, and low usage rates among households that nominally have access to LPG as a cooking fuel. There is no denying that the Indian government has done an outstanding job expanding household electricity and LPG access, but the substantial gains from extensive electricity use for productive purposes to transform rural economies, along with exclusive use of clean cooking fuels for large improvements in public health, remain elusive today.

There are no easy solutions to India's energy access problem. Governance of the power sector needs to improve to ensure that high-quality electricity supply will be available to rural households in the future, and that these households—along with agricultural producers—pay for their electricity. Improved governance, however, is very hard to achieve unless household incomes rise enough to sustain a virtuous cycle of higher electricity prices for better service. In India's kitchens, the growth in LPG connections has created an opportunity for major progress, but the high cost of LPG fuel relative to firewood, cow dung, and other alternatives discourages households from ending the dangerous practice of fuel stacking.

Over time, a combination of urbanization and rural development could help. Affordability is the most important barrier to improved energy access. Higher household incomes would increase willingness to pay for high-quality electricity service and clean cooking fuels, and this willingness to pay would enable the government to charge higher prices for better service. Urbanization would reduce the cost of service and create nonfarm employment opportunities. But because a fully urbanized India is not a realistic solution anytime soon, rural development is also very important.

ENERGY AND ENVIRONMENT IN MODERN INDIA

This chapter has reviewed three environmental problems and one energy access problem in India. The three environmental problems are relatively new and closely related to energy production and consumption. The energy access problem is ancient, but it turns out that India's newly found economic dynamism has not fully solved the problem. India continues to struggle with energy access and energy security, and these concerns are highly salient in contemporary Indian politics, as national schemes such as Saubhagya and Ujjwala for rural electrification and cooking fuel access, respectively, illustrate. India has not yet solved its conventional energy problems, and yet it faces pressure to reduce its climate impact. No other major emitter faces such a stark dilemma.

Energy and environment in India are closely intertwined. While many other environmental problems exist, it would be hard to argue that over a million deaths from air pollution, the existential threat of climate change in a poor society that depends heavily on agriculture, and rapid groundwater depletion would not feature among the most important for India to tackle. The contrast to historical environmental problems is stark. In India's post-reform era, the energy sector is a central driver of environmental degradation. India has reaped handsome benefits from increased use of modern energy, yet it has also paid a high price for this success.

In the meantime, the continued challenge of energy access shows that the environmental problems are not the flip side of a complete success in providing energy for economic development. India's energy access problem is not nearly as bad as it used to be, but rural electricity service continues to be poor and the quest for exclusive use of clean cooking fuels, as opposed to highly polluting biomass, still mostly elusive. These problems of energy access are, however, touching the lives of India's poor majority, which does not generate many greenhouse emissions beyond virtually unavoidable "survival" emissions.

In this sense, India's environmental challenges from energy have a Janus face. On the one hand, emissions from the Indian middle class, which is still a small minority of the population, grow. The middle class is also expanding, as poverty continues to retreat thanks to sustained economic growth over decades. On the other hand, hundreds of millions of Indians still have limited access to modern energy.

India's environmental problems are to a significant extent driven by the poorly regulated growth in energy use in the post-1991 reform era. Although they are for the most part only a few decades old, they are by now chronic in nature. There are no easy or rapid solutions on the horizon, and the problems continue to grow worse over time.

Why has India suffered from severe and chronic environmental problems with only partial progress in ending energy poverty? The next chapter investigates the societal and institutional origins of India's chronic crisis in energy and environment.

3

GOVERNANCE AND POLICY

The mobile phone is one of India's great success stories.[1] Mobile phones first arrived in India in the mid-1990s, and within a decade they had overtaken landlines by a comfortable margin. Besides the obvious advantages of the mobile phone, both before and after smartphones came to the market, India's success with mobile phones testified to the power of the private sector. India's landline connections had languished for decades, as the inefficient state monopoly failed to meet latent demand with affordable, high-quality service.[2]

But India's mobile phone revolution also highlighted deep problems in the country's energy sector. Because of India's unreliable electricity service, the telecom towers that made mobile telephony possible became reliant on diesel, at a high cost to the economy and environment alike.[3] In 2013 a report by Intelligent Energy estimated that over two-thirds of India's 400,000 telecom towers struggled with power outages in excess of eight hours a day. Forced to consume expensive and polluting diesel, telecom towers spent one-fourth of their entire operating expense in energy. This distorted pattern of energy consumption revealed a massive governance failure in Indian energy.

In more recent years, the solar revolution has found India. Over the years, the cost of solar power generation has decreased rapidly and made sunlight a compelling source of power. Combined with the practice of cross-subsidy in the Indian power sector, however, this golden opportunity has created new problems. This term, *cross-subsidy*, refers to the idea that some consumers pay higher prices to essentially subsidize lower prices for others. Industrial consumers, who currently pay very high electricity prices, now invest heavily in solar rooftop applications. This reduced reliance on the electric grid is a serious blow to the electricity distribution companies, as they face the danger of losing their best customers: industrial users that need large loads of energy and pay high prices for it.

Though very different on the surface, these two stories illustrate the challenge of governing energy and environment in India. On one hand, the explosive growth in mobile phone use and solar power generation demonstrate India's economic dynamism and ability to make things happen. The deep and seemingly intractable problems of the power sector, on the other hand, show the major difficulties of governing the world's largest democracy. India's dynamic entrepreneurs have produced economic growth, but this growth has generated a host of new problems because of limited state capacity.

India's environmental crisis today reflects this imbalance. In the past, poor economic performance minimized the potential for environmental degradation. Today, economic growth generates serious environmental problems, and the government's limited ability to mitigate the consequences results in a crisis.[4] India really needs a capable government to reverse environmental degradation, but the current institutions are unable address the problem.

In what follows, I refer to these core features of the Indian political economy as a *captive society*. Beginning with the ubiquitous diesel generator, which is widely used for "captive" generation at the site, wealthier Indians have found countless innovative private solutions to their problems. Where the state has failed to provide adequate public services, the private sector has supplied a suite of partial and imperfect solutions. These private solutions do not solve the problem, but they provide at least some relief to those with the wherewithal to purchase and deploy them.

As necessary as the private solutions are, they also have a role to play in perpetuating India's environmental crisis. The Indian middle class and industry focus on solving their own problems, instead of engaging in collective action to solve common problems. When someone installs their own groundwater pump, solar home system, or air purifier, their interest in engaging in collective action decreases. They have found relief to their own problem, so solving the country's problem is now less important.

This logic is compounded by weaknesses in the state apparatus. Effective collective action requires a glimmer of hope that things can change. In India, the barriers to effective public policy—whether prescribing desirable or proscribing undesirable behaviors—are high. The Indian state lacks the resources, skilled staff, and freedom from political interference to implement effective policies on the ground. Conflicts between the central government in Delhi and the state governments, along with India's complicated electoral calculus and strong incentives for opportunistic and populist policies, make administrative reform hard to achieve. As a result, India continues to "muddle through."[5] Economic growth produces real gains to the population, but the government faces serious difficulties in trying to direct or control the negative side effects of economic expansion. These include air pollution, carbon dioxide emissions, and groundwater depletion.

In the short and medium run, Indian policy makers have no choice but to accept the limits of policy in their current predicament. Policy making in India is more an art than a science, and there is an urgent need for innovative shortcuts. It is highly unlikely that India will find sustainable solutions to its energy and environmental crisis in the short run. It is far more likely that a patchwork of temporary solutions continues to evolve and prevent the system from collapsing under its own weight, though barely.

In the long run, the space of possibilities is far wider. As the Indian education system continues to move forward in fits and starts, the country's young population is in a far better position to demand public services than their parents were. India's elections have often revolved around caste and religion. A more educated and better informed electorate could put tremendous pressure on politicians to focus on public service delivery, instead of caste and communal politics. Such a change would make all the difference for India's ability to govern energy and environment. If India can take full advantage of its proud democratic tradition, over a billion people will have an unprecedented opportunity to enjoy the fruits of economic growth without a permanent state of environmental crisis.

For clarity, I will divide my discussion into two parts: environmental and energy policy. I separate these two interrelated fields because they serve very different purposes and are, therefore, structured differently. Environmental policy is focused on containing degradation. Energy policy can have huge impacts on environmental degradation, yet the primary goals tend to emphasize abundant and affordable energy.

The first of the sections to come focuses on environmental policy proper. I review the legislative and regulatory frameworks that pertain to air pollution, groundwater depletion, and climate change. The second section focuses on energy policy and related areas insofar they are pertinent to energy-related environmental problems. As we shall see, Indian environmental policies overall are simply too weak to address the problems; energy policies are often strong but poorly crafted and misguided despite the best of intentions.

ENVIRONMENTAL POLICY IN INDIA

In India's federal structure, energy and environmental policies are the responsibility of both the central and the state governments. Interestingly, India's constitution is one of the few in the world that specifically mention environmental protection.[6] The constitution does not specifically address environmental authority and instead allocates environmental subjects to the national and state levels in an ad hoc manner that reflects the political bargaining between proponents of centralized versus decentralized India. In an important revision, the Constitution of 1976 (Forty-Second Amendment) explicitly addresses environmental protection, listing the protection of natural environment as a "fundamental duty" of every Indian citizen. The amended constitution assigns environmental subjects such as sanitation, agriculture, water, and irrigation under state authority. These subjects are governed by state law. The list of subjects governed by federal law, in turn, include such environmentally important subjects as nuclear power, oil production, mining, and interstate rivers. Finally, the concurrent list includes subjects such as forests and, crucially for our purposes, the power sector.

The totality of India's environmental legislation remained thin until the Stockholm conference in 1972. As Dwivedi notes, "Prior to 1972 environmental concerns such as sewage disposal, sanitation, and public health were dealt with by different federal ministries, and each pursued these objectives in the absence of a proper coordination system at the federal or intergovernmental level."[7] This lack of attention, of course, is not surprising. When the Indian federal structure was created, the environment was not yet a topic of serious concern even in industrialized countries. While the Indian constitution has a great deal of specific instruction for the governance of specific sectors, from water to forests, it does not attempt to create a system of environmental governance.

The preparations for the Stockholm conference led to the establishment of a National Committee on Environmental Planning and Coordination (NCEPC), "an apex advisory body in all matters relating to environmental protection and improvement."[8] The creation of the NCEPC was the first concrete step toward the creation of a system of environmental policy under India's federal system. While the NCEPC itself was a weak body with little authority in the Indian political system, at the very least India now had a formal body in charge of designing a system of environmental governance.

The creation of the NCEPC did not, however, result in the kind of legislative activity that one saw in the United States when the Environmental Protection Agency was created. The 1970s were a difficult decade for India, as Indira Gandhi's government descended into authoritarianism under economic pressure and failed socialist policies. Environmental concerns, which mostly originated from the international arena, largely disappeared in the shadow of massive economic hardship and legitimate concerns about the future of Indian democracy under Prime Minister Gandhi's Emergency.

When politics and the economy stabilized in India, planning for environmental governance resumed. In 1981 the Indian government passed the Air (Prevention and Control of Pollution) Act.[9] Drawing on the international decisions of the 1972 Stockholm conference and the institutional architecture created for the Water Act of 1974, the Air Act of 1981 gave the Central and State Pollution Control Boards the authority to control air pollution. This legislation gave states the right to declare "air pollution control areas" and require industries operating within them to obtain permits for continued operation. Initially, the fines were rather modest, but an amendment in 1987 gave the Pollution Control Boards the authority to impose large penalties and even shut down noncompliant facilities. While enforcement remains challenging to this date, the 1987 amendment did allow citizens to initiate proceedings to deal with air pollution. In particular, the judiciary could now react to citizen complaints without waiting for a government request.

A real turning point for India's efforts to stop air pollution was the Bhopal chemical disaster in 1984.[10] Following a massive gas leak enabled by mismanagement and negligence on part of a Union Carbide pesticide plant in Bhopal, over half a million people were exposed to methyl isocyanate, a dangerous gas. Widely considered the world's worst industrial disaster, the Bhopal incident gave a boost to India's efforts to invest in environmental protection and regulate behaviors that might harm the environment and public health. Bhopal left a permanent scar and gave rise to a surge in popular concern about environmental health. It gave policy makers a strong mandate to regulate industrial emissions and impose stronger penalties on violators, who previously had escaped responsibility.

The Environment (Protection) Act of 1986 was an important advance insofar it specified the powers of different authorities to regulate air quality.[11] The act gave a legal foundation to imposing discharge standards on industry and enforcing procedural safeguards, along with "powers of entry and inspection." Failure to comply with the act could result in imprisonment for up to five years. The act also allows the central government to prohibit and restrict "the location of industries and the carrying of process and operations in different areas."

Now India's central and state government had the legal authority to impose rules on industry and act on infringements. Policy makers and regulators now had access to a wider range of instruments than pollution control areas and permits. Both existing and new plants could be regulated, and entry and inspection meant regulatory violations would have consequences. In practice, however, the enforcement of the act has proven difficult. In a field experiment conducted in Ahmedabad and Surat, Gujarat's largest cities, Duflo et al. found that according to audits under the state's environmental regulation model, 93 percent of plants with high pollution potential were in compliance with emission standards. In a back-check monitored by the research team, however, only 41 percent of the plants were in compliance. This is a difference of 53 percentage points, resulting from "auditors [fabricating] data to falsely report plants as narrowly compliant with the regulatory standard."[12]

While conducted in only two cities, there are good reasons to believe such problems are widespread. Gujarat is one of the wealthier states in India, with better regulatory capacity. The plants analyzed belonged to the high-pollution category, a natural focus area for regulators. Considering that the auditors were likely bribed to fabricate the emission audit, such a pattern would likely persistent in lower-capacity states and in industries that are considered less essential from a pollution perspective.

Indeed, environmentalists have criticized India's pollution control system for a weak mandate, inadequate human resources, and low budgets for a long time. In 2009, writing for CSE, Bhushan, Yadav, and Roy examined the functioning of three important State Pollution Control Boards—Maharashtra, Gujarat, and Karnataka—across a wide range of indicators. The analysis revealed a wide range of deficiencies. For example, none of these boards monitored on average even one emission stack per industry producing air pollution between 2001 and 2006. Similarly, the number of inspections per industry ranged from 0.3 (Maharasthra) to 2 (Gujarat).[13] With such low inspection numbers, noncompliant plants have little reason to worry about enforcement.

India's most iconic landmark, Taj Mahal, played an essential role in efforts to draw the public's attention to air pollution.[14] Made of white marble but turned yellow and green because of toxic fumes, Taj Mahal is one of India's most visible victims of air pollution. As Bergin et al. write, when particulate matter accumulates on the Taj's famous white marble surface, it becomes discolored.[15] While most air pollution problems are not highly visible, except when a winter smog descends on towns and villages, the discoloring of the Taj is visible—and deeply disturbing—to millions of domestic and foreign tourists alike.

As early as December 30, 1996, well over a decade before air pollution became a public concern in India, the Supreme Court of India delivered a ruling to protect the Taj from air pollution by banning the use of coal and coke in industry within what is known as the Taj Trapezium Zone (TTZ). An area of 10,400 square kilometers, the TTZ is a special air pollution control area within which industries are not to use coal or coke as a fuel. They must, instead, either secure natural gas supplies, relocate outside the trapezium-shaped area, or shut down. The TTZ is a good illustration of how Indian environmental policy making operates. We saw earlier that emissions audits in Gujarat's industrial hubs have resulted in weak results, as auditors have fabricated the data to protect industrialists from fines and imprisonment—likely in exchange for a lucrative bribe. In the TTZ, the blanket ban on certain fuels makes enforcement a lot easier, as hiding the use of coal and coke is far more difficult than manipulating specific end-of-pipe emissions numbers. Unfortunately the blanket ban has its own limitations. Although designed to maximize effectiveness by considering wind patterns, the trapezium does not fully remove the impact of coal and coke burning, as plants outside the trapezium will continue to emit. Worse, the TTZ's focus on industry in particular leaves other sources of air pollution largely intact.

Another interesting but not very effective experiment was Delhi's "odd-even" scheme. Following the lead of cities like Mexico City, Delhi's chief minister Arvind Kejriwal, who rode to office on an anticorruption wave, welcomed the year 2016 with a rule that allowed cars to run in the city depending on the last digit of their license plate. Vehicles with odd numbers would be allowed on odd dates; vehicles with even numbers would run only on even dates. The idea was to quickly reduce air pollution and congestion from road traffic through a visible rule that was certain to draw a lot of attention.

The results of the scheme were mixed. A study conducted by researchers at India's National Physical Laboratory and the Jawaharlal Nehru University in New Delhi found that air pollution levels continued to climb during and after the first implementation period of the scheme between January 1 and 15, 2016.[16] Delhi's PM2.5 concentration increased from 164 micrograms per cubic meter before the scheme to 187 during and 197 soon after it. While these results do not rule out the possibility of a marginal impact from the scheme, they clearly show that the scheme did not solve Delhi's air pollution problem.

And this, in fact, is the important point. The odd-even scheme illustrates a serious underlying problem with India's approach to air pollution. The problem has multiple sources, spread across many sectors and all of India. Chief Minister Kejriwal's solution focuses on one source in one city, using a blunt instrument. The results were disappointing for people who held unrealistic expectations about the nature of India's air pollution problem.

Fast-forward to 2018, and India had finally upgraded its air pollution policies and regulations.[17] These policies focused on dust control, new command-and-control limits on emissions from power plants, and strengthening of vehicular emission controls. India, finally, had air pollution technology standards for new power plants, technology standards and emission limits for industry, and more stringent automobile and two-wheeler emission standards. And yet India's air pollution framework was still lacking. Air pollution controls did not cover all sources of emissions, and enforcement was poor. Although air quality continued to deteriorate over time, the Indian government did not take action to address the problem. It simply did not face much pressure to take decisive and costly actions. The vast majority of Indians either were unaware of the air pollution problem, quietly accepted it as the price of doing business, or felt there was little they could do.

In late 2018 Prime Minister Modi's cabinet finally announced a National Clean Air Programme.[18] The NCAP consists of enhancements to the national air quality monitoring program, a tree planting drive, and other initiatives. Most important, the NCAP promises to develop city-specific action plans for 102 cities that currently fail to meet national air quality standards. Here the Indian government emphasizes urban areas, where air pollution is a salient problem and high population densities maximize the public health impact of the smog.

These plans are important in a symbolic sense, but their overall effectiveness is rather limited. Air quality monitoring and tree planting do not address the root cause of the problem: emissions. The NCAP does not offer a comprehensive solution that would reduce air pollution across key sectors, from power generation and industry to transportation and residential biomass burning. Focusing on a handful of cities is also hardly an appropriate strategy, when the sources of air pollution are diverse and dispersed across cities, towns, and villages. Considering that the 102 cities identified under the NCAP cover but a fraction of India's air pollution sources, it is unlikely that major reductions in urban air quality would be possible without targeting peri-urban and rural areas around the cities. Or, as researchers at the Centre for Policy Research in New Delhi put it,

> The National Clean Air Programme (NCAP), launched by the Ministry of Environment, Forest and Climate Change (MoEFCC) in January 2019, looms large over the newly elected government's policy landscape. The NCAP identified 102 non-attainment cities—which have particulate matter levels that exceed the annual standards—and set a reduction target of 20–30% by 2024. However, in its approach, the NCAP is a status quo-ist document, which adheres to city specific templates from the past, and wholly misses addressing governance gaps. It reinforces India's policy response to air pollution, which has largely been reactive and overly reliant on administrative solutions. The existing regulatory design has proved to be entirely inadequate to meet the scale of the problem, and the monitoring and enforcement capacity of government agencies (such as the pollution control boards) is insufficient, especially for dispersed sources of pollution like vehicles, stubble and waste burning. An effective air pollution control strategy must break away from

the status quo, and instead strategically prioritize key, implementable actions.[19]

To summarize, India is far from having a functioning system for dealing with the air pollution problem. While China, for example, has made major progress in its "war on pollution,"[20] India is only now taking steps. The Indian administrative system simply does not have a capable agency for dealing with air pollution. The government is not willing to impose harsh penalties on polluters or highly visible costs on consumers. As a result, the air pollution crisis continues, causing over one million premature deaths a year and taking a heavy toll on the country's economy.

While air pollution is a relatively new topic for India, legislation to manage groundwater use goes back to the colonial 1882 Indian Easement Act. The rules for groundwater allocation, initially set by British courts for colonial India, "were established in the context of disputes related to the use of land for mining or other industrial activities." The courts made a clear distinction between surface water and groundwater, thus giving "landowners virtually limitless control over groundwater."[21] This decision continues to characterize—or, better yet, haunt—India's groundwater rules to this date.

In 1970 the Indian government, observing the rapid expansion of irrigation under the Green Revolution, prepared a model bill to improve the management of groundwater. The bill was designed as a flexible framework that states could use to deal with their specific issues. Although revised multiple times between 1970 and 2005, the model bill gave state governments the right to notify areas that require a specific permit for groundwater use. The unfortunate reality is that India's groundwater legislation has even less tooth than its air pollution system. While the 1970/2005 model bill was a serious effort to address the limits of India's hopelessly outdated colonial legislation, it has had little effect on actual groundwater use. The fundamental principle of landowner rights remains intact and all but prevents rules to protect entire aquifers from depletion. Although state groundwater boards can monitor groundwater levels and issue recommendations, they cannot actually stop landowners from depleting aquifers connected to wells on their land. Indian states have, almost without exception, refrained from measures to actually constrain groundwater extraction by farmers and other users.

A particularly troubling feature of the 1970/2005 model bill is that it only requires registration and permits for new groundwater uses. Although new uses are plausible in some of the less developed states in eastern India, such as Bihar, these states tend to have abundant and largely untapped groundwater resources. Where groundwater depletion is already occurring, existing users are grandfathered in and can continue to deplete aquifers without any constraints. Considering that the Indian Green Revolution began already in the 1960s and grew rapidly over the next two decades, the vast majority of farms in India's modern agricultural states have used groundwater for decades. They cannot be subjected to registration and permit processes, even though these are the very areas where groundwater levels are the lowest because of decades of exploitation.

Such a system may have been necessary to build political support for the model bill, but it has made it almost entirely ineffective in solving the problem of groundwater depletion. Indian states are not even able to register existing groundwater uses. India needs to act swiftly and decisively in areas where the Green Revolution, amplified by the perverse incentives created by subsidies for electricity, fertilizer, and thirsty crops, has driven groundwater depletion. Unfortunately, India's groundwater legislation is ill-prepared to enable such action.

One problem India has faced is the legacy of groundwater development, as opposed to management, as the dominant paradigm.[22] When the Indian groundwater system began to grow during the Green Revolution, it had a simple mandate: to accelerate the use of groundwater for irrigation. This task was far simpler than the upcoming challenge of management, as it only required agricultural extension through a variety of subsidies and other support mechanisms.

The problem is that these institutions have, to this date, inherited an internal contradiction. They were originally designed to promote groundwater use, but now the pressure is building to manage it instead. An institution that was designed to enable groundwater extraction has limited ability to do exactly the opposite by preventing farmers, industry, and others from accessing groundwater. The contradiction between original mandate and current need is increasingly a cause of problems, as "the 'common pool' nature of groundwater has created a paradox of groundwater use and problems, particularly in India. While this has enabled a variety of people to access water for various purposes, often under various kinds of duress and hardship, groundwater access has focused on the creation of sources, increasingly running into resource-centric problems at scales of aquifers."[23] This strategy, which focused on expanding the use of groundwater, initially made sense in the context of an impending famine, but over time this approach has not produced good results. The impressive gains in food security and rural development have come at the long-run cost of sustainability.

States have also made various attempts to stop groundwater depletion. For example, in 2002, "Andhra Pradesh . . . adopted the Water, Land and Trees Act, 2002, which constitutes a state-level authority charged with promoting water conservation, regulating the exploitation of ground and surface water, advising the state government on legislative, administrative and economic measures to conserve natural resources, and advising the government on enhancing public participation in these matters."[24] The practical implementation of such principles has proven very difficult, however, and groundwater depletion in the state continues largely unabated. Indian states' limited ability to act on groundwater is a major problem, as the exact nature of the groundwater problem varies significantly across states. The agricultural powerhouses, such as Punjab in the North and Andhra Pradesh in the South, now face a groundwater emergency. Yet others, such as Bihar and Uttar Pradesh of the Hindi belt, would benefit from increased use of groundwater in irrigation. From a governance perspective, it would indeed be ideal if each state could adopt policies tailored to its problems. Alas, Indian states have, almost without exception, done a very poor job at managing their groundwater resources. And while some of this failure can be attributed to the center's weak legislative framework and agricultural pricing policies that drive the cultivation of water-thirsty crops, state governments could do a great deal to contain the damage. If a state like Punjab put a price on electricity, it would discourage excessive irrigation.

For India, climate change is the newest of three environmental problems covered in this volume. Until climate change found its way to the international agenda at the end of the Cold War, there was no discussion of climate change legislation in India. Where environmental problems such as groundwater depletion and air pollution received limited attention, climate change was not even a topic of conversation except in the realm of diplomacy. It is only in the past decade or so, after the Copenhagen climate summit in 2009, that climate change has emerged as a major topic of interest in Indian politics and society.

According to Dubash and Joseph, Indian climate policy can be divided into three periods: pre-2007, 2007–2009, and after 2009.[25] In the pre-2009 period, climate change was exclusively a diplomatic issue, to be handled by the Ministry of External Affairs. Environmental and energy specialists had little say over international negotiations. Career diplomats made decisions based on India's general foreign policy principles, which emphasized neutrality and opposition to Western dominance.

At the Earth Summit in Rio de Janeiro, Brazil, in 1992, India was forced to react to growing international concern about climate change. As Mohan notes, India's position was aligned with the broader Group of 77, the primary negotiation bloc of developing countries.[26] India did not yet see climate change as a real threat but instead focused on defending its sovereignty and accusing industrialized countries of using climate change as a political weapon to constrain development in the global South. In the Kyoto Protocol of 1997, India secured an important victory in that developing countries were entirely exempted from emission reductions. This decision, which I will dissect in the next chapter, legitimized India's emphasis on avoiding emissions commitments and reduced domestic pressure to act. At this time, India's domestic climate policies were nonexistent. As Gupta notes, "At the domestic political level, the climate change issue has been minimally discussed, although the level and depth of the discussions has increased over the years. There has been an implicit agreement that the government can represent the North-South issues, but should avoid discussions on energy, transport and agriculture. Government policy documents do not, in general, give climate change any importance."[27] Indeed, another decade was to go by before India would even actually begin to formulate a domestic policy response to climate change.

For India, one important mechanism enshrined in the 1997 Kyoto Protocol on climate change was the Clean Development Mechanism (CDM), which allowed developing countries to reduce emissions and sell carbon credits according to third-party estimates of the size of these reductions.[28] The CDM is one of the Kyoto Protocol's flexibility mechanisms, designed to reduce the cost of mitigation by allowing project developers to capitalize on low costs in developing countries. Given India's large size and considerable potential for low-cost greenhouse gas emissions, the country quickly established itself as a leading CDM market alongside China and Brazil.[29] The first project was implemented already in 2003, and in 2005 India started 192 new projects. Overall, between 2003 and 2011, India launched 2,178 CDM projects. Of these, 1,426 (65 percent) were based on renewable energy. The carbon credits from the CDM enhanced the profitability of renewable energy at a time when costs were still very high compared to coal-fired power generation.

A major problem with the CDM scheme was the challenge of establishing additionality: Did the carbon credits really contribute new projects that would have failed without the CDM, or did they just enhance the profitability of projects that would have gone ahead without the CDM? Although there is little doubt about the existence of Indian CDM projects, it is hard to establish whether the CDM enabled these projects. After all, it is possible that some of them would have been profitable without any carbon credits, and the CDM amounted to nothing more than an income transfer from industrialized countries to the project developer.

A report by Climate Strategies in 2007 analyzed a sample of fifty-two Indian CDM projects and found several weaknesses in additionality testing. Only half of the analyses explicitly considered alternative projects as a benchmark. Only one-third of them conducted an investment analysis to assess the financial implications of the CDM carbon credits. Other problems include the lack of independent data not originating from the project promoter and a comparison against common practices in the relevant industry. While this report was written using early projects, it highlights the difficulty of additionality considerations in the Indian context. The overall climate impact of CDM projects in India thus remains unclear. It was in the 2007–2009 period that India began developing domestic institutions to govern climate change. While developing countries continued to resist emissions reductions, India, alongside other major developing countries, began to face both domestic and international pressure to reduce emissions. In 2007 Prime Minister Manmohan Singh establish a Council on Climate Change that he personally chaired. The following year, in 2008, India issued a National Action Plan on Climate Change (NAPCC).[30] The document emphasized the priority of "economic and social development and poverty eradication" and proposed the approach of cobenefits, such as reduced air quality or green jobs, as a key pillar of India's climate policy. Recognizing these considerations as central, the plan established eight national missions to improve energy efficiency, promote renewable energy, and build capacity for climate research, but it did not introduce any specific plans or new targets.

Since 2010 Indian climate change institutions have continued to develop.[31] After the Copenhagen climate summit in 2009, the pressure to promise new emission reductions was off, as the failure to agree on a globally binding treaty sent negotiators to regroup. Instead, India's focus was on developing the domestic apparatus to act on Minister Ramesh's Copenhagen promises. A key development was the formulation of State Action Plans on Climate Change to complement the NAPCC. When Ramesh left the Ministry of Environment and Forests in 2011, progress stalled, and coordination between government agencies began to suffer.

In 2014 Prime Minister Modi's new government, which had obtained a majority in the May 2014 general election, added climate change to the portfolio of the small and underfunded Ministry of Environment and Forests. While the addition had symbolic value, adding yet another massive mandate on a small ministry's agenda would make effective implementation virtually impossible. Climate change is a massive challenge that would require significant changes across the entire Indian economy, and tasking one of the less powerful ministries without a major resource expansion suggests a somewhat frivolous attitude.

For India, the 2015 Paris agreement on climate change is an important international reference. India's Nationally Determined Contribution (NDC) emphasized investments in non–fossil fuel power generation capacity, offering to expand it to 40 percent of all capacity by 2030. Prime Minister Modi campaigned internationally for India's leadership position, and India emerged as one of the "good guys" in the Paris negotiations. The Modi administration repeated this performance in the Glasgow climate summit of 2021, announcing a net zero emissions target for India by 2070, only a decade after China's target, and aiming for 500 gigawatts of non–fossil fuel power generation capacity by 2030.

In practice, however, India's climate policies have had only limited impact on the ground. India's climate policies tend to be goals, plans, and announcements without a solid foundation for implementation. India's NDC under the Paris agreement is ultimately quite conservative and mostly reflects preexisting trends in the power sector, with a heavy emphasis on renewable power generation capacity. It does not put much pressure on the government or expose India to significant risk of failure. It also does not feature any new legislative or regulatory solutions that would boost India's weak climate policies.

Dubash and Jogesh evaluate India's state-level climate action plans focusing on Karnataka, Himachal Pradesh, Madhya Pradesh, Odisha, and Sikkim. Their overall conclusion is that these plans missed the opportunity to shape long-term development:

> These shortcomings are united by a common thread—a tendency to prematurely view state climate plans as vehicles for generating implementable actions rather than an opportunity to redirect development toward environmental sustainability and climate resilience. Thin conceptual frameworks, processes that provide no space for generating a vision of change, limited state capacity, and truncated time frames all reinforce this outcome. While concrete actions are indeed important, these may be of limited value unless informed by a broader vision of future directions in key climate-related sectors such as agriculture, water, and energy.[32]

Indeed, to speak of climate policy as an independent orientation is somewhat misleading in India. As Atteridge et al. note, "At each level of decision making in India, climate policy is embedded in wider policy concerns."[33] The central government is concerned about international image, the carbon budget, energy security, cost of energy, and economic development. State governments have less interest in international affairs or carbon budgets, but they are very sensitive to the local concerns of energy security, cost of energy, and economic development. Local governments have even more parochial interests, but similar to other levels of government, they use available opportunities to boost their image as climate leaders, as long as it is not expensive for them.

Similarly, Wu argues that India's climate policy can be understood as a combination of proactive energy security and economic development measures, such as renewable energy development, and shallow reactive measures aimed at mitigating international pressure at a low cost.[34] India has reduced emissions—or, at the very least, constrained their growth—where doing so has served more valued domestic priorities, notably energy security and energy for development. But where climate policy would compromise energy security and/or carry a high cost, such as reducing domestic coal use by using imported natural gas, Indian policy makers have not taken action.

The rapid expansion of renewable energy is a good example of this tendency. As noted, India's renewable energy journey got a major boost when the state of Gujarat began formulating supportive policies for grid-scale solar installations. These policies were motivated more by industrial and energy security concerns than by environmental issues. Similarly, when the central government in Delhi began to promote renewable energy with a variety of support mechanisms, ranging from solar parks to auctions, it did so to exploit falling costs and improve the country's power generation capacity. Renewable energy was a solution to a number of problems, of which climate change was not primary in the Indian policymaker's view.[35] But when renewable energy created a window of opportunity to craft an image of climate leadership, the media-savvy Modi government did not fail to use it on the global arena and in domestic politics.

India's renewable energy boom has not, however, led the Indian government to declare the end of coal. In India, a rapid growth of renewable power generation goes together with a steadfast commitment to the continued exploitation of domestic coal resources, as Indian energy policies do not aim to reduce greenhouse gas emissions or reduce reliance on fossil fuels. To the contrary, the government foresees growth in both coal-fired power generation and, crucially for energy security, domestic production of coal.

Curiously, this structural dependence on coal is partly driven by the various taxes and fees on coal.[36] State governments in eastern India are heavily dependent on coal royalties and other revenue for their budgets. Domestic coal is subject to a 14.5 percent royalty, a 5 percent Goods and Services Tax, and contributions to mineral development funds. There is also a fee for both domestic and imported coal.[37]

The Indian railways, the largest employer and most important transport enterprise in the country, uses coal freight fees to subsidize passenger transportation.[38] Railways transport the majority of all coal burned in India, and almost half of all railway revenue comes from coal freight. India's rapidly growing train passenger traffic is heavily subsidized and unprofitable, and the railway system's survival depends on equally rapid growth in coal freight. Should coal transports decrease in the future, the railways would either have to increase train ticket prices—a huge political problem, considering that the vast majority of Indians have few alternatives in long-distance travel—or request budgetary support from the central government.

In coal-mining areas, tens of millions of people depend on the coal industry for their livelihoods, either formally or informally.[39] Besides official employees of the coal companies, there are a large number of contractors and an even larger number of informal employees, such as people who collect and sell coal to street vendors in cities along India's coal belt. Each of these workers often supports an extended family with few other livelihood opportunities in India's least developed states like Jharkhand and Chhattisgarh. Rohit Chandra, who wrote his doctoral dissertation on the Indian coal industry, estimates that there are ten to fifteen million people in India's coal belt today whose livelihoods would be threatened by reductions in demand for domestic coal.[40] Finding alternative livelihoods for this group of people in some of India's least developed districts, often marred by Maoist insurgencies, is a major challenge.

Broadly speaking, India has had only limited success in formulating and implementing effective policy to mitigate the environmental effects of economic growth. Air pollution problem remains severe, and yet the government has not taken concrete action to address the root causes of the problem. Groundwater depletion has reached alarming levels and continues mostly unabated, yet the Indian groundwater management system continues to rely on outdated principles inherited from the colonial era. India does not have a climate policy to speak of but rather focuses on questions of economic development, public finances, and energy security.

In a recent working paper, Pillai and Dubash propose that "compensatory federalism" can help India navigate the challenge of climate policy. Recognizing India's "top-heavy" federalist structure, with states having limited institutional capabilities and financial resources, they argue that the central and state governments need to play complementary roles in formulating and implementing policies.[41] Implementation capacity at the state level needs to be strengthened, but the center's financial support will remain essential to policy success. Such compensatory action will, however, require a much stronger alignment of central and state interests.

Because of India's weak implementation capacity in environmental law, the judicial system has stepped in to interpret and enforce environmental rights. According to Ghosh, "As the legislature and the executive are underperforming, those affected by environmental degradation or otherwise dissatisfied by a regulatory decision or policy, look to a 'responsive' judiciary for relief."[42] The state apparatus lacks the will and ability to translate environmental principles into concrete rules and regulations, and activist judges fill the void. Mehta captures this sentiment well, writing that "an important way in which courts use environmental rights and principles is to define the role of executive authorities, and to demand that they take steps to remedy their improperly exercised discretion or inaction."[43]

The problem with this approach is that it cannot solve India's energy-environment problems. On the one hand, many of these problems do not have clear victims that would be able to sue polluters. Air pollution hurts almost everyone in India and is caused by hundreds of millions of dispersed sources. In such a context, who would sue whom? While an aggressive judiciary can achieve much in adjudicating large developmental projects, such as hydroelectric dams or mines, it cannot develop a systematic approach to a problem with diffuse and disperse sources.

On the other hand, and perhaps more important, a judiciary is always hamstrung by the law. While activist judges can interpret the law according to their preferences, they do not have the power to change the legislative framework itself. They cannot order government officials to improve legislation and enforcement across the board; their powers are limited to interpreting law in specific cases, with plaintiffs and defendants and competing claims. This piecemeal approach is not what India needs.

To sum up, India's environmental governance leaves a lot to be desired. Although noble environmental principles are enshrined in the constitution itself, their translation into legislation, regulation, and concrete action is wanting, to put it mildly. The judiciary is probably the most important arm of the state that has attempted to address the problem, but it faces a number of inherent limitations. The judiciary will never be able to solve the deeper problems unless the politics and governance of the environment change, with corresponding legislative action.

ENERGY POLICY IN INDIA

While India's environmental policies are mostly toothless, Indian energy policy suffers from a different problem: it does shape behavior, but not always in ways that are desirable. Understanding India's environmental challenges requires looking behind formal environmental policy, and into the formulation and implementation of energy policy. Even though this policy field is not motivated by environmental considerations, it has a profound impact on India's sustainable development (or lack thereof). The reality is that energy policy overrides environmental policy almost without exceptions. While we can dismiss Indian environmental policy as mostly ineffective and the primary policy recommendation is to have more stringent policies with adequate enforcement, the problem with energy policy is more nuanced than that.

Most important, one must understand the trials and tribulations of the Indian power sector. It consists of the generation, transmission, and distribution of electricity. Generation is about power plants; transmission, about high-voltage lines from power plants to distribution centers; and distribution, about reaching the consumers themselves. A key reason for the complexity of power sector governance is that these three very different sectors are linked but face different challenges. Power generation feeds into the transmission system, which in turn supplies distribution centers with electrical energy. The distribution system interfaces with a huge number of diverse consumers. If anything goes wrong downstream, in distribution, the transmission and generation segments must adjust. Conversely, consumers ultimately feel any generation or transmission problems.

In India, the power sector is mostly populated by state-owned enterprises. Although India has moved away from vertically integrated monopolies, historically known as State Electricity Boards, the only two jurisdictions that have truly privatized the power sector are the National Capital Territory of Delhi and the state of Odisha in eastern India. Everywhere else, the distribution segment, which turns out to be the lynchpin of India's woes, consists of state-owned distribution companies.

The fundamentals of governing the power sector are enshrined in the 1950 Constitution of India, which assigns responsibility both to the central and state governments by placing electricity on the "concurrent list" of subjects. This dual authority leaves the Ministry of Power as the highest authority, but each state has considerable power because the distribution companies are under state control. In practice, the central government has only limited ability to force states to change their behavior in the power sector. The Ministry of Power can negotiate a memorandum of understanding with a state government, but the ministry has no direct authority over rules and regulations in the state, let alone the day-to-day management of the distribution companies.

India's efforts to modernize a struggling power sector began in the early 1990s.[44] In 1991, at the time of the Singh reform budget, India amended the Electricity (Supply) Act of 1948 to allow private power generation. The goal was to increase power generation capacity and reduce cost at a time of poor technical performance and chronic financial trouble across the State Electricity Boards. At that time, the Indian power sector, similar to many other developing country power sectors, found itself in a crisis. Over time, a significant deterioration in financial performance contributed to poor performance, with outages and low quality of supply. Against this backdrop of worsening performance, growing electricity demand contributed to a widening gap between supply and demand. The Indian government had to confront the reality that the power sector's weak performance was a major roadblock to economic growth.

While the power sector's weak performance drove the reforms, India's broader economic woes added to the pressure. As the Indian government sought a way out of decades of macroeconomic trouble, it realized that a functioning power sector would be necessary for success. Virtually any modern economic activity, in both industry and services, requires a reliable supply of power. A failure to improve the power sector's performance would have compromised the effectiveness of other reforms. In this context, deregulating power generation was a natural next step. It was also a simple move that would not necessarily have ripple effects on consumers.

Building on the platform of legislative reforms of 1991, the World Bank developed a cooperation with the eastern state of Odisha to deregulate and privatize the power sector.[45] The World Bank's ideology at the time put a heavy emphasis on competition, liberalization, and markets. This ideology led the bank to condition concessional loans on deregulation and privatization, and the Odisha state government needed the money. The combination of poor performance and financial conditionalities drove the state government to a radical reform plan. The model consisted of vertical and horizontal unbundling, along with the formation of an Odisha State Regulatory Commission and privatization of the distribution companies. While other states were slowly introducing independent power production, often with disappointing results, Odisha moved to the other extreme and embraced a "shock therapy" approach to power sector reform. The results were at best mixed.[46] The key goals of the reform—private generation and transmission investments, lower technical and nontechnical losses, and improved financial performance in the distribution companies—were not met. At the same time, Odisha's rural electrification rate remained relatively low at 19 percent in the 2001 Census of India, as opposed to an all-India rural rate of 44 percent. The state's disappointing performance can be attributed to weak commitment of political leaders and parties, lack of careful reform planning, and opposition by stakeholders like labor unions and consumer groups. The reforms were motivated by external finance and poor technical performance, yet there was no serious commitment to difficult reforms with pain in the short run.

India's experimentation with privatization did not last long, however.[47] The Odisha model did not produce the expected results, and California's flawed restructuring experience, with Enron manipulating the power market, brought global privatization efforts to a standstill after 2001. India continued to reform the power sector, but instead of following the World Bank's standard "textbook" approach, it opted for a "hybrid" model based on state ownership and eschewing the more aggressive privatization and liberalization measures.[48] Under this model, generation was largely privatized with the entry of independent power producers under the watchful eye of regulators. Vertical monopolies were unbundled and utilities corporatized, but privatization stalled, and competition was not liberalized outside rare exceptions such as Odisha and New Delhi.

In 1998 India passed the Electricity Regulatory Commission Act, in an effort to ensure that independent regulators would protect consumers from monopoly behavior. The idea was to create regulatory bodies that would set electricity prices in a fair and transparent manner, with input from producers and consumers alike—and without political interference from the government. This legislation enabled India to create central and state regulatory bodies with powers to set electricity prices. It did not, however, force states to do so. The result was partial compliance. By 2003 ten states, including Bihar, still did not have a functioning regulatory body for the power sector.

At that time, five years later, India passed the Electricity Act of 2003. Key reforms included removing the licensing requirement for power generation, except in the cases of nuclear and very large hydroelectric facilities. The act also mandated the unbundling of vertical monopolies and the creation of state regulatory commissions. It enabled franchising for rural distribution, required metering of electricity connections, and enhanced measures against power theft. It also enabled "open access" by allowing larger consumers to seek electricity from sources other than the incumbent distribution company. The act was envisioned as a comprehensive roadmap to a more efficient, market-based system that would use a combination of good governance, independent regulation, liberalization, and competition to significantly improve India's power sector performance.

Today, India's power generation is about half private and half public in terms of ownership. While 46 percent of the generation was privately owned in May 2019, 24 percent was under state control and the remaining 29 percent was owned by the central government. Over time, private participation in generation has increased significantly. Although initial experiences with privatized generation were disappointing, the compound effect of private investment over time has made a big difference. In 1991 India did not allow private generation at all, and today the division between private and public generation is approximately even.

Transmission, as is true of virtually every country in the world, remains firmly under the central government's control. Less than 10 percent of transmission is in private hands, and private participation in transmission is a licensed activity. In this sector, public monopoly is not a problem, as creating competition for transmission is virtually impossible due to economies of scale. The challenge lies with strengthening transmission capacities and regulating interstate power transfer to fully leverage India's diverse geographic conditions. Meeting this challenge becomes particularly important as renewable energy penetration grows. Solar and wind conditions can vary widely across India, so transmission of renewable power from its source to the location of demand is an important way to deal with intermittency and optimize power supply over time.

By far the most troubled segment is distribution. This segment suffers from a wide range of problems, including low electricity prices—in some states, zero—for agricultural users, low billing and payment collection rates, widespread power theft, poor management, and frequent political manipulation for electoral purposes. As a result of these problems, India's distribution companies provide poor service and exist on the brink of default, only to be rescued by frequent state government bailouts.

Indeed, India's efforts have largely failed to address the underlying problems. The power sector continues to suffer from heavy technical and nontechnical (i.e., power theft and nonpayment) losses. In 2018 transmission and distribution losses amounted to 21 percent of all power generation, well above the government's target of reducing losses below 15 percent by March 2019.[49] At that time, distribution companies held a total debt of INR 38,240 crore (US$5.16 billion at the October 31, 2018, exchange rate) despite a recent scheme, UDAY, that was intended to improve their performance in exchange for a state government bailout. Although the scheme was intended to improve distribution company performance with a package of carrots and sticks, in reality the companies ate the carrots but were never hit with the stick. Because the state governments need the distribution companies for political purposes, they cannot credibly threaten to penalize them for weak performance. The resulting "soft budget constraint" is a strong disincentive to make major managerial or governance reforms for better performance.[50]

The consequences of India's power sector problems are serious. With low electricity prices and strong political incentives not to curb power theft, most Indian distribution companies have no realistic hope of breaking even. They are in chronic financial trouble and dependent on state governments for subsidies. Their leadership has little autonomy and independence from state governments, which use inexpensive electricity and rapid rural electrification as political weapons in India's highly competitive elections.[51] Distribution companies have little incentive to improve their performance, as managers have neither the freedom nor the material incentives to show superior performance.

One useful approach to understanding these problems is to focus on the aforementioned cross-subsidy.[52] In India, agricultural consumers tend to pay the lowest rates, often enjoying free power. Households also tend to benefit from subsidies, whereas commercial and industrial users often pay very high prices. While nominally intended to help the poor and marginalized gain access to electricity, this form of social policy has caused a great deal of trouble in the Indian power sector. On the one hand, agricultural users exploit free or almost free electricity to deplete groundwater resources. On the other hand, industrial and commercial users struggle because a key input is both expensive and unreliable at the same time.

These problems can be seen across the financial chain that is supposed to link electricity consumption to payments to generators through the distribution companies. Across India, rates of billing and payment collection remain troublingly low. In a survey that our team conducted with the Council on Energy, Environment and Water in the summer of 2018 in Uttar Pradesh, we found that only 39 percent of the state's household were metered, billed, and paying for their electricity consumption.[53] The rest—six out of ten—were either not electrified, not paying a fixed fee, not receiving a bill, not paying a bill, or stealing electricity. While the situation is better in many other states, the problem itself is widespread across India.

The impact has been alarming. It does not really matter how distribution companies price electricity if they cannot collect most of their dues. Without measures to improve metering, billing, and collection, distribution companies cannot realistically expect to bridge the gap between cost and revenues. The lack of these revenues, in turn, makes it hard to improve metering, collection, and billing because distribution companies lack the cash to invest in improvements and are unable to secure loans because of their poor credit ratings.

Regulation is another example of a governance deficit in the power sector.[54] In principle, India's electricity distribution companies are responsible for covering their costs and collecting payments under prices and rules set by autonomous regulators. In reality, regulators lack the ability to prevent governments from forcing distribution companies to lower electricity prices for political reasons. Governments exercise influence over regulators, who resign themselves to their fate and accept electricity prices that contribute to massive financial losses and poor technical performance. The problem is further compounded by widespread electricity theft and nonpayment of bills by consumers. All this activity occurs in the shadow of modern, streamlined legislation that mostly follows best practices laid out by the World Bank and other international bodies with an interest in the power sector.

India's federal framework for power sector regulation is crafted according to good practices from other countries, and it lays a solid foundation for regulatory autonomy. But because the Indian state has limited implementation capacity on the ground and in most states electoral politics outweighs good governance, India's regulators find themselves severely constrained by government power. They do not have the de facto authority to tell state-owned distribution companies to improve their performance. While they are autonomous and independent on paper, in reality they know that they cannot resist political pressure from the government. As a result, they allow electricity prices that result in major technical and financial difficulties. Is there a solution to these problems? In a remarkable case study, Balls shows how the mountain state of Uttarakhand, which was carved out of the larger state of Uttar Pradesh in 2000, became a stalwart in the Indian power sector. Although underdeveloped, Uttarakhand had plentiful hydroelectric generation capacity. It reduced industrial electricity prices and, with favorable financial subsidies from the central government, saw the tripling of industrial facilities in the state between 2000 and 2011. Unfortunately, this solution was feasible only because the state had access to abundant hydroelectric energy. In the meantime, industry in the far larger Uttar Pradesh, which no longer had substantial hydroelectric generation capacity, languished.[55]

From an environmental perspective, it is useful to note that India's power sector problems also hurt large-scale renewable energy. As a new industry, renewable energy faces barriers to growth from high cost of finance. Both Indian and international banks see risks in renewable energy finance, and the sorry state of the power sector is an important cause of this problem. With distribution companies facing financial difficulties and often falling behind on payments, these risks are compounded and slow down the growth of renewable power generation in India. If the distribution companies were in better shape, their payments to renewable power generators would be more reliable.

State governments compound this problem with short-sighted policies, such as forcing independent power generators to renegotiate existing contracts, renewable power or not. In 2019, for example, the southern state of Andhra Pradesh elected a new government led by the opposition's Y. S. Jaganmohan Reddy, chief of the YSR Congress Party. The son of a long-time political leader from a family dynasty,[56] as chief minister Reddy demanded that power generators reduce the prices negotiated under the previous chief minister, N. Chandrababu Naidu.[57] This demand provoked a firestorm of criticisms, as the renewable energy industry and proponents of clean energy sources expressed concern about the state governments' credibility. If state governments could renegotiate agreements, project developers would not have a reliable cash flow, and the bankability of their projects would further suffer.

In some sense, then, India's progress with renewable energy deployment itself is surprising. In addition to the aforementioned problems, the Indian renewable energy industry has suffered from a lack of a powerful government champion. The Ministry of New and Renewable Energy, although established already in 1992 as the Ministry of Non-Conventional Energy Sources, is far weaker than the Ministry of Power. While the latter has the authority to regulate the Indian power sector, the MNRE has a less comprehensive mandate, focused on promoting renewable energy under the ministry's broader energy plan. Thus the Ministry of Power has far more authority over the power sector, and the MNRE remains a narrowly focused, largely technical agency. This institutional weakness explains why political leaders at the highest levels, including Mr. Modi first as Gujarat chief minister and then as prime minister, have played such an important role.

India's power sector rules also contribute to groundwater depletion. Considering that irrigation is by far the most important driver of groundwater depletion, state policies that either heavily subsidize or make electricity free for agricultural users are nothing short of ruinous. Major agricultural states from Punjab to Tamil Nadu and Telangana offer free power to farmers at a very high economic and environmental cost. The northern state of Punjab, known as India's "bread basket," paid US$909 million (INR 6,260 crore) in subsidies to agricultural users in the financial year 2018–2019 alone.[58]

In a somewhat ironic way, India's power sector woes also protect the groundwater resource:

> What is notable for the purposes of this discussion is that "inefficiencies" in power supply to agriculture in India (rationing, erratic voltage and frequency, etc.) are having the unintended consequence of limiting the rate of groundwater exploitation. This point appears to be lost on the power sector reformers intent on advocating efficient supply without rationing. It is clear that the metered tariff increases required to take a bite out of pumping demand are politically infeasible. At the same time, if full supply at constant voltage were made available, the likely (short-term) outcome would be to quicken the pace of groundwater overdraft. The solution—perhaps interim in nature—appears to be to continue with strict rationing.[59]

While low electricity prices are motivated by social policy, in reality they contribute to low-quality rural electricity service. Because low electricity prices harm the financial and technical performance of distribution companies, they contribute to outages and voltage fluctuation. Even though India as a country has enough generating capacity to meet its peak power demand, the sorry state of distribution companies is such a weak link that poor service remains commonplace. Distribution companies have difficulty making ends meet, so they cannot make required infrastructural repairs and fail to pay generators for their power. State governments then bail out the distribution companies, contributing to the problem of "circular debt," which will ultimately be paid from the public coffer.

Harish and Tongia use detailed electricity supply data from the southern state of Karnataka to explore how distribution companies end up compromising rural electricity supply. Their findings, which predate Saubhagya by half a decade, show how problematic the rural situation is even in a dynamic, well-governed state: "The principal hypothesis tested in this study is that the rural residential consumers are load shed enough for the resultant supply procurement relief to the utility to overcompensate for any tariff subsidy extended to these consumers relative to their counterparts in urban areas. . . . Rural (R) feeders, and surprisingly non-Bangalore [Karnataka's capital] urban (NBU) feeders as well, receive supply that is worse than in Bangalore city (Bangalore Urban, or BU)."[60]

The problem here is that although rural households pay relatively low prices, they more than compensate for those gains with frequent loss of power. The distribution company prefers to supply electricity to urban, industrial, and commercial customers, who pay higher prices, consume larger amounts, and have fewer opportunities for stealing. The rural consumers may benefit from low electricity prices, but they suffer from lower reliability at that time of the day when the value of electrical lighting and air circulation would be the highest. This kind of "subsidy trap" is a common consequence of politically motivated, administrative pricing across the world.[61]

In 2019 the Ministry of New and Renewable Energy formulated an ambitious scheme to expand the use of solar power in irrigation. The Kisan Urja Suraksha evam Utthaan Mahabhiyan (KUSUM) scheme aimed to develop 26 gigawatts of solar power generation capacity for irrigation by 2022.[62] The scheme aimed to improve energy security and reduce the cost of irrigation for farmers by solarizing some of India's thirty million agricultural pumps, of which one-third run on diesel. The scheme would build solar power plants and offer capital subsidies to farmers for solar pump purchase, and allow farmers to sell some of the electricity generated back to the national grid.

The ambitious KUSUM scheme yet again demonstrates India's capabilities and weaknesses in energy policy. On the one hand, solarizing millions of pumps clearly improves energy security, reduces pollution, and provides distribution companies relief as the demand for heavily subsidized agricultural power decreases. But as solarization proceeds, the number of pumps will increase, and demand for groundwater grow. As the KUSUM scheme does not contain strict safeguards against enhanced groundwater exploitation, it risks further deterioration in India's water security situation. As Shah, India's leading scholar on groundwater depletion, notes, "Free electricity is blamed for groundwater over-exploitation from Punjab down to Tamil Nadu, but its destructive impact is limited by restricted hours and unreliable supply. With reliable day-time free solar power, [solar irrigation pumps] can be way more lethal for our aquifers."[63]

As the Saubhagya scheme brought India's household electrification rate close to 100 percent, it also added to the grid over twenty-five million households with limited income and often minimal electricity consumption. According to a study conducted by the Initiative for Sustainable Energy Policy and Smart Power India Foundation, both the typical household and the typical firm in a sample of ten thousand households and two thousand firms in northern India consumed fewer than 40 kWh of electricity per month, even when off-grid alternatives like solar mini-grids were considered along grid connections. That is less than 50 percent of India's average per capita consumption.[64] Serving such consumers is a major strain for distribution companies, and because of the limited electricity consumption it produces few financial returns to compensate for the cost.

The Saubhagya scheme highlights a longstanding coordination challenge in the Indian power sector. Over time, India has made considerable progress in rural electrification, first as a side product of the Green Revolution, which resulted in the wholesale deployment of electric pumps across villages with untapped groundwater resources.[65] Later, in 2004, Dr. Manmohan Singh's government launched the Rajiv Gandhi Rural Electrification Scheme, named after an Indian National Congress chief minister assassinated in May 1991. This scheme offered a 90 percent capital subsidy for rural electrification works in the states, and over a decade got India very close to 100 percent village electrification, setting the stage for Saubhagya three years after Prime Minister Modi's term began.

The problem with India's rural electrification schemes is that they have not been coordinated with broader power sector reforms. While the immediate financial cost of RGGVY and Saubhagya mostly fell on the central government, the challenge of serving hundreds of millions of new customers, many of whom were very poor and consumed minimal amounts of electrical energy, was never fully addressed. While universal household electrification itself is a laudable goal, and perhaps a sociopolitical necessity for an aspiring major power, it was not managed with an eye on the long-term prospects of the power sector as a whole.

The political economy behind India's power sector troubles is a good illustration of a broader concern. As state-owned enterprises, distribution companies are hesitant to increase electricity prices to cover the real cost of service and ensure a fair return, as they should do in a well-functioning regulated system.[66] For the same political reasons, distribution companies are unable to crack down on power theft.[67] These problems contribute to poor technical and financial performance, making it hard for distribution companies to improve their service or develop innovative solutions to their problems. The poor performance, in turn, encourages nonpayment and theft, along with hostility to higher electricity prices.

Three decades after the 1991 reforms, then, India's power sector remains little changed. Superficial reforms such as unbundling and pro forma regulatory authorities notwithstanding, the basic logic of politically motivated pricing, weak billing and collection, and widespread power theft continues to hamper the development of the sector.

But while India's overall power sector performance is poor, there is substantial variation across the states. In a sense, India's power sector problems are aggravated by an awkward division of responsibilities between the center and the states. Because states control electricity distribution, differences in per capita income, economic structure, and ability to govern generate massive gaps in performance across the states. Unfortunately, some of the largest states, notably Uttar Pradesh with a population in excess of 200 million and counting, have poorly performing power sectors.

The center's ability to intervene is constrained for the aforementioned constitutional reasons. While the central government can create incentives and, in some instances, threaten states with penalties for poor performance, the most important power sector decisions are made in the states. Electricity prices are set by state regulators based on distribution companies' proposals, and the final responsibility for metering, collection, and billing also lies with the distribution companies.

This constitutional challenge can be seen in the Ministry of Power's May 2019 five-year roadmap for the Indian power sector. While the roadmap sets a wide range of goals for generation, transmission, and distribution, it is conspicuously silent about electricity pricing and theft. The proposed solutions range from universal metering of connections to transmission infrastructure construction, along with text message reminders to consumers to pay their bills. They do not, however, address the root causes of the problem: low electricity prices, theft, and nonpayment. A lasting solution would require pricing reform and effective measures to reduce losses, but such solutions are difficult to execute. The central government has a limited mandate; state governments value their political control of the distribution companies. The vicious cycle continues.

In renewable energy, the same issues raise barriers to progress.[68] While the central government sets targets for deployment, it cannot force states to meet the targets, let alone enable renewable electricity generation. As a result, renewable energy capacity sits idle because of curtailment, whereby wind and solar power are not supplied to the electric grid even when they can be generated. Renewable energy generators also struggle with delayed payments by distribution companies, and again the central government has only limited capacity to address these violations and enforce power purchase contracts.

Compared to the power sector, India's oil and gas system is less dysfunctional. It is more tightly controlled by the Ministry of Petroleum and Natural Gas, with limited state participation. As a general rule, India no longer offers subsidies for gasoline or diesel consumption except on an ad hoc basis, such as to provide relief to farmers in times of high oil prices. These subsidies are nothing in comparison to the power sector; theft of petroleum products is a relatively minor nuisance.

The main exception to low subsidy rates is the LPG cooking program, which plays an important role in promoting clean cooking access. This subsidy is far less problematic than the electricity subsidy, as it is administered as a direct transfer to a bank account based on an LPG purchase. This system effectively deters leakage, as it would be difficult for individual LPG consumers to abuse the system. Because individual consumers purchase

LPG cylinders at an unsubsidized rate, the decision to resell fuel amounts to recovering the money spent on the purchase. This approach still constitutes abuse of the subsidy system, but the direct transfer approach makes systematic fraud far more difficult. For example, purchasing cylinders en masse using false personal identification is no longer possible.

The difference between the power sector and oil/gas is illuminating in two important respects. The first is the relative ease of managing the distribution of oil and gas products, which are first manufactured and then distributed to consumers, most of whom are wealthy by Indian standards, with the exception of household LPG users. The major difficulties of coordinating the generation, transmission, and distribution of power are not present, and this relative simplicity has helped the Indian oil/gas sector avoid the kinds of deep, systemic problems that characterize the power sector. The second point is the perhaps unforeseen benefit of retaining oil and gas under the central government's rule. The power sector's worst excesses are perpetuated by state governments.

The transportation sector, though not formally an energy subject, deserves a comment as well because it has a major impact on energy-related environmental problems in India. On the surface, India's governance structure for transportation planning is quite logical. The central government is responsible for interstate transportation, state governments handle transportation within their borders, and urban governments plan local transportation. The problem is that India's complex conditions have beaten this linear arrangement.[69] First, India's urbanization has occurred at breakneck speed and with very little formal coordination. Urban slums and peri-urban areas have expanded well beyond formal town boundaries, with the unfortunate result that either nobody has been in charge or too many jurisdictions have claimed authority for local planning. What is more, within large urban areas interagency competition has crowded out effectively coordinated, cooperative arrangements. Gandhi and Pethe, for example, note that in 2008 the city of Bangalore had master plans simultaneously prepared by "Bangalore Development Authority, Bangalore Metropolitan Region Development Authority, Bangalore Mysore Infrastructure Corridor Planning Authority, Bangalore International Airport Area Planning

Authority, etc."[70] All these plans overlapped and claimed priority over the others.

Although the National Urban Transport Policy of 2006 attempted to solve the problem by establishing a Unified Metropolitan Transport Authority for cities with over one million inhabitants, "in practice the transport authorities have not been able to successfully discharge their functions."[71] They lack the authority to enforce decisions and they are not represented by political leaders who could put pressure on other agencies to comply with coordination efforts.

To summarize, Indian energy policy suffers from an altogether different problem from environmental policy. India does have a variety of energy policies, and some of them are downright aggressive, such as offering free power to farmers. But these policies do not constitute an effective system of governance that would strike the right balance between consumer interests, producer interests, and cost to society. They tend to be politically motivated and often populist in orientation. While the central government's policies tend to be better than those of most state governments, India's federal structure and constitutional rules limit the center's ability to rein in underperforming states.

THE FLAILING STATE

The Indian state has for a long time been notorious for its weak implementation capacity. Over three decades before this book, Wade asked "why the Indian state is not better at development," pointing out that corruption and perverse incentives made the country's bureaucracy quite incapable of promoting development.[72] In a more recent volume, Kapur, Mehta, and Vaishnav demonstrate that India's underperformance in public service delivery is a chronic and systemic problem. As the authors put it, "Even a casual observer of the Indian state would be struck by its limitations. . . . While the state might be undermanned in terms of adequate personnel, it is most certainly as over-bureaucratized as it is understaffed."[73]

India's fundamental institutional problem is the lack of implementation capacity on the ground. While India has managed to break out of the license *raj* trap and the government is no longer an enemy of progress, Lant Pritchett's "flailing state" is an appropriate description of the Indian state.[74] The union government has the capacity to enact effective policies, but turning those policies into concrete action in India's twenty-nine states, ten thousand cities, and six hundred thousand villages is an altogether different matter. A combination of resource scarcity, lacking human capital, corruption, and perverse political incentives have time again defeated spirited plans to correct India's course.

This problem of lacking state capacity has many causes. From lack of fiscal bandwidth and inadequate education to corruption and political manipulation, the Indian state suffers from a number of chronic ailments. These weaknesses are best understood as systemic difficulties in governing a diverse and poor country with massive inequality. India's constitutional structure is impressive on paper, yet it has consistently failed to address major problems that hurt large segments of the population.

In the prereform era, the Indian state had a tight grip on the economy and society when it came to regulation. The notorious "license raj," whereby the Indian state made it very difficult for new players to enter industry or commerce, had a massive negative impact on India's economic performance.[75] A small number of inefficient monopolies dominated India's tiny formal economy, and bureaucrats tightly controlled both domestic and foreign competition.[76] In this environment, economic growth was muted and India's innovative private sector suppressed.

At the same time, the state had little ability to improve conditions on the ground. While government regulations suppressed private enterprise, the bureaucracy lacked the capacity to improve everyday life with effective public service delivery. From corruption to a lack of human capital and financial resources, the Indian administration had limited ways to improve lives and livelihoods in the country's cities and villages. The Indian government had few resources available to it and was heavily dependent on foreign assistance. The resources were also not effectively deployed because of political manipulation, corruption, and misaligned incentives.

From government procurement to infrastructure schemes and everyday public service delivery, corruption and political manipulation have been endemic in India for a long time. As Wade put it almost a decade before the economic reforms began, in India corruption's "effects are strongly regressive . . . it skews the output of departments far from the optimum almost however the optimum is defined."[77] Indian politicians transfer bureaucrats between posts, and bureaucrats pay bribes to obtain the most powerful posts. The bureaucrats, in turn, extract bribes from industry and the population. This administrative system of corruption produces major inefficiencies, as politicians can have arbitrary influence over bureaucrats, who in turn have little incentive to work hard to improve their jurisdiction's lot. As long as the system of assigning posts is chronically corrupt, an individual bureaucrat has little to gain from going beyond the call of duty.

This problem continues to exist to this date. According to the Corruption Perceptions Index published by Transparency International in 2017, India was number 81 among 180 countries when ranked by absence of corruption. For comparative purposes, China ranked number 77. While these rankings are far from suggesting a corruption crisis, they do indicate a serious problem. Improving public service delivery and the quality of public infrastructure projects would benefit from lower corruption, which would reduce procurement costs and improve vendor performance, as government agencies would select the most competitive offer on price and quality, not size of bribe. Similar problems with corruption are also found at the local level, as frontline public servants abuse their power to take bribes in exchange for ignoring nonpayments and even outright theft of electricity.

The combined effect of weak economic performance and lacking public service delivery was literally deadly in the prereform era. Extreme poverty contributed to morbidity and mortality, and a dysfunctional administrative structure prevented effective public sector intervention. Although India proudly presented itself as a socialist economy, in practice it was unable to offer the vast majority of its citizens even basic education or health care. As late as 1990, only a year before Prime Minister Singh's emergency budget, India's infant mortality rate stood at 89 per 1,000 births. By 2017 it had decreased to 32—a major improvement, even though India still has a long way to go.

The reform era kick-started economic growth, yet it also brought a host of new challenges. Most important, rapid growth in economic activity finally allowed large private and public investments into infrastructure. From roads and bridges to international airports, India's investments in basic economic infrastructure surged. The private sector, especially services, grew rapidly and created a middle class with purchasing power and aspirations for a better life. Major cities in South India boomed, with metropoles like Hyderabad and Bangalore joining Mumbai as centers of economic activity.

Ideally, the Indian state would have made better use of the fruits of economic growth. One of India's great problems is that economic growth at the national level does not always contribute to better lives for the population. India's human development indicators have, in fact, fallen behind economic development. In 1990, at the cusp of the all-important economic reforms, India's human development index stood at 0.427. By 2017 it had increased to 0.640. While this increase is itself welcome, it is actually quite slow. The annual growth in the human development index was only 1.51 percent between 1990 and 2017, a very slow rate in a time of unprecedented economic growth. In the meantime, the far poorer Bangladesh increased from 0.387 to 0.608, an annual growth rate of 1.69 percent.

The flailing state, then, made some progress toward, but did not achieve, the goal of broad social and economic betterment. While India has made a lot of progress, the Indian state's limitations have meant that those benefits are not evenly spread. The weakest strata of society have not benefited as much as their wealthier counterparts. India's economic growth is unequal in nature, and large segments of the Indian population have realized only modest gains from a massive expansion of the economy.

In the field of energy and environmental policy, the results are plain for everyone to see. Economic growth put tremendous pressure on India's scarce natural resources and ecological systems. Growth in production and consumption added to air pollution, groundwater depletion, and greenhouse gas emissions. Had the Indian state been better equipped to deal with these problems through effective policy and regulation, the country's environmental degradation might not have reached crisis proportions. In the prereform era, weak economic performance limited the effect of human activity on the environment; after the 1991 reforms, India's economy has grown rapidly, and the lack of effective environmental governance has led to an environmental crisis. Rapid economic growth has overall been a blessing for the Indian population, but the negative effects of uncontrolled economic expansion are by now a major threat to public health, as well as future growth itself.

On the other hand, India has made rapid, and sometimes historical, progress with public investments. Examples include the distribution of efficient LED lighting and solar power generation, and there is a good chance of similar achievements in electric vehicles, efficient electric appliances, and other technological improvements. Although India's track record is underwhelming, it is not all gloom and doom. There are pockets of success that warrant special attention.

These inconsistencies cannot be fully understood by looking at rules, regulations, and policies in the books. A review of formal legislation, policy, and regulation in India would lead one to conclude that India is doing quite well—and leave the reviewers scratching their heads when it comes to explaining the country's horrendous air quality, or persistent failures to reform the power sector. A review of actual implementation on the ground, however, would soon reveal the deep problems with getting the work done. Standards for air quality are not met, and many polluters get away with serious violations. Climate change action plans have no budgets or enforcement authority attached to them. Only the groundwater crisis can be mostly explained with reference to the rules and regulations on paper.

GOVERNING ENERGY AND ENVIRONMENT IN INDIA

Drip irrigation is a great idea. It produces the desired effect of plant growth with less water than conventional flooding techniques and thus offers a neat technological fix to a water scarcity problem. No wonder, then, that the Indian government has passed a series of policies to subsidize drip irrigation in the hopes of a revolution in groundwater management, but without the pain of higher water prices. Drip irrigation was already piloted in 1970 at the Tamil Nadu Agricultural University, and in 1988 the state of Maharashtra introduced the first set of capital subsidies.[78]

The problem with these drip irrigation subsidies is that despite their elegant logic and technical potential, they have not worked in real life. Although the technical potential for reductions is very large, in practice the human factor beats the engineer's solution. Many farmers use drip irrigation technologies inefficiently, as they would when the technology is heavily subsidized and water basically free. Others use the drip irrigation to complement traditional irrigation, expanding acreage under cultivation. In a study comparing theoretical potential and outcomes under realistic assumptions about behavior, Fishman, Devineni, and Raman find that excessive extraction would decrease by only one-third even if drip irrigation were adopted across all of India.[79] This result stands in stark contrast to the theoretical potential, with advanced technologies and no increase in acreage, which is a 90 percent decrease in excessive extraction.

The story of drip irrigation is a good summary of India's governance problem in the field of energy and environment. The Indian government tends to approach problems with subsidy schemes that would, under the best of conditions, produce highly desirable results. But because the subsidies do not correct the underlying incentive problem—in the case of drip irrigation, overuse of underpriced water—they tend to be far less effective in reality and often have unintended consequences. In the case of drip irrigation, farmers may choose inefficient technologies and use them in a way that fails to maximize their water conservation potential. This is an example of limited effectiveness.

Even worse might be the unintended consequences. Drip irrigation gives farmers access to capital that enables increased water consumption through expanded cultivation. Instead of replacing conventional water pumps, drip irrigation is added on top of them. Farmers use the government subsidy to increase their profits and in doing so defeat the purpose of the scheme itself.

Economist Albert O. Hirschman proposed a useful analytical approach to understanding governance of this captive society in his classic volume *Exit, Voice and Loyalty.*[80] When studying the failure of Nigeria's national railway system, Hirschman wondered why the railway monopoly did not improve its service despite trucking as a readily available substitute for consumers. His answer was that the consumer "exit" from railway freight to trucking left the railway management without consumer complaints and activism that would have forced transformative reforms. With easy exit, consumers had little reason to exercise "voice" and improve the railway service. Because the railways were a state-sponsored monopoly, they continued to survive despite poor performance.

Hirschman's analysis is based on three possible responses to distress and trouble in organizations and societies. The first, loyalty, means that people fail to react to the decline. In the Indian energy and environment scenario, loyal citizens would continue to behave and vote as before, without considering the environmental crisis. If enough people choose loyalty, things will continue to get worse. Loyalty is a plausible choice even under bad performance because it does not require action—people can continue to do what they have always done.

The second option is voice. In this scenario, Indians would demand change. They would vote for candidates that have effective and credible plans for solving the country's environmental crisis. They would sign petitions, organize protests, and run for office on environmental issues. Voice, unfortunately, is difficult to exercise. It requires collective action by committed individuals willing to incur a cost to turn a troubled system around. Such action is difficult in a huge and diverse population that faces many challenges and difficulties on a daily basis.

The third option, exit, refers to people who leave a failing organization. As an alternative, exit is easier than voice because it does not require collective action. Individuals and households can choose to abandon a dysfunctional system on their own, regardless of whether others join the mission. In this sense, exit is always an easier and more likely option. It is difficult to mobilize the stakeholders of an ailing organization to come together and effectively exercise voice; it is far easier for each stakeholder to individually leave the sinking ship behind.

In India, the state's poor performance has often left voice out and forced people of means to choose between exit and loyalty. In a troubling turn, exit dominates. Because India's middle class is still very small in number, it cannot realistically expect to shape politics. Instead, middle-class households look for private solutions to their problems. For the middle class, loyalty is not an option because the failure of public service delivery brings very real costs. Exit requires some private investment, but it does not require the kind of deep and sustained commitment that exercising voice in the world's largest democracy would require. As Sandipan Deb notes in his analysis of the phenomenon, which he calls a "mental exit," "the [Indian] middle class uses every means it can think of to avoid or evade taxes. It is also increasingly insulating itself . . . [creating] a collection of countless gated communities."[81]

Joseph provides an interesting view on this problem in her study of diesel generators and corruption. According to her study, "The decision of industrial consumers to exit the state-run system is in direct response to the adoption of only partial reforms in the sector. . . . The state utilities continue to operate with precarious financial positions, rendering them incapable of investing in needed infrastructural improvements, and thus unable to keep up with growing demand."[82] In the Indian context, industrial users have mostly chosen to invest in private alternatives to grid electricity service. High electricity prices for industrial users combined with low reliability have forced them to look for alternatives, but the sorry state of the power sector and the complex politics surrounding it have discouraged collective action to develop systemic solutions to the problem.

The diesel generation situation, similar to drip irrigation, exemplifies a second-order problem in the exit-voice-loyalty framework. Governments respond to societal demand for private solutions with subsidy schemes that reduce the cost of private solutions. These private solutions either fail to solve the social problem or make it worse. Because the private solutions remain out of reach for the poor and the marginalized, the subsidy-enhanced exit strategy exacerbates inequality.

The original impetus for free electricity, driven by a wave of farmers' movements across the country beginning in the 1970s, is itself an example of the troubling kind of voice.[83] Farmers mobilized to demand support for their livelihoods. This mobilization was a response to the Green Revolution, which necessitated large-scale agricultural inputs, notably water and fertilizer.[84] The mobilization was consistent with the idea of competing interests in a democratic system, and yet somehow it produced distorted policies that generated large benefits to a small group of wealthy landowners at everyone else's expense. Voice was used, but the results of this exercise did not lead to the betterment of the Indian condition. Rather, they created new long-term problems that would haunt the country for decades to come.

I have already given the examples of the diesel generator, rooftop solar, and private groundwater pumping. But similar examples of exit can be found in many other sectors as well. Dissatisfied with public transportation? Drive your own car, or call an Ola cab. Unhappy with the trains? Many airlines offer short flights to nearby cities now. Worried about security with an ineffective policy force? Move to a gated housing complex with private security.

As a result of India's institutional limitations in energy and environmental policy, policy makers face major difficulties in controlling the negative effects of economic expansion on humans and nature. It would be wrong to blame India's institutional problems on the appeal of the exit strategy. Instead, the woes run far deeper and were there decades before a wealthy middle class could begin devising exit strategies. But the exit option makes it very hard for India to solve the problems, as many of its more influential citizens have little reason to pay attention to politics and governance.

Groundwater use exemplifies these tendencies. India's groundwater regime does not impose any real constraints on use, as aquifers are considered to be common property. India's groundwater boards lack the authority to actually constrain groundwater use, while policy makers hesitate to increase electricity prices or encourage the cultivation of water-saving crops by lowering minimum support prices for thirsty crops such as rice and wheat. The problem is enormously complex and politicized, so individual farmers double down on groundwater depletion by investing in more powerful pumps. In cities, industry, commerce, and households also buy their own pumps to ensure water access in a scenario of worsening scarcity. Such behavior contributes to both depletion and inequality.

Measures against air pollution feature the same problem. India's air pollution policies of 2018 are somewhat effective on paper, but their enforcement is severely compromised by politics, corruption, and resource scarcity. As a result, effective measures to reduce emissions are lacking. Indian households and offices with resources invest in air purifiers to at least protect their members indoors, though this strategy is obviously at best partial because it means going outdoors is still dangerous.

In the case of climate change, the problem is somewhat different. Because there are few domestic drivers of action, climate policy becomes haphazard and reflects related goals, as in the case of renewable energy deployment for energy security. Those areas of climate policy that do not produce concrete cobenefits receive little, if any, attention.

While policy implementation languishes, there is no shortage of subsidies of all stripes in India. In reviewing India's policy successes in the area of energy and environment, it is striking how heavily they depend on subsidies and public procurement. While India lacks the capacity to effectively regulate social and economic behavior, its economic growth has produced enough surplus to either offer positive incentives or simply buy outcomes with tax revenue and public debt. India's renewable energy program is essentially a government auctioning scheme, as is the famed UJALA scheme that distributed LED lights across hundreds of millions of households. The Ujjwala scheme to promote LPG, in turn, is a subsidy scheme. So is the Saubhagya scheme to promote household electrification.

The problem with this strategy is that while subsidies and public procurement promote positive behaviors, they do little to curb negative behaviors. Renewable energy auctions do not constrain air pollution or carbon dioxide emissions from coal-fired power generation; LED lights to do not stop extensive waste of energy under heavily subsidized prices in many Indian states. Drip irrigation subsidies do little to stop farmers from flooding their fields when electricity is virtually free and groundwater use not regulated in any meaningful way. India has the capacity to promote positive behaviors, but the resulting policies tend to be ineffective because the incentives for bad behavior remain intact. In many cases, society also pays a high price for unintended consequences that overly generous subsidy programs produce.

To be sure, none of this is to say that India's weak state capacity has its origins in Hirschman's trilemma. As we have seen, India's institutional problems stem from deep structural constraints in the country's politics and society. But when the middle class chooses exit over voice, the prospects for change diminish. A shift from today's inconsistent performance to progressive improvement would require a wave of citizen activism not just in the nation's capital but across India's twenty-nine states. As private solutions—Hirschman's exit—continue to expand thanks to a dynamic private sector and technological progress, the deck is increasingly stacked against collective action, or Hirschman's voice. While this dynamic is not the root cause of India's governance problems, it contributes to a vicious cycle that makes the search for solutions difficult. Despite poor performance, India's policy makers simply do not face heavy pressure to correct course. Too many Indians choose the exit strategy and lose interest in the hard work of searching for sustainable solutions.

India's federal structure complicates these efforts. Authority over key elements of the energy puzzle remains divided between the center and the states. While the center has ambitious plans for renewable energy and other clean technologies, states remain conflicted. Some states, such as Gujarat or Tamil Nadu, recognize clean technology as a key element of future economic growth and job creation. In India's coal belt, states like Jharkhand and Chhattisgar are suspicious of new energy policies that slow down coal mining.

In these circumstances, Indian policy making to address energy-related environmental problems is an example of "muddling through."[85] The rather weak institutional structure does not face enough pressure to address increasingly serious problems because individuals and organizations look for private solutions to their problems. And because the institutional structure is weak for social and political reasons, it is difficult to reform without heavy pressure from crisis conditions.

While Manmohan Singh's government was able to ram through a transformative budget in 1991, at a time when the Indian economy was facing imminent collapse, environmental crises have not seen such a crisis. When the entire Indian economy stared into the abyss after the debt-fueled party of the 1980s, the government was forced into action, as it had to choose between breaking the rigid institutional structures of the license *raj* and a deep recession that would have almost certainly prompted an electoral disaster. In contrast, as the groundwater crisis worsens or millions die from air pollution, individual Indians can seek at least some relief from private solutions. Even where these solutions are far from perfect, they are in many ways a safer bet than dedicating one's efforts to effecting structural reforms in India's cumbersome and complicated political system.

So far, India's environmental plight has not brought the country to the precipice. It has, instead, generated a chronic background condition that has made life more dangerous and less productive for the population, with the worst effects concentrated on the poorest and least privileged. It has also generated short-lived crisis conditions, such as when Delhi becomes engulfed in smoke as millions of farmers burn their crop residue in North India, or when yet another record heat wave comes and goes. The problem with these events is that they have not yet had much lasting impact. As the smoke dissipates and the heat comes down, life goes back to normal—until the next environmental calamity strikes. Conversely, the temporary reduction in air pollution during the COVID-19 crisis in 2020 showed Indians what clean air is, but the public's memory is short, and solving the air quality problem will take years, if not decades.

The solution might lie with India's young voters. Breaking India's policy implementation paralysis will require a strong push, as the severity of the country's social problems has not provoked the state to take decisive action. If a new generation of voters refuse to support politicians who fail to take action, regardless of their religious and caste background, then the Indian state may for the first time face the kind of pressure that it cannot resist.

The barriers to change are high, however. The new generation of voters would have to coordinate their actions to exercise a good kind of voice in a diverse and polarized country. They would have to do so against the wishes of many in the older generations, and in the face of daunting odds in the world's largest democracy and a complex federation.

4

FLEXING MUSCLE IN GLOBAL ENVIRONMENTAL POLITICS

When Jairam Ramesh represented India at the much awaited United Nations climate change summit in Copenhagen, Denmark, in 2009—the climate summit that was to end all climate summits with a globally binding treaty mandating deep emission cuts but failed in a spectacular manner—it became clear to everyone that a new era had begun. In his capacity as the state minister of environment and forests, Ramesh abandoned India's traditional position in global climate negotiations and suggested that India would contribute to the global climate regime. Here is what he had to say about India's views on climate change on December 16, 2009, during the ministerial segment of the Conference of Parties:

> We are convinced that a low-carbon strategy is an essential aspect of sustainable development. While we already have one of the lowest emissions intensity of the economy, we will do more. We are targeting a further emissions intensity decline of 20–25% by 2020 on 2005 levels. This is significant given our huge developmental imperatives. . . . Deeply conscious of our international responsibilities as well, we have already

declared that our per capita emissions will never exceed the per capita emissions of the developed countries. We have recently unveiled projected GHG emissions profiles till the year 2030.[1]

Other negotiators were not used to hearing such language from the Indian delegation. Historically, India had accumulated a reputation for a hardline position against any commitments to climate mitigation for developing countries. India was known as one of the obstructionist parties in the negotiations, repeatedly hammering industrialized countries with their exclusive responsibility for causing, and solving, the problem of climate change. Minister Ramesh's view of India as "neither defensive nor obstructionist" came as a great surprise to the international community,[2] which was not used to India's engaging in pragmatic dealmaking to make progress in climate diplomacy.

It is fair to say that India's role in global environmental politics has undergone a dramatic transformation. If India was known as the reliable laggard, opposed to any proposal to mitigate global environmental problems, this simplistic understanding would no longer do. India's position in global environmental politics, rather, reflects the country's mixed record in dealing with energy and environmental problems. India would face the trials and tribulations of striking a fine balance between protecting its space for economic development and supporting fair and equitable approaches to avoiding environmental calamity.

The early years of India's participation in global environmental politics found the country in a defensive posture. It is only a slight exaggeration to say that India's framework for dealing with global environmental politics was colored by a colonial history, and the lingering distrust toward industrialized countries. Indian positions in global environmental negotiations were determined by broader diplomatic considerations. They had little to do with India's own environmental or energy policy.

As India itself began to change in the era of economic reform that began in 1991, the country's environmental rhetoric also changed. Initially, India's official position veered toward an even stronger emphasis on differences between developing and industrialized countries, even as the North-South gap in living standards was finally shrinking at a healthy pace. In an opportunistic move, India doubled down on the difference between luxury and survival emissions, emphasizing the global North's responsibility for causing, and by direct extension solving, the climate change problem. This framing was to characterize India's position for two decades.

In recent years, India has made the ambitious move of claiming leadership in environmental protection. Following Ramesh's course correction, India has sought to establish itself as a responsible major power in global climate negotiations. These changes reflect India's economic development and deepening domestic environmental crisis. The country is now a far more open economy and society than before, with a growing and increasingly vocal environmental civil society. It also faces serious environmental and resource challenges that undermine its prospects as a future superpower.

India's leadership claims have not, however, been unconditional. They have been opportunities, as the Indian government has highlighted those aspects of India's energy transition that have been relatively costless and politically unproblematic. Where the government has either failed to make progress or still sees an uncertain future, India has been notably absent.

To summarize, India's global environmental journey has taken the country from a traditional Third World position against colonial and imperial powers to a somewhat reluctant and inconsistent champion of environmental sustainability. The change has been slow and the transition is far from complete, yet India's energy and climate policies would be completely unrecognizable to an observer attending the Earth Summit of 1992 or the Kyoto Protocol negotiations in 1997.

AGAINST COLONIALISM AND IMPERIALISM

The first major conference on the global environment was the United Nations Conference on Human Development in Stockholm, Sweden, in 1972. India's prime minister, Indira Gandhi, was the global South's shining star in Stockholm. Her passionate oratory established India as the leader of the Third World coalition for decades to come. She acknowledged the importance of environmental problems but argued they could not be separated from economic development. She then went on to lambast industrialized countries for their excessive consumption and failure to reduce their footprint. She argued that while environmental stewardship is a common responsibility, industrialized countries need to move first considering their historical responsibility for the problem and capability to act. According to one of the most memorable lines of the conference, "poverty is the worst form of pollution."

This line of argumentation had a lot of appeal for the recently decolonized global South. In 1972 decolonization had produced a large number of desperately poor but sovereign countries. Krasner shows that the global South's international negotiation stances are best understood as a collective response to deep external and internal vulnerabilities.[3] Developing countries worried that environmentalism would allow industrialized countries to "pull the ladder" behind them and prevent the global South from fully participating in the world economy, instead of just supplying natural resources under volatile commodity prices. As a result, the global South as a negotiating bloc refused the notion.

For industrialized countries, India's position was an early warning of a rocky road ahead. India established itself as a leader in the Third World coalition with its "anti-North streak" that reflected a long history of colonial and imperial exploitation.[4] Earlier, in Stockholm, India had made it clear that it was adamantly opposed to any constraints imposed by industrialized countries. India saw global environmental problems as caused by industrialized countries and argued that these countries should accept responsibility for solving these problems. Countries like India should, instead, focus on poverty alleviation without any external constraints imposed by the wealthy and polluting countries.

Indeed, India's staunch rejection of Western dominance in global environmental politics and defense of national sovereignty were to be seen in other key negotiations of the late twentieth century.[5] Two good examples are the negotiations on ozone depletion and the governance of biodiversity.

In the negotiations on the Montreal Protocol of 1987 to stop ozone depletion to the United Nations Framework Convention on Climate Change in 1992, India established itself as a staunch defender of national sovereignty and poor countries' right to pursue economic development on their own terms. The problem of ozone depletion did not initially interest India much. India's own production and consumption of those ozone-depleting substances used in refrigeration, air-conditioning, and spray cans were minimal. Because India is an equatorial country and most of the population has a relatively dark skin, the worst effects of ozone depletion—in particular, skin cancer—would not harm India. Moreover, India had reason to worry about the future. Even though its current consumption and production were minimal, the future might be different. Fueled by external debt or not, India's economy was growing, and people needed fridges and air conditioners. Without access to advanced technology, India's contribution to the ozone problem might grow, and a treaty constraining India's options could prove costly. India saw efforts to phase out ozone-depleting substances as unfair and impractical for developing countries that were currently producing little but would see growing demand in industries like refrigeration and air-conditioning.

The Indian delegation did not participate in the early negotiations on ozone depletion at all, under the assumption that "scientific uncertainties about ozone depletion continued, there was no proof of any threat to India, and India's CFC production remained marginal to world production."[6] Most important, India had no delegation in the Vienna Conference in 1985. At this time, India's official position was still that ozone depletion was not a problem for India and that the country had little at stake in the negotiations. This strategy made sense for India, considering it was neither a major contributor nor a victim of the problem.[7]

As the negotiations continued, there was also "a sense amongst Indian policy makers that the Montreal Protocol was yet another example of Northern effects to dominate the South."[8] When industrialized countries embraced the fight against ozone depletion and tried to persuade Indian diplomats to join the Montreal Protocol in a conference in London in 1989, Environment Minister Z. A. Ansari rejected the proposal, arguing that

> ozone depletion had been caused by the North's profligate use of CFCs over many decades. . . . The North had a moral responsibility to assist the developing countries by transferring the technology. . . . Finally, given the grossly unequal production and consumption of CFCs by developed

and developing countries, any protocol that sought to place similar restrictions on the use of CFCs on all countries was iniquitous and therefore unacceptable.[9]

Over time, however, India's position began to shift. Scientific uncertainties around ozone depletion disappeared as research continued and, from a diplomatic perspective, industrialized countries' unified position made it difficult for India to continue opposition. Instead, the Indian delegation began to demand appropriate modifications, from financial aid to delayed phase-out schedules. By the June 1990 London conference, India was ready to join. The Indian delegation applauded the principle of differentiated responsibilities, the central role of financial assistance, and the emphasis on additionality in financial assistance.

While India's overall position and normative commitments had not changed, the combination of a unified OECD front and generous accommodations turned the tide. India had a credible enough exit option to extract concessions, yet it saw the diplomatic and economic costs of doubling down on obstructionism as too high. Considering that both the United States and the European Community were moving ahead with emissions reductions, and the Montreal Protocol had directed signatories to stop trade with non-members, India, along with China and other developing countries, decided to join the Montreal Protocol in exchange for modest financial support and extended timelines for phasing out ozone-depleting substances.

India's positioning in the negotiations on another key topic of the Earth Summit era, biodiversity, points to the same direction. Indeed, biodiversity as an issue in general has provoked bitter North-South conflicts.[10] Expanding human activity across the world contributed to habitat loss and species extinction, producing both economic damage (e.g., loss of potentially valuable biological resources) and a clear and present danger to indigenous livelihoods (e.g., forest peoples in Latin America), not to mention the intrinsic value of rich natural environments. Alas, the problem was that many of the habitats and species under threat were found in poorer countries that had not yet decimated their biota. Wealthy industrialized countries, which had destroyed their natural forests centuries earlier, were now asking countries like Brazil, Indonesia, and Malaysia not to do the same.

For India, this North-South setup was the perfect storm. In the early stages of the negotiations, leading up to the Earth Summit in Rio de Janeiro, Brazil, in 1992, "India's interests encompassed international assistance and incentives for the conservation of biodiversity; easy access to biotechnology; and the prevention of Northern intellectual property legislation from hindering the flow of technology and information to the South." The last point related to a broader conversation in India, where

> the government also saw a public interest role for itself in crucial sectors like pharmaceuticals and agriculture. Thus, in the case of pharmaceuticals, the need to make drugs cheaply and widely available to the predominantly poor population of India was the main logic behind the government's encouragement of local innovation and competition by allowing only process patents, as well as its retention of broad compulsory licensing powers in order to keep the prices of essential drugs under control. In the case of agriculture too, with India primarily an agrarian economy, and with the majority of farmers being subsistence or small producers, commercial farmers with exportable surpluses constituting a minuscule minority, the government saw a public interest role for itself, for instance in making seed cheaply and widely available and in encouraging national self-sufficiency and food security.[11]

Over time, these conflicts intensified, if anything. India's position reflected the broader concerns of the coalition of developing countries. When the Convention on Biological Diversity was finally negotiated, it was a relatively toothless instrument with no provisions for enforcement. The conflicts surrounding biodiversity made the negotiations very difficult from the beginning, as major developing countries with biodiversity hot spots realized their bargaining power, while industrialized countries refused to offer generous compensation for effective protection measures. As Harrop and Pritchard write, "The CBD imposes very limited commitments: the one strict unqualified obligation on Parties being that they submit national reports. . . . Most articles of the CBD contain provisions which are expressed in imprecise language or over-qualified terms which enable member states to implement these provisions in virtually any manner they wish, whether challenging or not."[12]

This weakness notwithstanding, or perhaps partly because of it, India's view of the negotiation outcome was positive. The Ministry of Environment and Forests argued:

This Convention can . . . be viewed as a gain for us since it not only supports the actions we are already taking for the conservation of our biodiversity, but also creates a firm link between the transfer of genetic resources and the return transfer of biotechnology which uses those resources. In addition, the Convention calls for a sharing of the profits derived from biotechnology which uses the genetic resources of developing countries. . . . Obligations on us . . . are essentially of a contractual nature and dependant [*sic*] on provision of finance and technology.[13]

Here India's defensive posture validated a weak negotiation outcome. For India, effective measures to reduce biodiversity loss were not key; rather, Indian policy makers wanted guarantees that any concrete action to protect biodiversity would be combined with profit sharing and access to biotechnology. By virtue of its very weakness, the CBD underscored national sovereignty over biological resources and reaffirmed India's control of its own biota and the systems that governed intellectual property rights.

Of all the different topics, population control was perhaps the most sensitive for India. During the twenty-one-month "Emergency" declared by Prime Minister Indira Gandhi in 1975, a poorly planned sterilization campaign resulted in widespread human rights violations. Here Weiner's analysis of the momentous importance of this campaign in the 1977 parliamentary elections is worth quoting at length:

Janata [opposition] party candidates campaigned on a single issue: ending the emergency and restoring democracy to India. Economic issues were secondary, except insofar as they illustrated the problems that arose when individuals were deprived of their rights to protest. In northern India a primary target of the opposition was the sterilization program that had been vigorously and in many areas forcibly pursued by state government chief ministers under the influence of Sanjay Gandhi. Word spread throughout India (including areas without a sterilization program) of some of the excesses committed by state governments aggressively carrying out the sterilization campaign: quotas assigned to local school teachers and other government officials; villagers who could not obtain loans or licenses unless they agreed to sterilization; government officials who, desperately seeking to meet their quotas (or paying the penalty of not receiving their dearness allowances) forcibly dragging villagers, young and old, to nearby sterilization camps; hastily constructed sterilization camps where some patients became infected or died; police firings at Turkman gate in Delhi and in parts of Uttar Pradesh when there were clashes between local people and government officials; slum dwellers who were told that their houses would be removed by government bulldozers unless they agreed to being sterilized.[14]

When democracy was restored in 1977, the Indian society was scarred for decades to come, and the idea of top-down population control had become a definite red flag. On this issue, India's international position was overdetermined from the beginning.

To summarize, India's first two decades in global environmental politics were about being against, not for, something. At home, a combination of widespread poverty and a history of British colonial exploitation made global environmental commitments an anathema. Internationally, India established itself as a vocal advocate for the Third World and felt that industrialized countries were not trustworthy.

Similar to other poor countries, India approached global environmental politics with a skeptical and suspicious attitude.[15] India positioned itself as the champion of an abused and disenfranchised global South, surrounded by former colonial and imperial masters bargaining in bad faith. It rarely sought specific environmental outcomes in negotiations but rather used global environmental politics as an opportunity to underscore its sovereignty and score points against its perceived opponents from the industrialized global North.

All this was to change only slowly, in fits and starts over a period of three decades. Climate change, although initially India's golden opportunity to lambast the industrialized world for hypocrisy, played a key role in the country's evolving position in global environmental politics.

LIFESTYLE EMISSIONS

In 1988 climate change appeared for the first time on the global political agenda. An unusually hot summer in the United States prompted the U.S. Senate to conduct an investigation, and famed scientist James Hansen argued for mounting evidence on global warming caused by greenhouse gas emissions. From this point on, climate change has increasingly come to dominate global environmental politics. For India, climate politics was a complicated challenge from the beginning. Global inequity in greenhouse gas emissions gave India a new rhetorical weapon against the global North, yet Indian policy makers were also concerned about possible international constraints on the country's "carbon budget" for economic growth. It was only later that Indians realized that the most dangerous threat to development was not some insidious form of carbon imperialism, but rather climate change itself.

At the time, formal international negotiations on climate change began in Toronto, Canada. As climate change was still a new phenomenon, there was much emphasis on establishing the Intergovernmental Panel on Climate Change to develop a basic understanding of the nature of the problem and possible solutions. But already at that time, politics began to poison the process. Different governments conducted their own investigations and tried to decide whether they should embrace or contest the emerging idea of global climate cooperation.

For India, the early climate change debate was a golden opportunity. If India today has low per capita emissions, then the country's contribution to the problem at the time of the 1992 Earth Summit must be considered absolutely minimal. In 1990 India's per capita emissions stood at a puny 0.7 tons. In contrast, the United States had per capita emissions of 19.3 tons. The average American emitted almost thirty times as much as the average Indian. As a result of this dramatic difference, India's share of global carbon dioxide fell below 3 percent in 1990. Every sixth human in the world was Indian, yet India emitted only about one in every forty tons of carbon dioxide.

Quite understandably, India's early position reflected concerns about constraints on economic development. In the April 1990 Conference of Select Developing Countries on Global Environmental issues in New Delhi, the Indian hosts argued that the problem of climate change was mostly caused by industrialized countries and that developing countries would not be in a position to slow down their emission growth without generous financial assistance and technological transfer. Poorer governments, the Indian hosts said, would need financing and clean technology to stop the growth of greenhouse gas emissions. The Indians also firmly rejected the notion that climate mitigation should be pursued when it would compromise economic development.[16]

Indian environmentalists were quick to join this call. In 1991 two Indian environmentalists at CSE, Anil Agarwal and Sunita Narain, published a pamphlet titled *Global Warming in an Unequal World*.[17] They argued that the industrialized countries were woefully ignorant of the Third World's plight:

> Behind the global rules and the global discipline that is being thrust upon the hapless Third World, there is precious little global sharing or even an effort by the West to understand the perspectives of the other two-thirds. How can we visualise any kind of global management, in a world so highly divided between the rich and the poor, the powerful and the powerless, which does not have a basic element of economic justice and equity. One American is equal to, god knows, how many Indians or Africans in terms of global resource consumption.

For Western environmentalists, Indian environmentalists' position was not welcome news. The Western environmental movement already faced pushback from a coalition of those worried about the cost of climate mitigation. When India's environmentalists failed to take a clear position in favor of environmental sustainability, they weakened the environmental movement's framing of climate change as a common issue. India's positioning also had an impact on other developing countries, which seized the opportunity to declare their opposition to any constraints on their economic development.

By the time the negotiations for what would be the Kyoto Protocol were in full swing, India's position had hardened. According to Raghunandan, the Indian posture "ossified into stonewalling of persistent developed country efforts to breach the developed-developing firewall, and belabouring concerns about funding and transfer of technology from developing countries."[18] Drawing on this hardline view, India scored a major victory in the Berlin conference in 1995, where countries agreed to formulate what would become the Kyoto Protocol only two years later. The negotiation outcome, the Berlin Mandate, explicitly codified a strict binary distinction between developed and developing countries. It gave an extreme interpretation to the idea of common but differentiated responsibilities by exempting developing countries from emission reductions:

> The Parties should protect the climate system for the benefit of present and future generations of humankind, on the basis of equity and in accordance with their common but differentiated responsibilities and respective capabilities. Accordingly, the developed country Parties should take the lead in combating climate change and the adverse effects thereof. . . . Not introduce any new commitments for Parties not included in Annex I, but reaffirm existing commitments in Article 4.1 and continue to advance the implementation of these commitments in order to achieve sustainable development, taking into account Article 4.3, 4.5 and 4.7.

This victory for developing countries proved impossible to reconcile with domestic politics in the United States. In particular, the Kyoto Protocol, negotiated in December 1997, reflected the impossibility of meeting all these goals at the same time.[19] In the United States, the Senate had unanimously passed a "sense of the Senate" motion to reject any climate agreement that would not impose binding constraints on countries like India. While Vice President Gore managed to salvage the negotiations themselves with his last-minute intervention, the United States never ratified the Kyoto Protocol. As the United States had promised to do much of the heavy lifting by reducing emissions by 6 percent relative to a 1990 baseline, U.S. nonratification made the Kyoto Protocol a rather toothless treaty.

During the first decade of the twenty-first century, the balance of power began to tilt toward emerging economies. China, India, and other emerging markets enjoyed the fruits of rapid economic growth. The world realized that these countries, led by China, were no longer vulnerable Third World economies. In response, China and India joined forces with Brazil and South Africa to form the BASIC alliance.[20] A key outcome of the alliance is that it made explicit the growing gap between a large number of least developed countries and large emerging economies. This increasingly visible gap forced the BASIC members to adjust their negotiation strategies, as they attempted to thwart calls for emissions reductions. Hiding behind the least developed countries would no longer do, even if India in particular still had some of the lowest per capita emissions on the planet. The country's economic dynamism and large size all but guaranteed the kind of attention that India's political leaders would rather have avoided.

India's position was still largely obstructionist, and the domestic elite's emphasis on national sovereignty made negotiations more difficult.[21] India was, indeed, widely considered a difficult negotiating partner in global climate talks. While other countries refrain from formally accusing India of obstructionism, negotiators from industrialized countries share a common view of India as one of the most combative and rigid negotiators. As an illustrative example, Vihma cites the Indian delegation's comment from the Dialogue Workshop at the Vienna climate talks in 2007 that mitigation commitments could "keep developing countries poor for another three generations."[22]

India was also vocal in insisting that industrialized countries offer generous climate finance to support mitigation and adaptation in poorer countries. In fact, "India has repeatedly outlined that Annex I parties have committed themselves to provide new, additional, adequate, and predictable financing to developing country parties to implement the UNFCCC."[23] Here India emphasized the need to finance clean technology and emissions reductions more broadly and also reminded the industrialized countries that they had already made concrete promises to that effect.

And yet while many saw India as a problem, the country's low per capita emissions are a fundamental reality. Although India's middle class contributes to the global climate crisis through unsustainable lifestyle choices, the vast majority of Indians produce few greenhouse gas emissions. Although India's per capita carbon dioxide emissions have grown sixfold in three decades, they remain far below the global average. If we exclude the wealthiest quartile of Indians, the remaining one billion people still generate minuscule amounts of carbon dioxide. In such a situation, to blame India for self-interested obstructionism does appear unreasonable. While high-income and upper-middle-income countries can reduce their fossil fuel use without sacrificing the well-being of their citizens, the best India can aim for is low-carbon growth. Zero-carbon development, let alone emission reductions, is impossible barring revolutionary advances in clean technology across many sectors of economic activity.

Overall, then, India's position was a mix of unproductive obstructionism and genuine concern for equity in defense of developmental space. India often made it hard for industrialized countries to make progress in negotiations and increase their ambition. Few politicians in the industrialized countries can promise deep cuts to emissions at an economic cost when major emerging economies such as India refuse to participate. On the other hand, India's leadership, if at times combative and disruptive, forced wealthier countries to make concessions to the developing world in the form of delayed emissions limits and green finance for mitigation and adaptation. In defending the interests of the poor against the wealthiest countries on the planet, India has been an effective advocate.

CLAIMS OF LEADERSHIP

India's environmental discourse began to shift at the time of the Copenhagen climate summit in 2009. By that time, a new generation of environmental activists, many with international experience, had begun to raise awareness about climate change as an essential problem for India's future.

As a result, India went to the summit with mixed feelings—and with an unusually open mind. As noted earlier, Environment Minister Ramesh acknowledged that India needs to embrace a low-carbon future and carry its weight, even though industrialized countries would need to lead the transition for decades to come.

This discourse did not upend India's vigorous defense of its right to economic development and poverty alleviation, but it did recognize environmental protection, and mitigation of climate change in particular, as a legitimate goal of international cooperation and national planning. Whereas India's earlier position was to downplay the problem and portray it as a devious ploy to control developing countries, now India began to recognize the problem. It continued, however, to assign blame on wealthier countries and insist that they refrain from shrinking India's carbon budget.

India's core position remained quite stable throughout.[24] The change that occurred between 2007 and 2011 was one of strategy, as the country moved from a purely defensive posture to a more dynamic and flexible framing of the issue. Especially during Jairam Ramesh's time, India has shown more willingness to compromise and make deals with other countries. Although the next environment minister, Jayanti Natrajan, did not prove as flexible and accommodating, "the general dynamics that have led to a more open negotiation strategy seem to be difficult to stop, as the underlying trends—both domestically and internationally persist. These trends include increasing pressure on domestic energy resources, the search for new business opportunities (e.g., in the CDM), and pressure from other developing countries."[25]

Within this broad outlook, more nuanced positions have emerged. According to Dubash, key positions in India's contemporary climate discourse—and, I would argue, environmental issues more generally—can be grouped under three categories.[26] First, "growth-first realists" emphasize the importance of economic growth and the threat that international climate cooperation, as opposed to climate change itself, presents to India's prospects. This frame is a modest revision of the historically dominant "equity" frame, which emphasizes India's poverty, low per capita emissions, and minimal historical contribution to the problem. While growth realists see climate change as a real problem, they do not consider it central to India's future.

The more significant departures from the past include "sustainable development realism" and "sustainable development internationalism." The former recognizes the importance of sustainable development for India but puts domestic cobenefits of climate policy ahead of solutions to the global problem itself. This narrative notes that there is much India can do to improve domestic conditions through activities that mitigate climate change, while reaping international reputational benefits as a bonus. This realist frame, for Dubash, dominates India's public discourse on climate change today.

The internationalist version emphasizes the importance of India's commitment to multilateralism and has only limited domestic support. This version is a radical departure from the two realist orientations, as it holds that India is responsible for mitigating climate change despite low per capita emissions. It does not give industrialized countries a free pass, but it maintains that India's best course of action is to play a constructive role in global climate mitigation, perhaps even as an example of climate leadership in the global South. This strategy would reap domestic cobenefits, facilitate clean technology development, enhance India's global reputation, and create opportunities for a truly sustainable path of development.

This classification is a far cry from the classic distinction between Gandhian, appropriate technology, and Marxist approaches that Guha proposed to characterize India's environmental movement before India's economic reforms began.[27] All these perspectives share a lot in common with the traditional equity frame, and none of them is entirely compatible with the three policy discourses that Dubash identifies in today's India. To put it bluntly, India's traditional environmentalism has given way to a new generation of thinkers that have far more in common with global debates than was true in the past. The world and India have both changed, and Indian environmentalism has adapted to changing social, economic, and political conditions.

Recognizing these new realities, India went to the Paris negotiation in 2015 with an optimistic outlook. Prime Minister Modi launched a publicity campaign to highlight India's renewable energy ambition and invited other countries to learn from India's success in reducing the cost of renewable power generation through reverse auctions that leveraged market competition to produce low-cost renewable power. As Mathur writes, this outlook originated from three mutually reinforcing streams of thought:

> (i) the crystallization of the thought that action was needed by all countries, including India (largely because it was seen that significant climate-related domestic action, with very strong development benefits, was possible at a low incremental cost that India could absorb because of the development gains); (ii) India could contribute by lowering its carbon intensity (though not by reducing its absolute carbon emissions); and (iii) there were opportunities to use the size of the Indian market to enhance the rate of adoption and simultaneously enable price reduction of low-carbon technologies as well to strengthen markets for these technologies in other developing countries. These led India to believe that a universal agreement to which it agreed would have to be based on self-prepared pledges by individual countries.[28]

The official discourse on India as a progressive climate leader was, again, carefully tailored to match domestic policy ambitions. When India announced its Nationally Determined Contribution (NDC) under the 2015 Paris Agreement on climate change, its most important commitment was to increase non–fossil fuel share of electricity generation capacity to 40 percent by 2030. This cornerstone commitment, which was made conditional on adequate climate finance from the industrialized countries, closely reflects the country's own power sector planning and does not constitute a major deviation from the baseline of domestic policy. India's domestic renewable energy target for 2022 was increased to 225 gigawatts in 2018. By 2030 the government expects renewables to be over 50 percent of total capacity. Compared to this plan, a 40 percent non–fossil fuel target is easy to reach.

In 2021, at a United Nations climate summit in Glasgow, Scotland, Prime Minister Modi surprised the global audience by announcing that India would commit to a 2070 net zero emission target. This target, which would have India reach carbon neutrality a decade after China, would be backed by 50 percent of renewable power generation capacity by 2030 and other power sector measures. Observers favorably received this combination of a relatively ambitious long-term goal and plausible short-term targets. As a hedge, Modi did state that the wealthy countries will need to contribute a whopping trillion dollars to support the transition.

India's most industrious state has led the way to a low-carbon future.[29] When the Bharatiya Janata Party (BJP) won the general election in 2014 and Narenda Modi became prime minister, he had years of experience promoting solar power in his home state, Gujarat. Blessed with abundant sunshine and a strong industrial sector, Gujarat was the first state to develop a solar policy in 2009. The Gujarati government encouraged investors to set up large solar projects for grid-scale power generation. For systems up to 500 megawatts—a very large system at the time—Gujarat's state policy offered a generous price of US$0.26/kWh for the first twelve years of a project. This generous price encouraged early movers to invest in Gujarat, and today prices are but a tiny fraction of the original announced price. The first-mover advantage, combined with excellent insolation and rapidly growing electricity demand, has made Gujarat a leader in solar power across all of India.

Where domestic policy has proven difficult or ineffective, India's international negotiation position remains cautious. Perhaps a case of putting the cart before the horse, India's international announcements have mostly followed perceived trends. A review of India's policy positions reveals the general pattern identified earlier, of little change in core position but a much more flexible and adaptive strategy to secure concrete gains from negotiations and avoid the reputation of a stubborn laggard. This logic can be seen by reading India's NDC to the Paris Agreement, which shows some overall ambition but with major variation across sectors, depending on whether Indian policy makers have reason to believe the challenge is an easy or a difficult one.

This dynamic is readily seen in the case of transportation emissions. India's NDC does not make any specific commitments to reducing transportation emissions, even though domestic policy makers are increasingly showing interest in electric vehicles. India's transportation emissions continue to grow, and the nascent EV market is years away from bending this emission curve in a way that would be certain enough to prompt a public promise. In such a setting, Indian policy makers have surmised, a conservative approach of underpromising, and possibly overdelivering, would be the right course action.

In the power sector, coal remains an important challenge for India's climate policy. While the updated NDC goal to increase non–fossil fuel share of generation capacity to 50 percent suggests increasing awareness of competitive renewable power among the Indian political elite, India's energy planners do not expect significant reductions in coal-fired power generation. India's National Electricity Plan of 2018 expects coal-fired power generation capacity to grow to 238 gigawatts from 192 gigawatts by 2027. This increase is modest compared to expected growth in electricity demand—a doubling of total demand by 2027—but is growth nonetheless. India's thermal power generation capacity, the vast majority of which is coal, would be 43 percent of total capacity instead of 67 percent today. The average capacity factor for coal-fired power plants would remain low but reach 60.5 percent by 2027.

This strategy would allow India to meet ambitious renewable energy targets yet significantly increase coal-fired power generation. Where the Indian government sees an opportunity for improved energy security and development, clean energy projects and policies are framed as solutions to climate change. Where such opportunity does not yet exist, the Indian government no longer adopts a hardline position but instead remains silent.

India's achievements cannot be discounted as purely opportunistic, however. Considering the country's low per capita emissions and the fact that outside the power sector fossil fuels continue to dominate over cleaner alternatives, it is implausible to expect anything except emissions growth from India for decades to come. The question is how fast emissions grow. India has already managed to bend the emissions curve with renewable energy and energy efficiency. It is also possible that India manages to accelerate its coal phaseout with battery storage, hydrogen, and improved transmission.

Global environmental concerns cannot be disentangled from domestic problems in India. Understanding the local cobenefits of dealing with global environmental problems is key to India's environmental strategy. Local problems such as air pollution and groundwater depletion have motivated the expansion of public interest in clean energy. As a vulnerable country with a growing population and economy, India has embraced the cause of climate mitigation. It has not, however, done so without tying climate mitigation to local fobenefits.[30] India's policy makers have found a way out of their obstructionist position by justifying climate mitigation with local cobenefits that make emissions reductions a smart move for India as a country, regardless of any international pressure from the industrialized countries. Institutional capacity remains an obstacle, but with a clear commitment to action we will likely see improvement over time.

This intimate connection between domestic and global environmental issues in the Indian discourse is essential to reconciling the apparent conflict between environmental awareness and a steadfast defense of the developmental space. India's position in global environmental policy began to change when the stark trade-offs between economy and environment lost their traction and Indian policy makers started to see opportunities in sustainable development. Because of this structural change, India no longer sees a need to maintain the traditional Third World position of hardline confrontation with the industrialized countries.

At the same time, however, Indian policy makers remain aware of the virtual impossibility of economic growth without higher greenhouse gas emissions. This reality makes it impossible for India to fully embrace a position that sets up hard constraints on economic activity on environmental grounds. India's climate and clean energy policy exploits opportunities for mitigation where the costs are relatively low and cobenefits available, yet government officials avoid making commitments that could prove costly or difficult to meet. Indian leaders sometimes announce wildly ambitious targets to the domestic audience, such as replacing all car sales with electric vehicles by 2030,[31] but retain a cautious position in international negotiations.

The point, then, is not to deny the reality of climate change but to vigorously defend India's carbon space for economic development. India recognizes climate change and other global environmental problems as real threats. It maintains, however, that solving these problems requires decisive leadership from wealthier countries for reasons of both efficacy and equity. There is considerable variation among Indian stakeholders' views of how much they think India should do unilaterally, with Dubash's growth realists insisting on minimal action and sustainable development internationalists aiming to lead the world. In government, the growth realist narrative continues to dominate, though the intermediate position of sustainable development realism has recently begun to gain ground.

This logic can be seen by investigating India's position on two global environmental agreements. The first one is the Minamata Convention of 2014, which aims to reduce dangerous mercury emissions from coal-fired power plants, mining, and other activities. Specifically, the convention banned some products containing mercury by the year 2020. Furthermore, it required the installation of best available technology and the application of best environmental practices within five years for all new sources of mercury.[32]

The Minamata Convention, which entered into force in August 2017, had a tumultuous negotiation history. For years, China and India refused to participate. Until the mid-2000s both countries argued against any legally binding rules. At the fifth and final round of negotiations in 2013, however, the Chinese delegation changed its position and announced a certain willingness to accept legally binding constraints. This 180-degree change was essential for a negotiation breakthrough and was driven by a combination of increased domestic awareness of the problem, higher wealth levels and willingness to pay, and domestic scientific and technical capacity to act.[33] China no longer saw mercury control as a net negative, but rather as a natural and feasible action to protect public health at an acceptable cost.

When China changed course and accepted the need to reduce mercury pollution, India was left alone and grudgingly accepted the deal—though with special exemptions and extended phaseout schedules. India was now alone, as all other major powers had subscribed to the notion of mercury control. Being the lone holdout would have been costly for India's image, so the government negotiated a compromise that allowed the treaty to form and, in a few years, enter into force.

The second agreement is the 2016 Kigali amendment to the Montreal Protocol on HFC emissions. This important amendment aims to ban the use of HCFC, which does not deplete the ozone layer but is a tremendously powerful greenhouse gas. India, again, was an important holdout but finally agreed to participate in exchange for additional time to phase out HFC, along with financial support. Because India was alone in opposition, it decided to accept a compromise that would buy it more time to find alternatives in the crucially important sectors of air-conditioning and refrigeration. When the United States and China agreed to collaborate on an HFC phaseout, India was left alone among the major economies, similar to the mercury negotiations. India recognized the necessity of accepting some kind of agreement but succeeded in securing a slower schedule for freezing HFC emissions by 2028, as opposed to 2019 (industrialized countries) or most developing countries, including China (2024).[34] Again, India was forced to adopt a more flexible position by China's changing position, yet the end outcome was not all that bad for India.

These agreements, along with India's marriage of climate mitigation and local cobenefits in the carbon space, show how India can play a constructive role in global environmental cooperation. For India, economic development and poverty alleviation are nonnegotiable priorities. As long as hundreds of millions continue to live in poverty, any approach that compromises India's economic development or constrains its carbon space is off the table. This logic is readily seen in the 2070 net zero commitment, which strikes a delicate balance between meeting global expectations while avoiding a premature shrinking of India's carbon space.

India's future in global environmental politics lies with the original spirit of sustainable development, with a strong equity focus. On the one hand, India's renewable energy boom has already demonstrated the benefits of adopting a proactive image. On the other hand, it is all but certain that India's greenhouse gas emissions, and environmental footprint more broadly, will continue to grow for over a decade. India thus faces the same challenge as China: focusing attention on the positive and away from the negative, as hiding behind the developing country bloc becomes more and more difficult.

5

THE FUTURE OF ENERGY AND ENVIRONMENT IN INDIA

What might India's energy and environment future look like? India is both full of potential and afflicted by greater problems than any other major economy. India's population will grow, but nobody can say with any certainty by how much. India's low-carbon transition has started, but nobody can say whether it will be swift or glacial. All these uncertainties compound one another and leave a bewildering range of possible outcomes to consider. Considering these uncertainties, I refrain from making any firm predictions in this concluding chapter and instead choose the more modest approach of qualitative scenario analysis. I describe and discuss three qualitative scenarios, each of which could plausibly capture the most important features of India's future. Table 5.1 summarizes these highly stylized scenarios for India—and, by direct extension, the world.

Of the three scenarios, the first sees India fall into chaos, as economic growth disappoints and environmental destruction drives over a billion people into despair. In this scenario, India fails to develop in a sustainable manner. A giant with clay feet, India slowly descends into authoritarian populism in an increasingly hostile South Asia and a world.

The second scenario is perhaps better news for India, but a potential disaster for the world. In this scenario, India's economic growth continues

TABLE 5.1 Three Stylized Scenarios for Demographic, Economic, Political, and Sustainable Development in India

SCENARIO	DEMOGRAPHY	ECONOMY	POLITICS	SUSTAINABILITY
A society in turmoil	Rapid population growth	Slow growth, widespread poverty	Authoritarian turn	Environmental degradation despite limited growth
Uncontrolled growth	Rapid population growth	Rapid growth, widespread poverty	Authoritarian turn	Rapid growth with major environmental degradation
A prosperous and sustainable India	A stable population	Rapid growth, reduced poverty	Vibrant civil society, robust democracy	Rapid growth with improved environmental quality

largely unabated for a few decades, but inequality grows, and badly needed investments in climate-proofing remain elusive. The Indian economy expands in size, but the current middle class reaps most of the gains. India's environmental footprint grows fast, and India plays a key role in contributing to ever-worsening climate disruption.

The last scenario, a prosperous and sustainable India, strikes the right balance. The economy grows, and the Indian state uses the growing resources to reduce poverty, enable climate adaptation, and gradually reduce the environmental footprint of the Indian economy. Although it is not an easy or linear process, India's governance capacity improves over time, and the country enjoys a golden age of social innovation in government, business, and civil society. While India's emissions grow, the country plays an important role in leading emerging economies to a more sustainable future, both by example and by arguing for sustainability in international negotiations.

Clearly, the implications for energy and environment are momentous both within and outside India. Here the causal arrow has two tips. On the one hand, India's ability to develop depends heavily on climate change. If global mitigation efforts continue to flounder and the worst outcomes are realized, large parts of South Asia will become uninhabitable. Climate disruption undermines the Indian economy, and those who are already poor and marginalized will suffer the most.

On the other hand, India's development patterns also drive greenhouse gas emissions. The large population and vast developmental space mean that India's contribution to climate change could grow rapidly and all but derail global efforts to avoid climate disruption. If India's economic dynamism continues to be fueled by fossil fuels without effective environmental management, the country might become the most important obstacle to effective climate mitigation in the critical decades leading to the year 2050.

The good news is that policy can avoid the worst outcomes in India's energy and environment. Despite population and economic growth, India is not doomed to a dystopian future described by continued extreme poverty, inequality, and irreversible environmental destruction. If India can break free of the trap of weak governance in a captive society, it can invest in sustainable economic growth and use the surplus from such growth to deal with the negative side effects of demographic and economic expansion. It all depends on improved governance, responsible resource allocation, and increased awareness of the need for sustainable development.

Nobody can say for sure which of these stylized scenarios best captures India's future. There are too many uncertainties related to population growth, economic development, social development, culture, and politics. By describing plausible scenarios in a qualitative manner, I hope to lay out the possibilities and underscore what is at stake when we debate sustainable development in the world's largest democracy.

A SOCIETY IN TURMOIL

The year is 2050. The world has failed to slow down global warming, and temperatures are on their way to increase by over 3 degrees Celsius by 2100 from preindustrial times. Despite some progress in the use of renewable energy in the power sector, the world economy continues to mostly run on fossil fuels. While the use of coal has decreased somewhat, national economies depend heavily on oil and gas. Deforestation and land degradation compromise food security and release vast amounts of carbon into the atmosphere every year.

In India, population growth continues at a rapid clip, with few signs of change. Although fertility rates have decreased, actual numbers continue to expand. India's population is close to two billion people, and the country faces chronic food security problems. Because social and educational development continues to lag, fertility rates among poor families remain high. India is closer to falling into the Malthusian trap than it has been since the onset of the Green Revolution almost a century ago.

In the meantime, India's energy transition sputters. Although renewable energy capacity has expanded, both technological and behavioral solutions to the problem of intermittency have proven disappointing. To meet the country's vast demand for power, coal-fired power generation has almost doubled. Climate change contributes to brutal heat waves that create a seemingly infinite demand for air conditioners. This vicious cycle contributes to massive increases in India's carbon dioxide emissions and exacerbates the bitter conflict over climate change among India and other countries.

Resource scarcity wreaks havoc in the Indian society. Indian agriculture can barely keep up with population growth, and the increasingly frequent and extreme droughts and heat waves have left large areas nonarable. Food security is a chronic problem, and because most Indians still rely on agriculture, progress in poverty alleviation has stalled. India's disappointing trajectory means that any hopes of ending poverty in the twenty-first century are all but guaranteed to fail.

These environmental disasters contribute to worsening inequality in India. The lack of water for irrigation, scarce land, and forest degradation hurt the rural poor the most. The Indian economy has tripled in size, but most of the gains have gone to the wealthiest decile, who increasingly import food and other goods from abroad.

India's social problems fuel domestic and international conflicts. Within India, rural insurgencies return as harvests fail and nonagricultural employment jobs remain unavailable to hundreds of millions in need. In South Asia, climate change contributes to growing vulnerability and sows the seeds of new conflicts between India and Pakistan. Other South Asian countries, such as Nepal and Bangladesh, increasingly see India as an unreliable bully that aggressively pursues opportunities to seize resources from them. Conflicts over water and migration have left India with very few friends in the region.

Over time, India's democratic foundations may prove unable to manage and contain these conflicts. Growing frustration among India's population results in the ascent of politicians that undermine the country's democratic institutions. The Indian democracy, which has beaten the odds since 1947, is closer to a permanent reversal to authoritarianism than ever before, except during the 1975–1977 emergency. The BJP's dominance raises the specter of authoritarian backsliding unless India's opposition parties find a way to challenge the Modi regime.

As a result, India's social and economic development is arrested. Poverty and inequality continue to worsen, and the glory days of rapid economic growth are long gone. COVID-19 leaves behind a weakened rural India. Poor economic performance is made worse by India's authoritarian turn. India continues to suffer from low institutional capacity, and now the lack of a robust democratic system makes things worse. Growing authoritarianism does not translate into effective state action, but rather an increasingly unaccountable and corrupt state apparatus. State governments frequently violate constitutional rules and clash with the increasingly incapable central administration.

For the rest of the world, India proves to be far less potent a force than many thought. Although India's population is massive and the energy transition has sputtered, India's greenhouse gas emissions remain low on a per capita basis. India remains the poor country it has always been. This monumental failure of social and economic development guarantees the failure of any grand schemes to end poverty. The vast majority of India's two billion people continue to live a wretched existence.

UNCONTROLLED GROWTH

Another difficult scenario is uncontrolled growth. In this scenario, India's economy continues on its current track. Growth is relatively fast, but its spoils are unevenly divided. Most of the gains go to the middle class, but there is enough left for extreme poverty to shrink. The problem is that India makes little progress with sustainability. The Indian government remains paralyzed with its intrinsic governance problems. The economy grows in spite of the government, and poverty alleviation is mostly driven by the market, with opportunities afforded by urbanization playing a key role.

India's population grows to about 1.7 billion. Rapid economic growth contributes to lower fertility rates, and this structural change reduces population growth. The reduction, however, is not fast enough to avoid a large increase in total population between 2020 and 2050. This rapid growth is not so fast as to bring India back to the brink of the Malthusian trap, but it does contribute to an outsized environmental burden that brings a dark cloud over India's future.

In this scenario, the good news is that the economy continues to grow despite resource scarcity and uncontrolled economic expansion. In a pattern reminiscent of India's first two decades of economic reform, private-sector dynamism overcomes resource and institutional constraints. India's entrepreneurial and innovative population continues to develop solutions to its problems, and some of those solutions do very well on the world market, too.

For large segments of the Indian population, economic growth produces both new opportunities and challenges. While the middle class gains, economic growth is a mixed bag for the poor. On the one hand, improvements in living standards continue. Much of the gains are made in growing rural areas, in particular smaller and medium-sized towns. But rural areas also develop with more nonfarm employment opportunities, productive use of new technology, and improved infrastructure from electricity to roads and water. The problem is that the country's environmental crisis continues to grow. Droughts, groundwater depletion, and air pollution harm the rural poor to a significant extent, undermining the gains from economic growth.

Inequality continues to expand, easily exceeding today's alarming levels. India's "billionaire raj" continues unabated, as most of the fruits of economic growth accrue to a small number of powerful tycoons who control both business and politics. The COVID-19 pandemic contributes to a growing rural-urban gap in economic fortunes. Over time, although everyone gains, environmental constraints corrode the rural poor's living standards. And because the rural poor gain less than the largely urban middle class to begin with, the gap between the rich and the poor widens.

For the Indian democracy, challenges abound. The Indian state's legitimacy hits rock bottom, as the country's majority grows frustrated with the government's failure to solve even the most basic problems. Improved education, largely stemming from growth in high-quality private schools, does not contribute to a more aware citizenry but rather provokes cynicism and hostility. India's political institutions, in turn, continue to direct economic activity toward rent seeking and worsen already severe inequality. When Indian citizens lose their faith in government, they perpetuate the pattern of voting based on caste, religion, and handouts.

In regional politics, India would be a hegemon—but not a benevolent or benign one. India's structural power continues to grow, and neighboring countries have no choice but to adjust to a mighty hegemon's regional order. But because of India's domestic problems and growing environmental crisis, the region becomes engulfed in conflicts over scarce resources, notably water.

In this scenario, India would be both a major contributor to and a victim of climate change. As India's economy continues to grow without much success in limiting environmental destruction, the country's greenhouse gas emissions surge. India plays a key role in propelling the world well above an increase of 3 degrees Celsius in global average temperature. The resulting heat waves, droughts, and floods wreak havoc among India's poor. Although higher income levels enhance adaptation capacity, continued institutional failure means that the poorest half a billion Indians have little recourse. The human costs of climate change in India become extreme, and climate change counts as among the five most important causes of mortality and morbidity in the country.

In international negotiations, India would be a roadblock to real progress. India's surging greenhouse gas emissions produce a negotiating tactic that is best described as flagrant obstructionism. India's primary goal in negotiations is to avoid any limitations whatsoever on industrial activity and fossil fuel consumption. Diplomatic relations with other countries would become increasingly strained, as India would lead the world toward irreversible climate disruption and stubbornly refuse to make a serious effort to stop this development.

A PROSPEROUS AND SUSTAINABLE INDIA

India's future need not be unsustainable. The two previous scenarios are driven by failures of economic development and government policy. If India manages to continue its business dynamism and add a layer of effective public policy in the environmental and social realms, the future may look very different. I end this book on a positive note, exploring what a prosperous and sustainable India might look like.

In this scenario, rapid social change brings population growth under control. Building on a trend of decreasing fertility rates, the Indian population stabilizes sooner than most people expected, and, if anything, policy makers begin to focus their attention on the challenge of supporting older people in a population that is no longer so young. Key drivers of this important transition include progress in education for women, increased female participation in the labor market, and a more liberal social atmosphere. These trends are already observed in some of the socially progressive states, such as Kerala, and in the decades to come they will spread across India.

India's economy continues to develop, as smart policies support a healthy mix of agricultural expansion, industrial development, and continued excellence in services. Despite the specter of automatization, India manages to strengthen its industrial base and gain ground from China as the world's factory. Low labor costs, improving infrastructure, favorable investment environment, and rule of law drive industrial FDI to record heights. At the same time, India's agricultural productivity grows fast. Despite challenges related to climate change and water scarcity, agricultural productivity in India improves over time. This productivity, combined with growing off-farm employment opportunities and urbanization, greatly enhances the rural economy and plays a critical role in suppressing the growth of economic inequality. Finally, the Indian service sector continues to thrive. India's entrepreneurial population breaks free of constraints of tradition, and India rises to compete with the United States and China as one of the world's entrepreneurial powerhouses.

Thanks to growing political pressure, social policy allocates a substantial portion of the fruits of economic growth to benefit India's vast population. Despite India's institutional challenges, governments find creative solutions to important social problems over time. Even the worst-performing state governments improve their effectiveness. Because they used to be India's weakest link, their success is of particular import. Although the COVID-19 pandemic is a setback, prompt action by central and state governments enables a rapid recovery.

These changes are driven by an accountability revolution in India. As educational outcomes improve, people across the country escape the trap of voting based on factors like religion and caste. Instead, they begin to vote based on performance and policy platforms. Indian voters, increasingly, reward good performance, regardless of the communal and caste identity of politicians. As a result, India's intensely competitive elections produce ever more impressive results, and troubling phenomena such as convicted criminals winning office lose traction.[1]

This social revolution means less inequality. More tolerant and less rigid social attitudes directly contribute to social mobility, and government policy focused on delivering good public services helps those who are less fortunate. Because of the good results, government legitimacy increases, and problems like corruption and leakage all but disappear. Government social budgets grow, and most of that money is effectively deployed where it is needed the most. The bad old days of administrative corruption are over, as civil servants take pride in doing the right thing and the public has no patience with corrupt bureaucrats or politicians. Another key outcome of effective policy is resource efficiency. While slowing population growth and stabilization help with India's sustainability problem, the real solution lies with more effective policy. Both the central and state governments become far savvier in policy formulation and move away from blunt instruments such as bans and subsidies. India leads the world with public innovation programs, market-based environmental policies, public-private partnerships, and stringent constraints on depleting resources. While this wave of new policy and regulation hurts vested interests, such as industrialists and large landowners, in the short run, over time it produces such incontrovertible public health and economic benefits that there is no turning back.

In regional and global politics, India will be increasingly recognized as a benign hegemon and an example for other countries struggling with development in the twenty-first century. India's domestic success inspires other countries in South Asia and beyond, and Indian policy innovations diffuse across countries. India's international image improves, and business and government leaders across the world admire Indians for their resourcefulness and innovativeness. In global environmental and energy policy, India's ambitious goals, including aggressive decarbonization plans with detailed decadal targets, inspire awe. India leads the developing-country coalition, but with a strong bias in favor of sustainability.

Strong democratic and constitutional institutions underpin India's entry into the regional and global limelight. India's judicial system and free media continue to thrive, while corruption and resource constraints in bureaucracy and legislature become things of the past. Indian democratic institutions have never been as robust, and a vibrant civil society takes full advantage of the opportunities. Indians debate great social questions of the day and important government policies in a vigorous but respectful manner, across all levels of society and government, from Gandhi's village republics to national politics.

Even in this scenario, India faces a difficult challenge in mitigating and adapting to climate change because climate change continues and India is highly vulnerable to it. Indians pay a steep price for the world's failure to tackle the problem on time. However, a combination of growing awareness and enhanced government capacity help India avoid the worst consequences. Its success with adaptation to climate change becomes an important example for the rest of the world, and Indian experts tour the world's capitals to inform other governments of how to do it.

India's net contribution to solving the climate change problem is clearly positive. India's new energy and environmental policies are effective and efficient. They give credibility to India's claims for global leadership. Industrialized countries welcome India's pivotal contributions to slowing down climate disruption, while other developing countries eagerly follow India's example.

BREAKING FREE

For policy makers and civil society, the key question is how to steer India toward a benign scenario of economic growth, social development, and environmental sustainability. The three scenarios described are idealized archetypes, and if there is anything we have learned about India, it must be that archetypes rarely apply. But having a sense of a direction toward a goal, no matter how unrealistic, is important for securing the "small wins" that constitute tangible progress over time.[2] Goals can inspire, motivate, and guide.

To achieve the goal of sustainable development, India needs to break free from the captive society. India has, for the longest time, sought private solutions to a variety of ills. It has even harnessed government to pursue those private solutions. This dynamic of favoring exit over voice, especially among the more fortunate, has handicapped the government and made India's progress toward a sustainable and equitable society slower than it should have been. India needs to prioritize policies and regulations that simultaneously encourage positive behaviors and constrain negative behaviors. While the latter mode of action is far harder politically, there is no alternative to it. Positive behaviors can only go so far when unscrupulous choices go unpunished.

To me, the most important source of hope is India's young population, no longer chained by the karma of the past. India is by a wide margin the youngest of all major economies in the world. Its young cohorts have grown in a world of modern telecommunications, where smartphones and the internet have found their way into the hands of illiterate men and women in the smallest and most remote villages. If India exemplified a "modernity of tradition" for most of the twentieth century,[3] the twenty-first century has tilted the balance in favor of modernity. Nobody can say how close India is to a true tipping point, but clearly it is closer than ever before and moving in that direction at a rapid pace.

For India's elites, the challenge is to channel this potential into concrete action under a functioning governance framework. Assuming that the Indian society will over time find ways to hold governments accountable, elites face a new challenge, as winning elections will no longer be possible without sustainable human development. India's political leaders need to quickly learn how to formulate effective policies, and to resist the temptation to exempt the mighty and the powerful from common rules. The path of least resistance will unlikely lead anywhere except a disaster, considering how daunting India's future challenges are.

To achieve the goal of sustainable human development, India needs massive investments in human capital. Societal trends favor the transformation, but the political elite's wisdom is now badly needed to accelerate the transition. If the government has foresight, wisdom, and empathy, it contributes to ending the ways of the old with investments that help Indians break free of the captive society and hold their leaders accountable for good performance, brought about by responsible and prudent policies. Improvements in education, social security, and health care ensure that all Indians can contribute to building a prosperous and sustainable India for centuries to come.

More important than strengthening capacity for national policy in Delhi are improvements aimed to strengthen policy formulation in state capitals. India's fundamental challenge has, at least since the economic reforms in 1991, been the uneven performance of the states. Even in the fields of energy and environmental policy, we have seen remarkable variation in outcomes across states. If all Indian states performed at the level of the best Indian state in addressing the country's great challenges in energy and environment, the outlook would be far more optimistic. Researchers and activists need to prioritize action in the Indian states, with a clear focus on supporting the growth of local capacity. That is hard work and not always so rewarding in the short run, but in the long run it will make all the difference.

Even a bold quest for a sustainable India of the future must avoid the temptation to undermine or override democratic institutions. One of India's great strengths as a country is that every Indian citizen can vote, and a relatively free media monitors and criticizes government and business elites. While India's institutional challenges might lead some commentators to argue for a more authoritarian solution, it is hard to see how a Chinese or Singaporean regime could ever produce fair, equitable, and sustainable outcomes for almost two billion diverse and argumentative Indians. Instead of an authoritarian turn, India must strive for a sustainable future through democratic means. If it manages to do so, it can be a source of great inspiration for other countries facing the same challenges. Such is the power of homegrown democratic constitutionalism.

NOTES

INTRODUCTION

1. Agrawal et al. 2021.
2. "India Air Took 6 Hours Off Obama's Life," *The Hill*, January 27, 2015, http://thehill.com /policy/ energy-environment/230829-india-air-took-6-hours-off-obamas-life.
3. GBD 2018.
4. Pritchett 2009.
5. Unless otherwise noted, all numbers cited in this chapter are from the World Development Indicators, https://data.worldbank.org/products/wdi.
6. See "My Fridge Versus Power Africa," blogpost, Center for Global Development, September 9, 2013, https://www.cgdev.org/blog/my-fridge-versus-power-africa.
7. See DTE staff, "Looking Back at Stockholm 1972: What Indira Gandhi Said Half a Century Ago on Man & Environment," *Down to Earth*, May 31, 2022, https://www .downtoearth.org.in/news/environment/looking-back-at-stockholm-1972-what-indira -gandhi-said-half-a-century-ago-on-man-environment-83060#.
8. Lin, Cai, and Li 2003.
9. IEA 2017; BP 2018a.
10. IEA 2021.
11. "Corp India's 'Jugaad' Defies Blackouts," *Indian Express*, August 8, 2012, http:// indianexpress.com/ article/news-archive/web/corp-indias-jugaad-defies-blackouts/.
12. Costello 2015.

13. See Government of India, Ministry of Power, Gram Ujala Dashboard, https://gramujala .convergence.co.in/, accessed May 11, 2018.
14. See Ministry of New and Renewable Energy, "Physical Progress," September 9, 2022, https://mnre.gov.in/the-ministry/physical-progress.
15. Podishetti 2022.
16. Ahluwalia 2002; Drèze and Sen 2002; Panagariya 2008.

1. FOUNDATIONS AND HISTORY

1. Some regional classifications also include Afghanistan as part of South Asia.
2. Khan 2017.
3. Bayly 2001; Jaffrelot 2003; Jensenius 2017.
4. Kapur et al. 2010.
5. Jensenius 2015.
6. Kopas et al. 2020.
7. Ang 2016; Nahm and Steinfeld 2014. At the time of this writing, the Indian government aims to increase manufacturing to 25 percent of total GDP.
8. See Salvatore Babones, "Long-term Stagnation in Uttar Pradesh Is Modi's Biggest Challenge Ahead of India's 2019 Elections," *Forbes*, May 13, 2018, https://tinyurl.com /8e3ykh4w.
9. Some areas of India also have another monsoon season in the winter, known as the northeast monsoon.
10. Asif and Muneer 2007; Bhaskar 2013.
11. Wu 2018.
12. As I discuss India before independence, it bears remembering that the statistics are largely based on colonial records. Before India's decolonization in 1947, India still included both modern Pakistan and Bangladesh but excluded Bhutan, Maldives, Nepal, and Sri Lanka. The most important practical consequence of this distinction is that population and economic numbers are not directly comparable to those in independent India.
13. Gadgil and Guha 1993, 72, 78.
14. Bayly 2001, 13.
15. Bayly 2001, 25–26.
16. Gadgil and Guha 1993, 91–110.
17. Cassen 1978, 3.
18. Gadgil and Guha 1993, 107–8.
19. Gadgil and Guha 1993, 115–18.
20. Gadgil and Guha 1993, 119.
21. Gadgil and Guha 1993, 135.
22. Gadgil and Guha 1993, 120–22.
23. Cassen 1978, 3.

24. See Rema Nagarajan, "The Myth of India's Population Explosion," *Times of India*, June 23, 2016, https://timesofindia.indiatimes.com/blogs/staying-alive/the-myth-of-indias -population-explosion.
25. See Plowden 1883.
26. See Bishnupriya Gupta, "Falling Behind: India Under Colonial Rule," *Ideas for India*, February 21, 2018, https://www.ideasforindia.in/topics/poverty-inequality/falling-behind -india-under-colonial-rule.
27. Manish 2011, 205.
28. Cassen 1978, 210.
29. See Rossella Calvi and Federico Mantovanelli, "The Long-term Consequences of Medical Missions in Colonia India," *VoxDev*, September 20, 1919, https://voxdev.org/topic /health-education/long-term-consequences-medical-missions-colonial-india.
30. See Max Hannah Ritchie, and Bernadeta Dadonaite, "Child and Infant Mortality," *Our World in Data*, November 2019, https://ourworldindata.org/child-mortality.
31. See World Bank, "Energy Use (kg of Oil Equivalent per Capita)," https://data.worldbank .org/indicator/EG.USE.PCAP.KG.OE?locations=IN.
32. See World Bank, "Energy Use."
33. Cassen 1978, 211.
34. Cassen 1978, 212–13.
35. Hazell 2009.
36. Parayil 1992, 752, 746.
37. Wharton 1969, 464.
38. Pingali 2012.
39. Veeman 1978.
40. Cassen 1978, 215.
41. Chibber 2003.
42. CSE 1982, 122.
43. See OGD PMU Team, "Composition of Vehicle Population in India from 1951 to 2015," Community.data.gov, June 16, 2017, https://community.data.gov.in/composition-of -vehicle-population-in-india-from-1951-to-2015/.
44. Ghosh 2010.
45. Aklin et al. 2018, chap. 4.
46. Gadgil and Guha 1993, 87–103.
47. Gadgil and Guha 1993, 102–3.
48. Misra 2007, 134.
49. Gadgil and Guha 1993, 116–23.
50. Moolakkattu 2010.
51. Gadgil and Guha 2013, 23.
52. Rangan 2000, 1.
53. Baviskar 1995.
54. Pallas and Urpelainen 2013.
55. E.g., Upadhyaya 2018.

56. Guha 1988, 2580.

57. Guha 1988, 2580.

58. Guha 1988, 2580.

59. Gadgil and Guha 1994.

60. Dubash et al. 2018.

2. ECONOMIC GROWTH AND ENVIRONMENTAL DEGRADATION

1. "Sri Lankan Bowler Vomits in Delhi Cricket Match Due to Polluted Air," *The Guardian*, December 5, 2017.

2. CDKN 2014.

3. Shah 2009.

4. Central Ground Water Board 2017.

5. Hsu 2018.

6. "One More Push," *The Economist*, July 21, 2011.

7. Crabtree 2018, 87.

8. "India Jumps Higher in World Bank's Ranking of How Easy It Is to Do Business," *CNBC*, https://www.cnbc.com/2018/11/01/world-bank-india-improves-ease-of-doing -business.html.

9. Ahluwalia 2002, 67.

10. Crabtree 2018, 15.

11. World Inequality Dataset, https://wid.world/country/india/.

12. Oxfam India, 2018.

13. "India Records Its Hottest Day Ever with a Blistering 123.8°F," *Time*, May 20, 2016.

14. "As Countries Crank Up the AC, Emissions of Potent Greenhouse Gases Are Likely to Skyrocket," *Science*, March 8, 2018.

15. Bery et al. 2017.

16. NITI-Aayog 2017.

17. Hallström, Carlsson-Kanyama, and Börjesson 2015.

18. Netra Mittal, "What's in Store for the Meat Industry in India as the Country's 2000-Year-Old Tradition of Vegetarianism May Be About to Change," *Qrius*, March 30, 2022, https://qrius.com/meat-industry-india-tradition-change/.

19. Mihir Sharma, "Why India's Airlines Struggle to Take Off," *Bloomberg*, December 2, 2018, https://www.bloomberg.com/opinion/articles/2018-12-02/why-india-s-airlines-can -t-turn-growth-into-profits.

20. Alkon, Harish, and Urpelainen 2016; Cheng and Urpelainen 2014.

21. Craig Morris, "High German Power Prices, Low Monthly Bills?," *Energy Transition*, February 5, 2018, https://energytransition.org/2018/ 02/high-german-power-prices-low -monthly-bills/.

22. Baquié and Urpelainen 2017; Agrawal et al. 2021.

23. Alkon, Harish, and Urpelainen, 2016.

24. IEA 2021.
25. To be sure, India faces many other environmental problems as well, from forest degradation to urban waste. Because these problems are only loosely related to the energy sector, I do not consider them in this book.
26. WHO 2018.
27. See "The Lancet Commission on Pollution and Health," October 20, 2017, https://www.thelancet.com/commissions/pollution-and-health.
28. GBD 2018.
29. WB 2018.
30. Singh 2018, 35–36.
31. Tanushree Ganguly, "Understanding North India's Pollution Crisis," May 4, 2018, DownToEarth, https://www.downtoearth.org.in/blog/understanding-north-india-s-pollution-crisis-60426.
32. Singh 2018, 38–39.
33. Urban Emissions Info, "What's Polluting Delhi's Air?" March 2016, http://www.urbanemissions.info/blog-pieces/whats-polluting-delhis-air/.
34. "How Car Ownership Is Changing Rapidly and Irreversibly in India," *Economic Times*, October 21, 2018.
35. NITI Aayog and RMI 2017.
36. "India's Coal Power Plants 'Unhealthiest' in World: Study," *Economic Times*, February 21, 2019.
37. "Coal-Based Power Units Flouting Emission Control Norms: Report," *Business Standard*, December 7, 2017.
38. CSTEP 2018.
39. Yang and Urpelainen 2019.
40. AWC 2018, 4.
41. AWC 2018, 2.
42. Centre for Science and Environment, "On the Dust Haze Over North India," https://www.cseindia.org/on-the-dust-haze-over-north-india-8790.
43. GBD 2018.
44. Smith 2000; Shupler et al. 2018.
45. "Air Pollution Linked to 12.4L Deaths in India in '17: Report," *Times of India*, December 7, 2018.
46. Cheng and Urpelainen 2014; Gould and Urpelainen 2018.
47. "Delhi Pollution: City a 'Gas Chamber,' CM Arvind Kejriwal Blames Neighbours," *Indian Express*, November 6, 2016.
48. Singh 2018, 153–61.
49. AWC 2018.
50. Purohit et al. 2019.
51. Observable, at https://www.youtube.com/watch?v=kCmwKbVFbWg.
52. Hubacek et al. 2017.
53. Tongia and Gross 2018.

54. Buckley et al. 2019.

55. See Andy Colthorpe, "India's Grid Storage Sector a Big Driver for Forecasted 260 GWh of Annual Battery Demand by 2039," *Energy Storage News*, February 16, 2022, https://www.energy-storage.news/indias-grid-storage-sector-a-big-driver-for-forecasted-260gwh-of.

56. Balachandra, Ravindranath, and Ravindranath 2010; Chaudhary, Krishna, and Sagar 2015; Nandi and Basu 2008.

57. International Energy Agency, "Energy Conservation Act," https://www.iea.org/policies/1975-energy-conservation-act.

58. See "Energy Efficiency Progress Recovers in 2021 but Needs to Double for Net Zero by 2050," IEA, https://www.iea.org/topics/energyefficiency/e4/india/, accessed November 17, 2022.

59. Gupta and Paul 2019.

60. Singh, Mishra, and Banerjee 2019, 201.

61. CSTEP 2014.

62. Olivier, Schure, and Peters 2017.

63. Busby and Shidore 2017.

64. Sapkota et al. 2019.

65. Sapkota et al. 2019.

66. CDKN 2014, 18.

67. CDKN 2014, 21.

68. Srinivasan 2019, 41.

69. Pink 2016.

70. Garg, Mishra, and Dholakia 2015.

71. Merriott 2016.

72. Carleton 2017.

73. UNEP 2016.

74. ADB 2017.

75. Garg, Mishra, and Dholakia 2015.

76. *Moody's* 2019.

77. O'Brien et al. 2004.

78. Shankar, Kulkarni, and Krishnan 2011.

79. "Punjab's Water Deficit," *Tribune*, August 10, 2017.

80. Shah 2009.

81. Shah 2009.

82. Dasgupta 1977.

83. Singh 2000.

84. FAO, "The Fertilizer Sector," http://www.fao.org/docrep/009/a0257e/A0257E03.htm.

85. Shah 2009, 37.

86. Rud 2012; Aklin et al. 2018.

87. Kale 2014.

88. Birner, Gupta, and Sharma 2011, 40.

89. Birner, Gupta, and Sharma 2011, 109–10.

90. Shah 2009; Birner, Gupta, and Sharma 2011.

91. Zaveri et al. 2016.
92. Sekhri 2014.
93. Aklin et al. 2018.
94. Alkon, Harish, and Urpelainen 2016.
95. The Indian government defines a village as electrified if 10 percent of households have connections, along with public facilities. Thus an electrified village can have a vast majority of its households without power.
96. Aklin et al. 2016.
97. Chakravorty, Pelli, and Marchand 2014.
98. Blankenship, Wong, and Urpelainen 2019.
99. Agrawal, Bali, and Urpelainen 2019.
100. Burgess et al. 2019.
101. Blankenship, Wong, and Urpelainen 2019.
102. Kennedy, Mahajan, and Urpelainen 2019.
103. "Revenue Model for Energy," *Telegraph India*, July 6, 2015.
104. Burgess et al. 2019.
105. Urpelainen 2014.
106. Aklin et al. 2018, chap. 4.
107. Zerriffi and Wilson 2010.
108. "India Added 1.7 GW of Solar PV in Q1 2019, Rooftop Installations Declined," Mercom India, June 4, 2019, https://mercomindia.com/india-solar-pv-q1-2019-rooftop-installations/.
109. GOGLA 2019.
110. This number does not include sales of unbranded solar panels, which are ubiquitous in rural India.
111. Cheng and Urpelainen 2014.
112. Alkon, Harish, and Urpelainen 2016.
113. See official website at https://pmuy.gov.in/.
114. "82% of Ujjwala Families Return for LPG Refill," *Times of India*, March 8, 2019.
115. "Ujjwala Connections Get Three Refills Annually on an Average," *The Hindu*, December 21, 2018.
116. Cameron et al. 2016.
117. "India Becomes World's 2nd Largest LPG Consumer After Government's Ujjawla Push," *Economic Times*, February 5, 2019.
118. Khandelwal et al. 2017.

3. GOVERNANCE AND POLICY

1. Singh 2008; Agrawal 2018.
2. One must note, however, that India's mobile telecommunications revolution was itself fraught with inefficiency and corruption, such as in the case of broadband spectrum auctions (Thakurta and Kaushal 2010).

3. Intelligent Energy 2012.

4. For an illustration of how state capacity shapes important environmental policies, see Meckling and Nahm 2018; Gopinathan, Subramanian, and Urpelainen 2019.

5. Lindblom 1959.

6. Divan and Rosencranz 2001, 41.

7. Dwivedi 1997.

8. Kumar 2009, 7.

9. Divan and Rosencranz 2001, 60.

10. Kurzman 1987.

11. See Ministry of Environment, Forest and Climate Change, https://cpcb.nic.in/env -protection-act/, accessed March 1, 2020.

12. Duflo et al. 2013.

13. Bhushan, Yadav, and Roy 2009.

14. Divan and Rosencranz 2001, 261.

15. Bergin et al. 2014.

16. Rayies Altaf, "Odd-Even Scheme Had Little Impact on Air Pollution: Study," *Hindu Businessline*, August 16, 2018, https://www.thehindubusinessline.com/news/science/odd -even-scheme-had-little-impact-on-air-pollutio article24706635.ece

17. Purohit et al. 2019.

18. Ministry of Environment, "National Clean Air Programme (NCAP), *India Environmental Portal*, October 1, 2019, http://www.indiaenvironmentportal.org.in/content /460562/national-clean-air-programme-ncap/.

19. Santosh Harish, Shibani Ghosh, and Navroz K. Dubash, "Clearing Our Air of Pollution," Centre for Policy Research, June 11, 2019, https://www.cprindia.org/news /7874.

20. Wong and Karplus 2017.

21. Cullet 2014.

22. Kulkarni, Shah, and Shankar 2015.

23. Kulkarni, Shah, and Shankar 2015, 180.

24. Scott and Shah 2004, 152–54.

25. Dubash and Joseph 2016.

26. Mohan 2017.

27. Gupta 2001.

28. Benecke 2009.

29. Bayer, Urpelainen, and Xu 2014.

30. Wu 2018, 240, 245.

31. Dubash and Joseph 2016, 49.

32. Dubash and Jogesh 2014.

33. Atteridge et al. 2012, 68.

34. Wu 2018.

35. Chaudhary, Krishna, and Sagar 2015.

36. Kamboj and Tongia 2018.

37. In 2017 the 2010 Clean Energy Cess on coal, which was to support the National Clean Energy and Environment Fund for sustainable energy innovation, was abolished under the Goods and Services Tax reform. Funds collected from the cess were transferred to general govenrment expenditure.
38. Kamboj and Tongia 2018.
39. Pai et al. 2020.
40. Chandra 2018.
41. Pillai and Dubash 202.
42. Ghosh 2019, 2.
43. Mehta 2019, 272.
44. Singh 2006.
45. Rajan 2000.
46. Dash and Sangita 2011.
47. Tongia 2004.
48. Gratwick and Eberhard 2008.
49. See FE Bureau, "A Quarter Before Deadline, AT&C Losses Far Higher than UDAY Target," *Financial Express*, February 20, 2019, https://www.financialexpress.com/economy/a-quarter-before-deadline-atc-losses-far-higher-than-ud-target/1492814/.
50. Kornai 1986.
51. Min 2015; Aklin et al. 2018.
52. Chattopadhyay 2004.
53. Ganesan, Bharadwaj, and Balani 2019.
54. Dubash and Rao 2008.
55. Balls 2018.
56. Vaishnav 2017.
57. "Solar Storm: AP Govt's Bid to Renegotiate Renewable Contracts Could Have Serious Repercussions," *The Hindu*, August 2, 2019.
58. Manish Sirhindi, "Punjab Government Clears Rs 8,949 Crore Power Subsidy Bill for Last Fiscal," *Times of India*, May 26, 2019, https://tinyurl.com/y8rdah3z.
59. Scott and Shah 2004, 155.
60. Harish and Tongia 2014, 5.
61. McRae 2015.
62. See Ayush Verma, "8 Key Points from KUSUM Scheme Implementation Guidelines," Saur Energy International, July 25, 2019, https://tinyurl.com/y7a9tbyt.
63. Shah 2018.
64. Agrawal, Bali, and Urpelainen 2019.
65. Rud 2012.
66. Bhattacharyya 2007; Hirsh 1999.
67. Min and Golden 2014.
68. Interviews with Central Electricity Authority officers, January 2020, New Delhi.
69. Gandhi and Pethe 2017.
70. Gandhi and Pethe 2017, 59.

71. Gandhi and Pethe 2017, 59.
72. Wade 1985.
73. Kapur, Mehta, and Vaishnav 2018, 5–6.
74. Pritchett 2009.
75. Panagariya 2008.
76. Bhagwati and Panagariya 2013.
77. Wade 1985.
78. Malik, Giordano, and Rathore 2018.
79. Fishman, Devineni, and Raman 2015.
80. Hirschman 1970.
81. Sandipan Dey, "The Exit of the Middle Class," *The Mint*, July 11, 2013.
82. Joseph 2010, 510.
83. Birner, Gupta, and Sharma 2011.
84. Dasgupta 2018.
85. Lindblom 1959.

4. FLEXING MUSCLE IN GLOBAL ENVIRONMENTAL POLITICS

1. See Ministry of Environment, Forest and Climate Change, "Speech of Jairam Ramesh at Copenhagen on Climate Change," December 17, 2009, http://www.pib.nic.in/newsite/erelcontent.aspx?relid=56217.
2. Vihma 2011, 75.
3. Krasner 1985.
4. Vihma 2011, 74.
5. Rajan 1997.
6. Rajan 1997, 59.
7. Sprinz and Vaahtoranta 1994.
8. Rajan 1997, 64.
9. Rajan 1997, 63.
10. Rajan 1997.
11. Rajan 1997, 201, 199.
12. Harrop and Pritchard 2011, 476.
13. Rajan 1997, 240.
14. Weiner 1977.
15. Najam 2005.
16. Rajan 1997, 104.
17. Agarwal and Narain 1991.
18. Raghunandan 2019, 191.
19. Eckersley 2007.
20. Mohan 2017.
21. Vihma 2011.

22. Vihma 2011, 75.
23. Vihma 2011, 75.
24. Michaelowa and Michaelowa 2012.
25. Michaelowa and Michaelowa 2012, 587.
26. Dubash 2013.
27. Guha 1988.
28. Mathur 2019, 226–27.
29. Yenneti 2014.
30. Dubash 2013.
31. See "India Aims to Become 100% E-Vehicle Nation by 2030: Piyush Goyal," *Economic Times*, March 26, 2016, https://tinyurl.com/y765bd8e.
32. Stokes, Giang, and Selin 2016.
33. Stokes, Giang, and Selin 2016, 16, 19.
34. Ghosh 2019, 240–41.

5. THE FUTURE OF ENERGY AND ENVIRONMENT IN INDIA

1. Vaishnav 2017.
2. Weick 1984; Urpelainen 2013.
3. Rudolph and Rudolph 1984.

BIBLIOGRAPHY

Agarwal, Anil, and Sunita Narain. 1991. *Global Warming in an Unequal World: A Case of Environmental Colonialism.* New Delhi: Centre for Science and Environment.

Agrawal, Ravi. 2018. *India Connected: How the Smartphone Is Transforming the World's Largest Democracy.* New York: Oxford University Press.

Agrawal, Shalu, Nidhi Bali, and Johannes Urpelainen. 2019. "Rural Electrification in India: Customer Behaviour and Demand." New Delhi: Smart Power India and Initiative for Sustainable Energy Policy.

Agrawal, Shalu, Sunil Mani, Abhishek Jain, Karthik Ganesan, and Johannes Urpelainen. 2021. "India Residential Energy Survey (IRES) 2020." Harvard Dataverse. https://doi.org/10.7910/DVN/U8NYUP.

Ahluwalia, Montek S. 2002. "Economic Reforms in India Since 1991: Has Gradualism Worked?" *Journal of Economic Perspectives* 16, no. 3: 67–88.

Air-Weather-Climate (AWC). 2018. "Source Apportionment, Health Effects and Potential Reduction of Fine Particulate Matter (PM2.5) in India." AWC Research Group, Louisiana State University.

Aklin, Michaël, Patrick Bayer, S. P. Harish, and Johannes Urpelainen. 2018. *Escaping the Energy Poverty Trap: When and How Governments Power the Lives of the Poor.* Cambridge, Mass.: MIT Press.

Aklin, Michaël, Chao-yo Cheng, Johannes Urpelainen, Karthik Ganesan, and Abhishek Jain. 2016. "Factors Affecting Household Satisfaction with Electricity Supply in Rural India." *Nature Energy* 1: 16170.

Alkon, Meir, S. P. Harish, and Johannes Urpelainen. 2016. "Household Energy Access and Expenditure in Developing Countries: Evidence from India, 1987–2010." *Energy for Sustainable Development* 35: 25–34.

Ang, Yuen Yuen. 2016. *How China Escaped the Poverty Trap.* Ithaca, N.Y.: Cornell University Press.

Asian Development Bank (ADB). 2017. "A Region at Risk: The Human Dimensions of Climate Change in Asia and the Pacific." Manila: ADB.

Asif, M., and T. Muneer. 2007. "Energy Supply, Its Demand and Security Issues for Developed and Emerging Economies." *Renewable and Sustainable Energy Reviews* 11, no. 7: 1388–1413.

Atteridge, Aaron, Manish Kumar Shrivastava, Neha Pahuja, and Himani Upadhyay. 2012. "Climate Policy in India: What Shapes International, National and State Policy?" *Ambio* 41, no. 1: 68–77.

Balachandra, Patil, Darshini Ravindranath, and N. H. Ravindranath. 2010. "Energy Efficiency in India: Assessing the Policy Regimes and Their Impacts." *Energy Policy* 38, no. 11: 6428–38.

Balls, Jonathan. 2018. "Uttarakhand: The Golden Combination of Cheap Energy and a Large Industrial Base." In *Mapping Power: The Political Economy of Electricity in India's States.* New Delhi: Oxford University Press.

Baquié, Sandra, and Johannes Urpelainen. 2017. "Access to Modern Fuels and Satisfaction with Cooking Arrangements: Survey Evidence from Rural India." *Energy for Sustainable Development* 38: 34–47.

Baviskar, Amita. 1995. *In the Belly of the River: Tribal Conflicts Over Development in the Narmada Valley.* New York: Oxford University Press.

Bayer, Patrick, Johannes Urpelainen, and Alice Xu. 2014. "Laissez Faire and the Clean Development Mechanism: Determinants of Project Implementation in Indian States, 2003–2011." *Clean Technologies and Environmental Policy* 16, no. 8: 1687–1701.

Bayly, Susan. 2001. *Caste, Society and Politics in India from the Eighteenth Century to the Modern Age.* New York: Cambridge University Press.

Benecke, Gudrun. 2009. "Varieties of Carbon Governance: Taking Stock of the Local Carbon Market in India." *Journal of Environment and Development* 18, no. 4: 346–70.

Bergin, Mike H., Sachi Nand Tripathi, J. Jai Devi, Tarun Gupta, Michael McKenzie, K. S. Rana, Martin M. Shafer, Ana M. Villalobos, and James J. Schauer. 2014. "The Discoloration of the Taj Mahal Due to Particulate Carbon and Dust Deposition." *Environmental Science & Technology* 49, no. 2: 808–12.

Bery, Suman, Arunabha Ghosh, Ritu Mathur, Subrata Basu, Karthik Ganesan, and Rhodri Owen-Jones. 2017. *Energizing India: Towards a Resilient and Equitable Energy System.* New Delhi: Sage Publications.

Bhagwati, Jagdish, and Arvind Panagariya. 2013. *Why Growth Matters: How Economic Growth in India Reduced Poverty and the Lessons for Other Developing Countries.* New York: PublicAffairs.

Bhaskar, Bala. 2013. *Energy Security and Economic Development in India: A Holistic Approach.* New Delhi: Energy and Resources Institute.

Bhattacharyya, Subhes C. 2007. "Power Sector Reform in South Asia: Why Slow and Limited so Far?" *Energy Policy* 35, no. 1: 317–32.

Bhushan, Chandra, Nivit Yadav, and Anil Roy. 2009. "Turnaround: Reform Agenda for India's Environmental Regulators." New Delhi: Centre for Science and Environment.

Birner, Regina, Surupa Gupta, and Neeru Sharma. 2011. *The Political Economy of Agricultural Policy Reform in India: Fertilizers and Electricity for Irrigation*. Washington, D.C.: International Food Policy Research Institute.

Blankenship, Brian, Jason Chun Yu Wong, and Johannes Urpelainen. 2019. "Explaining Willingness to Pay for Pricing Reforms That Improve Electricity Service in India." *Energy Policy* 128: 459–69.

BP. 2018a. *BP Energy Outlook 2018*. London: BP.

——. 2018b. *BP Statistical Review of World Energy June 2018*. London: BP.

——. 2021. *BP Statistical Review of World Energy June 2021*. London: BP.

Buckley, Tim, Anil Gupta, Vibhuti Garg, and Kashish Shah. 2019. "Flexing India's Energy System: Making the Case for the Right Price Signals Through Time-of-Day Pricing." Lakewood, Ohio: Institute for Energy Economics and Financial Analysis.

Burgess, Robin, Michael Greenstone, Nicholas Ryan, and Anant Sudarshan. 2019. "Electricity Is Not a Right." Research Note. London: International Growth Centre.

Busby, Joshua W., and Sarang Shidore. 2017. "When Decarbonization Meets Development: The Sectoral Feasibility of Greenhouse Gas Mitigation in India." *Energy Research and Social Science* 23: 60–73.

Cameron, Colin, Shonali Pachauri, Narasimha D. Rao, David McCollum, Joeri Rogelj, and Keywan Riahi. 2016. "Policy Trade-offs Between Climate Mitigation and Clean Cook-Stove Access in South Asia." *Nature Energy* 1: 15010.

Carleton, Tamma A. 2017. "Crop-Damaging Temperatures Increase Suicide Rates in India." *Proceedings of the National Academy of Sciences* 114, no. 33: 8746–51.

Cassen, R. H. 1978. *India: Population, Economy, Society*. London: Palgrave Macmillan.

Central Ground Water Board. 2017. *Dynamic Ground Water Resources of India*. Faridabad: Government of India.

Centre for Science and Environment (CSE). 1982. *The State of India's Environment: The First Citizen's Report*. New Delhi: CSE.

Centre for Study of Science, Technology and Policy (CSTEP). 2014. "Review of Urban Transport in India." Bangalore: CSTEP.

——. 2018. "Benefit Cost Analysis of Emission Standards for Coal-Based Thermal Power Plants in India." Bangalore: CSTEP.

Chakravorty, Ujjayant, Martino Pelli, and Beyza Ural Marchand. 2014. "Does the Quality of Electricity Matter? Evidence from Rural India." *Journal of Economic Behavior and Organization* 107: 228–47.

Chandra, Rohit. 2018. "Embeddedness and Persistence: India's Coal Industry." Policy Brief 2018/1. Washington, D.C.: Initiative for Sustainable Energy Policy.

Chattopadhyay, Pradip. 2004. "Cross-Subsidy in Electricity Tariffs: Evidence from India." *Energy Policy* 32, no. 5: 673–84.

Chaudhary, Ankur, Chetan Krishna, and Ambuj Sagar. 2015. "Policy Making for Renewable Energy in India: Lessons from Wind and Solar Power Sectors." *Climate Policy* 15, no. 1: 58–87.

Cheng, Chao-yo, and Johannes Urpelainen. 2014. "Fuel Stacking in India: Changes in the Cooking and Lighting Mix, 1987–2010." *Energy* 76: 306–17.

Chibber, Vivek. 2003. *Locked in Place: State-Building and Late Industrialization in India.* Princeton, N.J.: Princeton University Press.

Climate and Development Knowledge Network (CDKN). 2014. "The IPCC's Fifth Assessment Report: What's in It for South Asia?" London: CDKN, Overseas Development Institute.

Costello, Kenneth W. 2015. "Major Challenges of Distributed Generation for State Utility Regulators." *Electricity Journal* 28, no. 3: 8–25.

Crabtree, James. 2018. *The Billionaire Raj: A Journal Through India's New Gilded Age.* New York: Tim Duggan Books.

Cullet, Philippe. 2014. "Groundwater Law In India: Towards a Framework Ensuring Equitable Access and Aquifer Protection." *Journal of Environmental Law* 26, no. 1: 55–81.

Dasgupta, Aditya. 2018. "Technological Change and Political Turnover: The Democratizing Effects of the Green Revolution in India." *American Political Science Review* 112, no. 4: 918–38.

Dasgupta, Biplab. 1977. "India's Green Revolution." *Economic and Political Weekly* 12: 241–60.

Dash, Bikash Chandra, and S. N. Sangita. 2011. "Governance Reforms in Power Sector: Initiatives and Outcomes in Orissa." Bangalore: Institute for Social and Economic Change.

Divan, Shyam, and Armin Rosencranz. 2001. *Environmental Law and Policy in India: Cases, Materials, and Statutes.* New Delhi: Oxford University Press.

Drèze, Jean, and Amartya K. Sen. 2002. *India: Development and Participation.* Second ed. New York: Oxford University Press.

Dubash, Navroz K. 2013. "The Politics of Climate Change in India: Narratives of Equity and Cobenefits." *Wiley Interdisciplinary Reviews: Climate Change* 4, no. 3: 191–201.

Dubash, Navroz K., and Anu Jogesh. 2014. "From Margins to Mainstream? State Climate Change Planning in India as a 'Door Opener' to a Sustainable Future." New Delhi: Centre for Policy Research.

Dubash, Navroz K., and Neha B. Joseph. 2016. "Evolution of Institutions for Climate Policy in India." *Economic and Political Weekly* 51, no. 3: 44–54.

Dubash, Navroz K., Radhika Khosla, Ulka Kelkar, and Sharachchandra Lele. 2018. "India and Climate Change: Evolving Ideas and Increasing Policy Engagement." *Annual Review of Environment and Resources* 43: 12.1–12.30.

Dubash, Navroz K., and D. Narasimha Rao. 2008. "Regulatory Practice and Politics: Lessons from Independent Regulation in Indian Electricity." *Utilities Policy* 16, no. 4: 321–31.

Duflo, Esther, Michael Greenstone, Rohini Pande, and Nicholas Ryan. 2013. "Truth-telling by Third-Party Auditors and the Response of Polluting Firms: Experimental Evidence from India." *Quarterly Journal of Economics* 128, no. 4: 1499–1545.

Dwivedi, O. P. 1997. "Environmental Protection Policies and Programmes in India, 1972–95." In *India's Environmental Policies, Programmes and Stewardship*, 51–78. London: Palgrave Macmillan.

Eckersley, Robyn. 2007. "Ambushed: The Kyoto Protocol, the Bush Administration's Climate Policy and the Erosion of Legitimacy." *International Politics* 44, no. 2–3: 306–24.

Fishman, Ram, Naresh Devineni, and Swaminathan Raman. 2015. "Can Improved Agricultural Water Use Efficiency Save India's Groundwater?" *Environmental Research Letters* 10, no. 8: 084022.

Gadgil, Madhav, and Ramachandra Guha. 1993. *This Fissured Land: An Ecological History of India*. Berkeley: University of California Press.

——. 1994. "Ecological Conflicts and the Environmental Movement in India." *Development and Change* 25, no. 1: 101–36.

——. 2013. *Ecology and Equity: The Use and Abuse of Nature in Contemporary India*. New York: Routledge.

Gandhi, Sahil, and Abhay Pethe. 2017. "Emerging Challenges of Metropolitan Governance in India." *Economic and Political Weekly* 52, no. 27: 55.

Ganesan, Karthik, Kapardhi Bharadwaj, and Kanika Balani. 2019. "Electricity Consumers and Compliance: Trust, Reciprocity, and Socio-economic Factors in Uttar Pradesh." New Delhi: Council on Energy, Environment and Water.

Garg, Amit, Vimal Mishra, and Hem H. Dholakia. 2015. "Climate Change and India: Adaptation Gap." Working Paper 2015-11-01. Ahmedabad: Indian Institute of Management.

GBD. 2018. "Burden of Disease Attributable to Major Air Pollution Sources in India." GDB Maps Working Group. Boston: Health Effects Institute. https://www.healtheffects.org/publication/gbd-air-pollution-india.

Ghosh, Shibani. 2019. "Introduction." In *Indian Environmental Law: Key Concepts and Principles*, ed. Shibani Ghosh. Hyderabad: Orient Blackswan.

Ghosh, Subhodip. 2010. "Status of Thermal Power Generation in India: Perspectives on Capacity, Generation and Carbon Dioxide Emissions." *Energy Policy* 38, no. 11: 6886–99.

GOGLA. 2019. "Peering Into the Future: India and the Distributed Standalone Solar Products Market." New Delhi: Global Off-Grid Lighting Association and cKinetics.

Gopinathan, Narayan, Narayan S. Subramanian, and Johannes Urpelainen. 2019. "Mid-century Strategies: Pathways to a Low-Carbon Future?" *Climate Policy* 19, no. 9: 1088–1101.

Gould, Carlos F., and Johannes Urpelainen. 2018. "LPG as a Clean Cooking Fuel: Adoption, Use, and Impact in Rural India." *Energy Policy* 122: 395–408.

Gratwick, Katharine Nawaal, and Anton Eberhard. 2008. "Demise of the Standard Model for Power Sector Reform and the Emergence of Hybrid Power Markets." *Energy Policy* 36, no. 10: 3948–60.

Guha, Ramachandra. 1988. "Ideological Trends in Indian Environmentalism." *Economic and Political Weekly* 23, no. 49: 2578–81.

Guo, Hao, Sri Harsha Kota, Kaiyu Chen, Shovan Kumar Sahu, Jianlin Hu, Qi Ying, Yuan Wang, and Hongliang Zhang. 2018. "Source Contributions and Potential Reductions to

Health Effects of Particulate Matter in India." *Atmospheric Chemistry and Physics* 18, no. 20: 15219–29.

Gupta, Abhishek, and Akshoy Paul. 2019. "Carbon Capture and Sequestration Potential in India: A Comprehensive Review." *Energy Procedia* 160: 848–55.

Gupta, Joyeeta. 2001. "India and Climate Change Policy: Between Diplomatic Defensiveness and Industrial Transformation." *Energy & Environment* 12, no. 2–3: 217–36.

Hallström, E., A. Carlsson-Kanyama, and P. Börjesson. 2015. "Environmental Impact of Dietary Change: A Systematic Review." *Journal of Cleaner Production* 91: 1–11.

Harish, Santosh M., and Rahul Tongia. 2014. "Do Rural Residential Electricity Consumers Cross-Subsidize Their Urban Counterparts? Exploring the Inequity in Supply in the Indian Power Sector." Working Paper 04-2014. New Delhi: Brookings India.

Harrop, Stuart R., and Diana J. Pritchard. 2011. "A Hard Instrument Goes Soft: The Implications of the Convention on Biological Diversity's Current Trajectory." *Global Environmental Change* 21, no. 2: 474–80.

Hazell, Peter B. R. 2009. "The Asian Green Revolution." IFPRI Discussion Paper 00911. Washington, D.C.: International Food Policy Research Institute.

Hirschman, Albert O. 1970. *Exit, Voice, and Loyalty: Response to Decline in Firms, Organizations, and States.* Cambridge, Mass.: Harvard University Press.

Hirsh, Richard F. 1999. *Power Loss: The Origins of Deregulation and Restructuring in the American Electric Utility System.* Cambridge, Mass.: MIT Press.

Hsu, Angel. 2018. "The 2018 Environmental Performance Index." New Haven, Conn.: Yale Center for Environmental Law and Policy.

Hubacek, Klaus, Giovanni Baiocchi, Kuishuang Feng, Raúl Munoz Castillo, Laixiang Sun, and Jinjun Xue. 2017. "Global Carbon Inequality." *Energy, Ecology and Environment* 2, no. 6: 361–69.

Intelligent Energy. 2012. "The True Cost of Providing Energy to Telecom Towers in India." White Paper, August 2012.

International Energy Agency (IEA). 2017. "Energy Access Outlook 2017: From Poverty to Prosperity." World Energy Outlook Special Report.

——. 2021. *India Energy Outlook.* Paris: IEA.

Jaffrelot, Christophe. 2003. *India's Silent Revolution: The Rise of the Lower Castes in North India.* New York: Columbia University Press.

Jensenius, Francesca R. 2017. *Social Justice through Inclusion: The Consequences of Electoral Quotas in India.* New York: Oxford University Press.

Jensenius, Francesca Refsum. 2015. "Development from Representation? A Study of Quotas for Scheduled Castes in India." *American Economic Journal: Applied Economics* 7, no. 3: 196–220.

Joseph, Kelli L. 2010. "The Politics of Power: Electricity Reform in India." *Energy Policy* 38, no. 1: 503–11.

Kale, Sunila S. 2014. *Electrifying India: Regional Political Economies of Development.* Stanford, Calif.: Stanford University Press.

Kamboj, Puneet, and Rahul Tongia. 2018. "Indian Railways and Coal: An Unsustainable Interdependency." New Delhi: Brookings India.

Kapur, Devesh, Chandra Bhan Prasad, Lant Pritchett, and D. Shyam Babu. 2010. "Rethinking Inequality: Dalits in Uttar Pradesh in the Market Reform Era." *Economic and Political Weekly* 45, no. 35: 39–49.

Kapur, Devesh, Pratap Bhanu Mehta, and Milan Vaishnav. 2018. *Rethinking Public Institutions in India.* New York: Oxford University Press.

Kennedy, Ryan, Aseem Mahajan, and Johannes Urpelainen. 2019. "Quality of Service Predicts Willingness to Pay for Household Electricity Connections in Rural India." *Energy Policy* 129: 319–26.

Khan, Yasmin. 2017. *The Great Partition: The Making of India and Pakistan.* New Haven, Conn.: Yale University Press.

Khandelwal, Meena, Matthew E. Hill Jr., Paul Greenough, Jerry Anthony, Misha Quill, Marc Linderman, and H. S. Udaykumar. 2017. "Why Have Improved Cook-stove Initiatives in India Failed?" *World Development* 92: 13–27.

Kopas, Jacob, Erin York, Xiaomeng Jin, S. P. Harish, Ryan Kennedy, Shiran Victoria Shen, and Johannes Urpelainen. 2020. "Environmental Justice in India: Incidence of Air Pollution from Coal-Fired Power Plants." Working Paper. Washington, D.C.: Initiative for Sustainable Energy Policy.

Kornai, János. 1986. "The Soft Budget Constraint." *Kyklos* 39, no. 1: 3–30.

Krasner, Stephen D. 1985. Structural Conflict: The Third World Against Global Liberalism. Berkeley: University of California Press.

Kulkarni, Himanshu, Mihir Shah, and P. S. Vijay Shankar. 2015. "Shaping the Contours of Groundwater Governance in India." *Journal of Hydrology: Regional Studies* 4: 172–92.

Kumar, Surendra. 2009. *Environmental Protection.* New Delhi: Northern Book Centre.

Kurzman, Dan. 1987. *A Killing Wind: Inside Union Carbide and the Bhopal Catastrophe.* New York: McGraw-Hill.

Lanjouw, Peter, and Nicholas Stern. 1998. *Economic Development in Palanpur Over Five Decades.* New York: Oxford University Press.

Lin, Justin Yifu, Fang Cai, and Zhou Li. 2003. *The China Miracle: Development Strategy and Economic Reform.* Hong Kong: Chinese University Press.

Lindblom, Charles E. 1959. "The Science of 'Muddling Through.'" *Public Administration Review* 19, no. 2: 79–88.

Maddison, Angus. 2010. "Statistics on World Population, GDP and Per Capita GDP, 1–2008 A.D." *Historical Statistics* 3: 1–36.

Malik, Ravinder Paul Singh, Mark Giordano, and M. S. Rathore. 2018. "The Negative Impact of Subsidies on the Adoption of Drip Irrigation in India: Evidence from Madhya Pradesh." *International Journal of Water Resources Development* 34, no. 1: 66–77.

Manish, G. P. 2011. "Central Economic Planning and India's Economic Performance, 1951–1965." *Independent Review* 16, no. 2: 199–219.

Mathur, Ajay. 2019. "India and Paris: A Pragmatic Way Forward." In *India in a Warming World: Integrating Climate Change and Development.* New Delhi: Oxford University Press.

McRae, Shaun. 2015. "Infrastructure Quality and the Subsidy Trap." *American Economic Review* 105, no. 1: 35–66.

Meckling, Jonas, and Jonas Nahm. 2018. "The Power of Process: State Capacity and Climate Policy." *Governance* 31, no. 4: 741–57.

Mehta, Dhvani. 2019. "The Judicial Implementation of Environmental Law in India." In *Indian Environmental Law: Key Concepts and Principles*, ed. Shibani Ghosh. Hyderabad: Orient Blackswan.

Merriott, Dominic. 2016. "Factors Associated with the Farmer Suicide Crisis in India. *Journal of Epidemiology and Global Health* 6, no. 4: 217–27.

Michaelowa, Katharina, and Axel Michaelowa. 2012. "India as an Emerging Power in International Climate Negotiations." *Climate Policy* 12, no. 5: 575–90.

Min, Brian. 2015. *Power and the Vote: Electricity and Politics in the Developing World*. New York: Cambridge University Press.

Min, Brian, and Miriam Golden. 2014. "Electoral Cycles in Electricity Losses in India." *Energy Policy* 65: 619–25.

Misra, Shalini. 2007. "Spirituality, Culture and the Politics of Environmentalism in India." *Journal of Entrepreneurship* 16, no. 2: 131–45.

Mohan, Aniruddh. 2017. "From Rio to Paris: India in Global Climate Politics." *Rising Powers Quarterly* 2, no. 3: 39–61.

Moody's. 2019. "The Economic Implications of Climate Change." *Moody's Analytics*, June.

Moolakkattu, John S. 2010. "Gandhi as a Human Ecologist." *Journal of Human Ecology* 29, no. 3: 151–58.

Nahm, Jonas, and Edward S Steinfeld. 2014. "Scale-Up Nation: China's Specialization in Innovative Manufacturing." *World Development* 54: 288–300.

Najam, Adil. 2005. "Developing Countries and Global Environmental Governance: From Contestation to Participation to Engagement." *International Environmental Agreements* 5, no. 3: 303–21.

Nandi, Paritosh, and Sujay Basu. 2008. "A Review of Energy Conservation Initiatives by the Government of India." *Renewable and Sustainable Energy Reviews* 12, no. 2: 518–30.

NITI Aayog. 2017. "Draft National Energy Policy for Public Comments." New Delhi: Government of India. http://niti.gov.in/content/draft-national-energy-policy-public-comments.

NITI Aayog and Rocky Mountain Institute (RMI). 2017. "India Leaps Ahead: Transformative Mobility Solutions for All." New Delhi: NITI Aayog and Basalt, Colo.: RMI.

O'Brien, Karen, Robin Leichenko, Ulka Kelkar, Henry Venema, Guro Aandahl, Heather Tompkins, Akram Javed, Suruchi Bhadwal, Stephan Barg, Lynn Nygaard, et al. 2004. "Mapping Vulnerability to Multiple Stressors: Climate Change and Globalization in India." *Global Environmental Change* 14, no. 4: 303–13.

Olivier, J. G. J., K. M. Schure, and J. A. H. W. Peters. 2017. "Trends in Global CO_2 and Total Greenhouse Gas Emissions." The Hague: PBL Netherlands Environmental Assessment Agency.

Oxfam India. 2018. "Widening Gaps: India Inequality Report 2018." New Delhi: Oxfam India, 2018.

Pai, Sandeep, Hisham Zerriffi, Jessica Jewell, and Jaivik Pathak. 2020. "Solar Has Greater Techno-economic Resource Suitability than Wind for Replacing Coal Mining Jobs." *Environmental Research Letters* 15, no. 3: 034065.

Pallas, Christopher L., and Johannes Urpelainen. 2013. "Mission and Interests: The Strategic Formation and Function of North-South NGO Campaigns." *Global Governance: A Review of Multilateralism and International Organizations* 19, no. 3: 401–23.

Panagariya, Arvind. 2008. *India: The Emerging Giant.* New York: Oxford University Press.

Parayil, Govindan. 1992. "The Green Revolution in India: A Case Study of Technological Change." *Technology and Culture* 33, no. 4: 737–56.

Pillai, Aditya Valiathan, and Navroz K Dubash. 2021. "The Limits of Opportunism: The Uneven Emergence of Climate Institutions in India." *Environmental Politics* 30: 93–117.

Pingali, Prabhu L. 2012. "Green Revolution: Impacts, Limits, and the Path Ahead." *Proceedings of the National Academy of Sciences* 109, no. 31: 12302–8.

Pink, Ross Michael. 2016. *Water Rights in Southeast Asia and India.* New York: Palgrave Macmillan.

Plowden W. Chichele. 1883. *Report on the Census of British India Taken on the 17th February 1881.* London: Eyre and Spottiswoode

Podishetti, Akash. 2022. "How Wind Power Fell Behind Solar in India?" *Business Standard,* October 11. https://www.business-standard.com/podcast/economy-policy/how-wind-power -fell-behind-solar-in-india-122101100159_1.html.

Pritchett, Lant. 2009. "Is India a Flailing State?: Detours on the Four Lane Highway to Modernization." HKS Working Paper RWP09-013. Cambridge, Mass.: John F. Kennedy School of Government, Harvard University.

Purohit, Pallav, Markus Amann, Gregor Kiesewetter, Vaibhav Chaturvedi, Peter Rafaj, Hem H. Dholakia, Poonam Nagar Koti, Zbigniew Klimont, Jens Borken-Kleefeld, Adriana Gómez-Sanabria, et al. 2019. "Pathways to Achieve National Ambient Air Quality Standards (NAAQS) in India." Laxenburg, Austria: International Institute for Applied Systems Analysis and New Delhi: Council on Energy, Environment and Water.

Raghunandan, D. 2019. "India in International Climate Negotiations: Chequered Trajectory." In *India in a Warming World: Integrating Climate Change and Development.* New Delhi: Oxford University Press.

Rajan, A. Thillai. 2000. "Power Sector Reform in Orissa: An Ex-Post Analysis of the Causal Factors." *Energy Policy* 28, no. 10: 657–69.

Rajan, Mukund Govind. 1997. *Global Environmental Politics: India and the North-South Politics of Global Environmental Issues.* New Delhi: Oxford University Press.

Rangan, Haripriya. 2000. *Of Myths and Movements: Rewriting Chipko into Himalayan History.* New York: Verso.

Rud, Juan Pablo. 2012. "Electricity Provision and Industrial Development: Evidence from India." *Journal of Development Economics* 97, no. 2: 352–67.

Rudolph, Lloyd I., and Susanne Hoeber Rudolph. 1984. *The Modernity of Tradition: Political Development in India.* Chicago: University of Chicago Press.

Sapkota, Tek B., Sylvia H. Vetter, M. L. Jat, Smita Sirohi, Paresh B. Shirsath, Rajbir Singh, Hanuman S. Jat, Pete Smith, Jon Hillier, and Clare M. Stirling. 2019. "Cost-effective Opportunities for Climate Change Mitigation in Indian Agriculture." *Science of the Total Environment* 655: 1342–54.

Scott, Christopher A., and Tushaar Shah. 2004. "Groundwater Overdraft Reduction Through Agricultural Energy Policy: Insights from India and Mexico." *International Journal of Water Resources Development* 20, no. 2: 149–64.

Sekhri, Sheetal. 2014. "Wells, Water, and Welfare: The Impact of Access to Groundwater on Rural Poverty and Conflict." *American Economic Journal: Applied Economics* 6, no. 3: 76–102.

Shah, Tushaar. 2009. *Taming the Anarchy: Groundwater Governance in South Asia*. Washington DC: RFF Press.

——. 2018. "Kick-Starting KUSUM." Anand, Gujarat, India: IWMI-TATA Water Policy Program.

Shankar, P. S. Vijay, Himanshu Kulkarni, and Sunderrajan Krishnan. 2011. "India's Groundwater Challenge and the Way Forward." *Economic and Political Weekly* 46, no. 2: 37–45.

Shupler, Matthew, William Godwin, Joseph Frostad, Paul Gustafson, Raphael E. Arku, and Michael Brauer. 2018. "Global Estimation of Exposure to Fine Particulate Matter (PM2.5) from Household Air Pollution." *Environment International* 120: 354–63.

Singh, Anoop. 2006. "Power Sector Reform in India: Current Issues and Prospects." *Energy Policy* 34, no. 16: 2480–90.

Singh, Namita, Trupti Mishra, and Rangan Banerjee. 2019. "Greenhouse Gas Emissions in India's Road Transport Sector." In *Climate Change Signals and Response: A Strategic Knowledge Compendium for India*, ed. Chandra Venkataraman, Trupti Mishra, Subimal Ghosh, and Subhankar Karnakar. Singapore: Springer.

Singh, R. B. 2000. "Environmental Consequences of Agricultural Development: A Case Study from the Green Revolution State of Haryana, India." *Agriculture, Ecosystems and Environment* 82, no. 1–3: 97–103.

Singh, Sanjay Kumar. 2008. "The Diffusion of Mobile Phones in India." *Telecommunications Policy* 32, no. 9–10: 642–51.

Singh, Siddharth. 2018. *The Great Smog of India*. New Delhi: Penguin.

Smith, Kirk R. 2000. "National Burden of Disease in India from Indoor Air Pollution." *Proceedings of the National Academy of Sciences* 97, no. 24: 13286–93.

Soonee, Sushil K., Samir C. Saxena, K. V. S. Baba, S. R. Narasimhan, K. V. N. Pawan Kumar, Praveen K Agarwal, Pankaj Batra, and Subrata Mukhopadhyay. 2019. "Renewable Energy Integration in India: Present State and Long-Term Perspective." In *2019 IEEE Milan PowerTech*. IEEE, 1–6.

Sprinz, Detlef, and Tapani Vaahtoranta. 1994. "The Interest-Based Explanation of International Environmental Policy." *International Organization* 48, no. 1: 77–105.

Srinivasan, J. 2019. "Impact of Climate Change on India." In *India in a Warming World: Integrating Climate Change and Development*. New Delhi: Oxford University Press.

Stokes, Leah C., Amanda Giang, and Noelle E. Selin. 2016. "Splitting the South: Explaining China and India's Divergence in International Environmental Negotiations." *Global Environmental Politics* 14, no. 4: 12–31.

Thakurta, Paranjoy Guha, and Akshat Kaushal. 2010. "Underbelly of the Great Indian Telecom Revolution." *Economic and Political Weekly* 45, no. 49: 49–55.

Tongia, Rahul. 2004. "The Political Economy of Indian Power Sector Reforms." Working Paper 4. Stanford, Calif.: Program on Energy and Sustainable Development, Stanford University.

Tongia, Rahul, and Samantha Gross. 2018. "Working to Turn Ambition Into Reality: The Politics and Economics of India's Turn to Renewable Power." New Delhi: Brookings India.

United Nations Environment Programme (UNEP). 2016. "Global Environmental Outlook: Regional Assessment for Asia and the Pacific." Nairobi: UNEP.

Upadhyaya, Himanshu. 2018. "Large Dams as 'Temples of Modern India'? An Obituary to Nehruvian Techno-political Dreams and a Plea for Gandhian Ethics." In *Intractable Conflicts in Contemporary India*, ed. Savyasaachi, 100–117. New York: Routledge.

Urpelainen, Johannes. 2013. "A Model of Dynamic Climate Governance: Dream Big, Win Small." *International Environmental Agreements* 13, no. 2: 107–25.

——. 2014. "Grid and Off-Grid Electrification: An Integrated Model with Applications to India." *Energy for Sustainable Development* 19: 66–71.

Vaishnav, Milan. 2017. *When Crime Pays: Money and Muscle in Indian Politics*. New Haven, Conn.: Yale University Press.

Veeman, Terrence S. 1978. "Water Policy and Water Institutions in Northern India: The Case of Groundwater Rights." *Natural Resources Journal* 18: 569.

Vihma, Antto. 2011. "India and the Global Climate Governance: Between Principles and Pragmatism." *Journal of Environment and Development* 20, no. 1: 69–94.

Wade, Robert. 1985. "The Market for Public Office: Why the Indian State Is Not Better at Development." *World Development* 13, no. 4: 467–97.

Weick, Karl E. 1984. "Small Wins: Redefining the Scale of Social Problems." *American Psychologist* 39, no. 1: 40–49.

Weiner, Myron. 1977. "The 1977 Parliamentary Elections in India." *Asian Survey* 17, no. 7: 619–26.

Wharton, Clifton R. 1969. "The Green Revolution: Cornucopia or Pandora's Box?" *Foreign Affairs* 47, no. 3: 464–76.

Wong, Christine, and Valerie J Karplus. 2017. "China's War on Air Pollution: Can Existing Governance Structures Support New Ambitions?" *China Quarterly* 231: 662–84.

World Bank (WB). 2018. "The Cost of Air Pollution: Strengthening the Economic Case for Action." Seattle: WB and Institute for Health Metrics and Evaluation, University of Washington.

World Health Organization (WHO). 2018. "WHO Global Ambient Air Quality Database." WHO. http://www.who.int/airpollution/data/cities/en/.

Wu, Fuzuo. 2018. *Energy and Climate Policies in China and India: A Two-Level Comparative Study*. New York: Cambridge University Press.

Yang, Joonseok, and Johannes Urpelainen. 2019. "The Future of India's Coal-Fired Power Generation Capacity." *Journal of Cleaner Production* 226: 904–12.

Yenneti, Komalirani. 2014. "What Makes Gujarat a Hotspot for Solar Energy Investments?" *Current Science* 106, no. 5: 665–67.

Zaveri, Esha, Danielle S. Grogan, Karen Fisher-Vanden, Steve Frolking, Richard B. Lammers, Douglas H. Wrenn, Alexander Prusevich, and Robert E. Nicholas. 2016. "Invisible Water, Visible Impact: Groundwater Use and Indian Agriculture Under Climate Change." *Environmental Research Letters* 11, no. 8: 084005.

Zerriffi, Hisham, and Elizabeth Wilson. 2010. "Leapfrogging Over Development? Promoting Rural Renewables for Climate Change Mitigation." *Energy Policy* 38, no. 4: 1689–1700.

INDEX

International Energy Agency (IEA), 7, 49, 52, 73
International Institute for Applied Systems Analysis (IIASA), 64
investments, capital, in heavy industry, 32–33
Iraq, U.S. invasion of, 44
irrigation, 20, 32; drip, 140–41; during Green Revolution, 111, 112; groundwater depletion from, 43, 83–84, 88, 129–30; KUSUM scheme for, 131
ISEP. *See* Initiative for Sustainable Energy Policy

Jahangir, of Mughal Empire, 24
Jainism, 35
Japan, 5, 20
Jawaharlal Nehru University, 109
Jinnah, Muhammad Ali, 16
Jogesh, Anu, 117
Joseph, Neha B., 114, 143
judicial system, response to environmental degradation, 120–21
jugaad (hack), as response to resource scarcity, 9, 10

Kanpur, Uttar Pradesh, 53
Karnataka, India, 130–31
Kashmir, 16
Kejriwal, Arvind, 62, 108, 109
Kerala, India, 178
Khandelwal, Meena, 98
Kigali amendment, to Montreal Protocol, 170
Kisan Urja Suraksha evam Utthaan Mahabhiyan (KUSUM), 131–32
Kolkata, India, 24
Kopas, Jacob, 19
Krasner, Stephen D., 152
KUSUM. *See* Kisan Urja Suraksha evam Utthaan Mahabhiyan
Kyoto Protocol, on climate change, 5, 114, 115, 151; U.S. reaction to, 160–61

Lahore Resolution, 16
Lakmal, Suranga, 41
land availability, population growth effect on, 31–32, 34
Lanjouw, Peter, 31
LED lights, 140; UJALA for, 10–11, 145
liberalization, 7, 8
license raj, 137, 147
liquefied petroleum gas (LPG), 33–34, 89, 98; biomass compared to, 62, 95–96, 99; rural-urban difference in, 50; subsidies for, 134–35; Ujjwala scheme for, 96–97, 99, 145
London, England, 25
Los Angeles, California, air pollution in, 56
Louisiana State University, 63–64
loyalty, in captive society, 142–43
LPG. *See* liquefied petroleum gas
Lucknow, Uttar Pradesh, 42

Maddison, Angus, 28
Maharashtra, India, 93–94, 141
Make in India scheme, 76
Malthusian trap theory, 26, 31, 32, 174, 176
Mao Zedong, 7
Marxism, 38, 164
Mathur, Ajay, 165
Mauryan Empire, 22
meat, 49, 76–77
media, in Delhi, 65
Mehta, Dhvani, 120
mercury, emissions of, 169
middle class, 3–4, 12, 162, 172; emissions of, 43, 100; energy consumption of, 29; exit of, 143, 144
Minamata Convention (2014), 169
minimum support price (MSP), 87
Ministry of Environment, Forest and Climate Change (MoEFCC), 110, 156
Ministry of Environment and Forests, 116
Ministry of External Affairs, 114

INDEX

Printed and bound by CPI Group (UK) Ltd, Croydon, CR0 4YY

23/04/2025

14660942-0002